MW01014258

THE
DIVINE
MESSIAH
OF THE
TANAKH

ERIC E. ENGLEMAN

innovo
PUBLISHING

Published by Innovo Publishing, LLC
www.innovopublishing.com
1-888-546-2111

Providing Full-Service Publishing Services for Christian Authors, Artists & Ministries: Hardbacks, Paperbacks, eBooks, Audiobooks, Music, Screenplays & Curricula

THE DIVINE MESSIAH OF THE TANAKH

Copyright © 2022 by Eric E. Engleman
All rights reserved.

No part of this publication may be reproduced, stored in a retrieval system, or transmitted in any form or by any means electronic, mechanical, photocopying, recording, or otherwise, without the prior written permission of the author.

Unless otherwise noted, all Scripture quotations taken from the New American Standard Bible® (NASB), Copyright © 1960, 1962, 1963, 1968, 1971, 1972, 1973, 1975, 1977, 1995 by The Lockman Foundation. Used by permission. www.Lockman.org.

The Holy Bible, Berean Study Bible, BSB. Copyright ©2016, 2020 by Bible Hub. Used by Permission. All Rights Reserved Worldwide.

The Christian Standard Bible. Copyright © 2017 by Holman Bible Publishers. Used by permission. Christian Standard Bible®, and CSB® are federally registered trademarks of Holman Bible Publishers, all rights reserved.

Scripture quotations are from The ESV® Bible (The Holy Bible, English Standard Version®), copyright © 2001 by Crossway, a publishing ministry of Good News Publishers. Used by permission. All rights reserved.

Copyright © 1995-2014 by ISV Foundation. ALL RIGHTS RESERVED INTERNATIONALLY. Used by permission of Davidson Press, LLC.

Jewish Publication Society (JPS) 1917; King James Version; Public domain.

Jewish Publication Society (JPS) 1985, Judaica Press, and Artscroll English Tanakh. Quotes used under "Fair Use."

Holy Bible, New International Version®, NIV® Copyright ©1973, 1978, 1984, 2011 by Biblica, Inc.® Used by permission. All rights reserved worldwide.

Scripture taken from the New King James Version®. Copyright © 1982 by Thomas Nelson. Used by permission. All rights reserved.

Library of Congress Control Number: 2022934455
ISBN: 978-1-61314-811-2

Cover Design & Interior Layout: Innovo Publishing, LLC
Cover Painting: Christ's Entry into Jerusalem by Hippolyte Flandrin ca. 1842

Printed in the United States of America
U.S. Printing History
First Edition: 2022

Has God called you to create a Christian book, eBook, audiobook, music album, screenplay, film, or curricula? If so, visit the ChristianPublishingPortal.com to learn how to accomplish your calling with excellence. Learn to do everything yourself, or hire trusted Christian Experts from our Marketplace to help.

ABBREVIATIONS

BDB—Brown Driver Briggs Hebrew Lexicon
BHS—Biblia Hebraica Stuttgartensia
BSB—Berean Study Bible
CSB—Christian Standard Bible
ESV—English Standard Version
ISV—International Standard Version
JPS—Jewish Publication Society
KJV—King James Version
MT—Masoretic Text
NASB—New American Standard Bible
NIV—New International Version
NKJV—New King James Version

TABLE OF CONTENTS

PREFACE

As I look at the log burning in the fireplace, I ponder the fact that all men and women are either on a path to heaven or to hell, and that the words that I now commence to write may influence them to take one path or the other. Because we are not unthinking lichens on the bottom of a rock, but rational self-aware "wondrously made" human beings, it is plain to me that God *is*, that he cares about his exquisitely made creation infinitely much, and that he has given me certain solemn responsibilities. My first responsibility is to love God as God really is, whether manifested in heaven or here within the physical creation. As I watch the log burn orange-hot, I know that some men, according to the Scripture, will burn like that forever, without hope of relief. And some—not many percentage-wise—will escape that punishment, but only because they bowed the knee to God and submitted to his will. So as I write these first words, I understand that I had better hold God first in my heart and make sure I am obedient to his holy Word, for woe to me if I should lead men and women away from the Almighty and his truth, such that they are directed to take the path more travelled and suffer God's wrath forever.

For the average Jewish person, the mission of this book, as implied in the title, necessarily puts me in the category that I profess to be trying to avoid. That is, the case presented here for a suffering Messiah *who is divine* necessarily must lead people down "the path more travelled." But right at the beginning, let me take issue with this supposed necessity, and base it upon holy Scripture: Regardless of what we may eventually decide to make of the substance and nature of God and "his Anointed," it is a fact that God not only made earth and man, but he also came to earth to visit men, and he visited them on numerous occasions in the form of man for the purpose of revealing himself to men and women who are made in his image. A compelling example of this is YHWH's visit to Abraham and Sarah whilst they camped by the trees of Mamre (Gen 18). Long before the Sinai Law, Abraham bowed with his face to the ground before the "three men," and had the doubting Sara (i.e., not doubting of God, but doubting of his goodness) prepare a meal for them, which they subsequently ate. Abraham "believed in the LORD; and [the LORD] reckoned it to him as righteousness" (Gen 15:6). At the trees of Mamre, Abraham believed in YHWH as the eternally and infinitely existing God who came to him in the flesh, who ate with him, and to whom he could appeal for mercy concerning the lives of those few righteous souls in Sodom. It is hard to believe that Abraham would have been credited with righteousness if he had turned away the three men who came to him, and, worse yet, sent armed men after them to kill them. No, a man coming in the name of YHWH, in the power of YHWH, and professing the substance of YHWH, is not—biblically speaking—*necessarily* disqualified. This book shows that, in fact, the Tanakh records that God came to men in some sort of physical manifestation (including as a "man" and the "Angel of YHWH") on many occasions, and that there are many signs and prophecies in the Tanakh that point to God ruling the world someday in the form of the Messiah—whom both the Old Covenant and New Covenant (i.e., the Tanakh and the New Testament) testify is the Son of God. The question that I attempt to answer in this book is this: Does the Old Covenant build, so to speak, a "forensic picture" of a divine Messiah such that when he would one day come, men and women would recognize him and exclaim, "That's him!" I think that the Scripture existing at the time of the coming of Jesus (the Tanakh) did indeed contain this "forensic picture," and, so, that is what this book will attempt to demonstrate.

I praise God for Mr. Nick Geiger (now with the Lord), and his wife Donna, as well as for Pastor Randy Burk, and his wife Sandy, for their unfailing kindness and friendship while this book was in the making. Mr. Lance Saltzmann helped in research, idea formulation, and proofreading, and Dr. Todd Bolen offered several valuable insights. Fuel for the project was regularly provided by Mrs. Lucy Pronenko's Borsch Suppe and prayers. Internet Archive has been a regularly-employed tool to access old written works—a tool that has been immensely helpful. This book is dedicated to Dr. Richard Rigsby (now with the Lord) and his wife, Donna, who together gave me a heart for Israel and for Israel's Messiah.

INTRODUCTION

Now therefore, O kings, be wise; be warned, O rulers of the earth. Serve the LORD with fear, and rejoice with trembling. Kiss the Son, lest he be angry, and you perish in the way, for his wrath is quickly kindled. Blessed are all who take refuge in him. (Psalm 2:10-12 ESV)

All the prophets prophesied only of the days of the Messiah. (Sanhedrin 99a)

When Jesus, the night before he was killed, was put on trial before the Sanhedrin, Caiaphas, the chief priest, demanded of him: "I adjure You by the living God, that You tell us whether You are the Christ, the Son of God?"[1] Jesus answered directly: "I am; and you shall see the Son of Man sitting at the right hand of Power, and coming with the clouds of heaven."[2] Given Caiaphas' motives, but more important for our subject, his and most others' understanding of Jewish religion, there was little chance of acquittal for Jesus regardless of whether he was truly the Messiah or not. By saying "I am," Jesus affirmed that he was the "Anointed One" spoken of in the Scriptures. This affirmative acknowledgment alone was probably enough to warrant his death. But by using the first person present tense "I AM," emphasized with connections to Psalm 110 and Daniel 7, Jesus ensured that the sentence passed upon him would be death—a horrible lingering death of Roman crucifixion because the Jews then had no right of capital punishment.

The Oral Law, what Jesus called "the traditions of the elders," first emerged in the intertestamental period, and through the times of domination by the Greeks and Romans grew in volume and importance, to the point of achieving an authority equal to, and, to some, greater than the written Scriptures. The Tanakh emphasized the sins of Judah and Israel, the need for a new heart and repentance, and the coming of a super-human Messiah to rule over a world remade. But in the Oral Law, as well as in the written works that were produced during the intertestamental era and later ("Apocrypha," "Pseudepigrapha," and sectarian writings found at Qumran), the Messiah was eclipsed by the subject of messianic times, and the subject of messianic times was dominated by the prospect of Israel once and for all gaining independence

---

[1] Matt 26:63
[2] Mark 14:62

from its gentile oppressors.[3] This resulted in the Jewish leadership at the time of Jesus looking forward to national independence and worldwide respect and influence, but not so much looking forward to the coming of the new leader who would put them under authority far more absolute than that experienced under the Roman Caesars.[4]

Nevertheless, many of the common people in Judah and in the Jewish dispersion looked forward more to the Messiah, knowing that the most wonderful thing about the coming messianic kingdom was not the kingdom, but the king. The New Testament historical record shows that this hope existed among at least a few. Zechariah, a Levitical priest who was the father of John the Baptist, knew that his son—in accordance with prophecies in Isaiah and Malachi—would prepare the way for the son of David who would redeem mankind and thereby make salvation possible. When his son was born, Zechariah prophesied (Luke 1:76-79):

> And you, child, will be called the prophet of the Most High; for you will go on before the Lord to prepare His ways; to give to His people the knowledge of salvation by the forgiveness of their sins, because of the tender mercy of our God, with which the Sunrise from on high will visit us, to shine upon those who sit in darkness and the shadow of death, to guide our feet into the way of peace.

Then there was Simeon to whom God had promised that he would not taste death until he had seen the Messiah. When God made good on his promise, and the aged man took the baby Jesus into his arms, he said (Luke 2:29-32): "Now Lord, You are releasing Your bond-servant to depart in peace, according to Your word; for my eyes have seen Your salvation, which You have prepared in the presence of all peoples, a light of revelation to the gentiles, and the glory of Your people Israel." Note here that for Zechariah and Simeon, their joy was

---

[3] The Dead Sea Scrolls documents just preceding the time of Jesus demonstrate that the Qumran sect was eschatologically minded; but, as Wolter's shows, messianic concerns were "sparse and ambiguous" and spoke "very little of an eschatological messiah." Nevertheless, he says this: "It is beyond dispute that the Qumran sectarians, like many of their Jewish contemporaries, understood their Scriptures to predict a future royal messiah who would deliver Israel from its enemies." (Al Wolters, "The Messiah in the Qumran Documents," in *The Messiah in the Old and New Testaments*, ed. Stanley E. Porter [Grand Rapids: Eerdmans, 2007], 80.)

[4] Alfred Edersheim says that there was much OT-based messianic awareness at the time of Jesus of Nazareth "among all classes, thoroughgoing Sadducees perhaps excepted"; but this awareness, which was largely a misunderstanding of the OT, did little to prepare them for the divine person of Jesus or his mission to provide the atonement needed for men's sins. They expected a conquering human king, but Jesus came as the divine "lamb of God." The intertestamental literature in general reflected this nationalistic hope. (See Alfred Edersheim, *Prophecy and History in Relation to the Messiah* [New York: Anson D. F. Randolf, 1885], lectures I and II.)

in response to the arrival of the Messiah and the salvation that he would bring, not only to Israel, but to all peoples. We could also consider John the Baptist who, once he was involved in his God-given ministry, described himself (John 1:23) as the "voice of one crying in the wilderness," whose mission it was to "make straight the way of the LORD." This, of course, was a quotation and fulfillment of Isaiah 40:3. When Jesus came to be baptized by John, John felt like next-to-nothing in comparison with him whom John called "the Lamb of God who takes away the sin of the world" (John 1:29)—thus identifying him with YHWH as well as the suffering servant of Isaiah 52 and 53 upon whom "the iniquity of us all" is laid. The great numbers who came to John and responded to his calls for repentance also indicate that there was significant eschatological concern among the people at the time of the beginning of Jesus' ministry.[5]

The point is that while the rabbis had changed the focus of eschatology from Messiah to Messiah's kingdom, and their oral word had become the highest authority, there still were some rabbis whose understanding of eschatology was mainly influenced by Scripture: their "Scripture" was the Tanakh, not what the scribes and rabbis said about the Tanakh. Even so, the Gospels' writers portray not only the people and their religious leaders, but Jesus' disciples as well, as being extremely slow to comprehend that the Messiah would be divine and would atone for the sins of all men through the voluntary giving of his own life. Even after the resurrection Jesus' disciples in general still did not fully get who Jesus was or fathom the significance of his death. When Jesus, a few days after the resurrection, walked along the road to Emmaus with two confused disciples (who didn't know, until later, who he was), he gently rebuked their unbelief with these words (Luke 24:25-26): "O foolish men and slow of heart to believe in all that the prophets have spoken! Was it not necessary for the Christ to suffer these things and to enter into His glory?" Luke goes on to say: "Then beginning with Moses and with all the prophets, He explained to them the things concerning Himself in all the Scriptures." When Jesus soon thereafter encountered the same mindset among his gathered disciples, after showing them his scarred hands and feet and taking a few minutes to eat a piece of broiled fish, he said (Luke 24:44): "These are My words which I spoke to you while I was still with you, that all things which are written about Me in the Law of Moses and the Prophets and the Psalms must be fulfilled." Jesus' conception of right religion, as well as how it was understood by Zechariah, Simeon, and John the Baptist, was obviously a product of the Tanakh—"the Law of Moses and the Prophets and the Psalms"—and not a product of the

---

[5] A fact recorded by the New Testament Gospels as well as Josephus (see *Jewish Antiquities*, book 18, chapter 5).

traditions of the rabbis, whose descriptions of the Messiah, in comparison to Scripture descriptions, were, as Alfred Edersheim put it, "indistinct, incoherent, unexplained, and from a much lower standpoint."[6] But once the eyes of the disciples were opened to the Scripture and how Jesus fulfilled them, they enthusiastically preached a Christ who was human *and* divine, and who suffered and died in order to atone for the sins of all mankind.

For the purposes of this book, I humbly ask the reader to walk with me on a perusal of the Old Covenant—which I'll usually call, in keeping with Jewish practice, the Tanakh—in order to shed the greatest inspired light on the Messiah question, and thereby make a biblically-based judgment regarding Jesus of Nazareth. Other than occasional insights, I will not consider the works of the rabbis (Christian-era Talmud, which is commentary on the Mishna, which itself is an early-Christian-era compendium of ostensibly pre-Christian-era Jewish Oral Law).[7] I do not believe that the God, who is love, would require his children to master such a vast ocean of rabbinic literature (or Christian literature, for that matter) in order for them to recognize the true Messiah and to be saved;[8] rather, God would have us read and understand the marvelous and obviously inspired book we call the Bible, for it can be apprehended in a mercifully short time for the purposes of wisdom and salvation. And that is what the merciful God really cares about, for he is not "wishing for any to perish but for all to come to repentance."[9] So in this question of Jesus' fulfillment of the Tanakh's teaching about the Messiah, let us decide the question "in the days of [our] youth, before the evil days come" (Eccl 12:1), by considering the highest source—God's holy Word.

Making the case for the divinity of the Messiah will be, in any case, an uphill task, for we naturally think of God as one person, and there is much in the Tanakh that appears to affirm this. With only relatively few hints and circumstances and prophecies that seem to teach something otherwise (these will comprise the contents of much of this book), the main sweep of Scripture teaches and presents God historically as one. And YHWH is emphatic: "I am

---

[6] Alfred Edersheim, *Life and Times of Jesus the Messiah* (New York: E. R. Herrick and Co., 1886), 164. Edersheim was a Jew who grew up in Vienna, attended the university there, converted to Christianity, pastored for many years, and lectured at Oxford. He was an expert in rabbinic literature and the conditions that obtained in Palestine at the time of Jesus.

[7] It should be noted that the "rabbis" of Scripture refer to the inspiration and authority of earlier *written* Scripture. David referred to Moses; Jeremiah referred to David; Daniel referred to Jeremiah; etc.

[8] "Then Rabbi Eliezer raised both of his arms and lay them on his chest, and said: Oy, these two arms of mine are like two Torah scrolls that will vanish from the world! For if all the seas were ink, and all the reeds were quills, and every person was a scribe, they still could not write down everything that I have read and taught." ("Avot of Rabbi Natan," 25, 3 [minor tractate of the Babylonian Talmud], www.sefaria.org.)

[9] 2 Peter 3:9

the LORD, and there is no other; besides Me there is no God" (Isa 45:5); and "Hear, O Israel! The LORD is our God, the LORD is one!" (Deut 6:4). Here, God tells us that he alone is God, that there are no other gods, and so, as he taught us from Sinai (Exod 20:3), we "shall have no other gods" before him— "him" being YHWH.

We should notice, though, that God does not literally say here, or elsewhere in the Tanakh (nor in the New Testament), that he is *one person.* Rather, the emphasis is on YHWH being *one God,* and that there are no other gods. From our human standpoint, we tend to naturally understand God as a person, or perhaps better, as a single self-aware cell of awareness. But here we are faced with the fact that we are limited in our understanding of our own personhood, and even more pertinent, we know, really, very little about God. "For who has known the mind of the LORD, or who became His counselor?" (Rom 11:34, quoting Isaiah 40:13). And God told us point blank: "'My thoughts are not your thoughts, nor are your ways My ways,' declares the LORD. 'For as the heavens are higher than the earth, so are My ways higher than your ways and My thoughts than your thoughts'" (Isaiah 55:8-9). We are finite, God is infinite. I can barely tie my shoelaces in the morning, but God by his Wisdom and Word made and sustains the universe. The fundamental substance of YHWH is God. In his God-ness, or Divinity, he may be a person in some ways like us (and surely is, since we are made in his image and likeness), but his personhood necessarily must be far, far beyond our ability to experience and comprehend.[10] My point here is that, when it comes to God and God's will, we should be open to more than what meets the eye, so to speak, for the eye, necessarily, cannot see itself nor see infinitely outside itself.[11] We are, as the Bible says, "worms" who, as the ancients said, cannot step over our own shadows.[12] If we are going to learn about things beyond our tiny sphere of

---

[10] Whether we say God is one person or three, we are in any case on speculative ground if just for the reason that Scripture testifies that God "is not a man that He should change His mind" (1 Samuel 15:29). Referred to here is not the physical nature of man, but the spiritual (i.e., conscious) nature of man which is fickle. This is very close to saying that he is not like human persons who are flawed in their thinking. Inasmuch as personhood is inherent in God's substance, it is only remotely like human personhood and in any case not subject to its flaws.

[11] In a related concept, Ps 94 points out how the One who made the eye and ear must necessarily be able to see and hear (v. 9): "He who planted the ear, does He not hear? He who formed the eye, does He not see?"

[12] Gregory Nazianzus (4th century AD) spoke of the human inability to fully conceive God: "To us who are (as Jeremiah saith), 'prisoners of the earth,' and covered with the denseness of carnal nature, this at all events is known, that as it is impossible for a man to step over his own shadow, however fast he may move (for the shadow will always move on as fast as it is being overtaken) or, as it is impossible for the eye to draw near to visible objects apart from the intervening air and light, or for a fish to glide about outside of the waters; so it is quite impracticable for those who are in the body to be conversant with objects of pure thought apart altogether from bodily objects. For something in our own environment is ever creeping in, even

personal experience, we must be told—and what we are told will necessarily surprise and amaze us. And that's just what God's revelation, as given in the Bible, does. For example, right at the start we are surprised to find God speaking in the first person plural: "Let *Us* make man" (Gen 1:26), and "Behold, the man has become like one of *Us*, knowing good and evil" (Gen 3:22). We also learn that while the basic Hebrew word for "God" is *El*, the plural of that word, *Elohim*, is far and away the preferred word for The Almighty in the Tanakh. Then there is the enigmatic Angel of YHWH who makes irregular appearances: sometimes he speaks as God, and sometimes as one speaking on behalf of God. And, of course, there is the mysterious Messiah concept that slowly develops in the Tanakh. But all this will be discussed in due course.

For now, just let it be known that the truth about God must surprise us, and that the Bible does indeed offer many surprises. God requires us first to honor his Word as given to us in Scripture. But this does not mean that we are thereby exempt from using our rational faculties. The Bible says, "Come now, and let us reason together" (Isaiah 1:18). Before we submit to God and his Word, after all, we must employ our God-given minds in order to come to the right decision of choosing to believe in God, and believe that the Bible is his Word. We also use reason to reject other religious systems because, in large degree, they don't "make sense." Now here a Jewish reader of this introduction may reject the Trinity doctrine out of hand as being irrational (and many would also say, unbiblical). But I would ask the reader to be patient and consider the following couple of thoughts for now: We can all agree that we are made in God's image and likeness, and agree that this mainly, perhaps entirely, has to do with the spirit and not the flesh—that is, has to do with the mind and not the physical body. And we can probably agree that our psychological makeup is necessarily to some degree a reflection of the mind of God, however faint that reflection might be. Now we know enough about ourselves to know that we, as persons, are complex. Yes, each of us is a solitary *cell* of awareness, but within that cell is a complexity that has fascinated studiers of the mind for millennia. A man, for example, is not only aware, but self-aware. He can introduce himself to another person, something that a dog or cat cannot do (as far as we know). He can talk with himself and ask himself if a certain course of action is the best way to go. This unique ability of a man to be aware of himself and to converse with himself (and thereby have a "conscience") is perhaps the core characteristic that reflects the image and likeness of God. Some of the early churchmen

---

when the mind has most fully detached itself from the visible, and collected itself, and is attempting to apply itself to those invisible things which are akin to itself." (Gregory Nazianzen, *Select Orations of Saint Gregory Nazianzen* 28.12 [*NPNF* 2/7:293]. www.ccel.org.)

pondered this human psychology analogy.[13] If this complexity is a trait of *finite* human beings made in the image and likeness of God, what would this complexity be within the *infinite* Godhead?[14] Anyway, just something to ponder as we proceed to consider the biblical data.

So our search for messianic truth will be in the Bible, a holy book which vastly outshines all other holy books, for it is the only one that answers man's ultimate questions: Who is God? How did mankind come to be? Why are we separated from God? Why do we suffer? Is there an afterlife and judgment after death? How can men and women find peace with God? We will discover that the Tanakh slowly builds a "forensic picture" of the one who will one day be the solution to the great problems of mankind. This "picture," as we will see, begins right at the beginning of the grand narrative that takes account of the godly "seed" that descends from Adam and Eve and is said to end many generations later in the Messiah—the Messiah who is responsible for reconciling men and women back to God, thereby giving them the possibility of escaping the unending punishment that is the necessary result of human evil. It is critical, right from the start, for us to know that the bloodline that the Tanakh tracks—from Adam and Eve through Abraham and David—*is going somewhere*, and going somewhere of supreme importance to man. The preeminent purpose of the Bible is to glorify the Almighty God through, first,

---

[13] Concerning this analogy, Tertullian of Carthage (2nd-3rd centuries AD) wrote the following: "And that you may the more readily understand this, consider first of all, from your own self, who are made 'in the image and likeness of God,' for what purpose it is that you also possess reason in yourself, who are a rational creature, as being not only made by a rational Artificer, but actually animated out of His substance. Observe, then, that when you are silently conversing with yourself, this very process is carried on within you by your reason, which meets you with a word at every movement of your thought, at every impulse of your conception. Whatever you think, there is a word; whatever you conceive, there is reason. You must needs speak it in your mind; and while you are speaking, you admit speech as an interlocutor with you, involved in which there is this very reason, whereby, while in thought you are holding converse with your word, you are (by reciprocal action) producing thought by means of that converse with your word. Thus, in a certain sense, the word is a second *person* within you, through which in thinking you utter speech, and through which also, (by reciprocity of process) in uttering speech you generate thought. The word is itself a different thing from yourself. Now how much more fully is all this transacted in God, whose image and likeness even you are regarded as being, inasmuch as He has reason within Himself even while He is silent, and involved in that Reason His Word! I may therefore without rashness first lay this down (as a fixed principle) that even then before the creation of the universe God was not alone, since He had within Himself both Reason, and, inherent in Reason, His Word, which He made second to Himself by agitating it within Himself." (Tertullian, *Against Praxeas* 2.7.5 [ANF 3:600-601]. www.ccel.org.)

[14] My thoughts here are due much to reflecting upon Shedd's explanation about how the Godhead necessarily contains three personalities. See Chapter I ("Nature and Definition of God") and Chapter IV ("Trinity in Unity") in third main section ("Theology [Doctrine of God]") of vol. 1 of William G. T. Shedd, *Dogmatic Theology* (New York: C. Scribner's Sons, 1888), especially pp. 178-194, 255-256. Accessible at www.archive.org.

a recording of his deeds in this cosmos, and, second, through providing men and women information whereby they can know God and be saved, and thereby come to worship him. The Bible describes the sinful and desperate plight of mankind, and describes the way by which men and women can escape their hopeless predicament. Thus the Bible is ultimately about God's concern for man and his love for man, most marvelously displayed in his willingness to atone for their sins. The bloodline is the means through which God works his miraculous and infinitely loving purpose—a purpose that is in the final analysis fulfilled by the Messiah, who is the son of David and the Son of God.

In the name of keeping things "mercifully short," we will not consider many of the types and symbols that prefigure the Messiah. Much could be said about this topic, and it is a worthwhile and thought-provoking one. The sacrificial systems of the Mosaic and patriarchal eras (and even before: e.g., God clothed Adam and Eve with animal skins upon their expulsion from the Garden) which prefigure the need for blood atonement will in general not be considered. And the many persons in the Torah whose lives in some ways typified the life of the Messiah (like Abraham, Jacob, Joseph, Moses, Joshua, David and Solomon) we may mention only in passing. The focus here will be mainly on the prophecies that speak with some clarity about the Messiah— some spoken to, or by, patriarchs, some contained within the Psalms, and not a few spoken by prophets who ministered at various times between King David and the rebuilding of Jerusalem after the Babylonian exile. Chapter 1 will cover the main prophecies from the time of the creation till the time of David and Solomon. Here, we will see that the "forensic picture" is slow to develop up to the time of David whose psalms (and others' psalms) fill out the picture greatly. In chapter 2 we will consider what the prophets, from Solomon's time till the return from exile, said about the Messiah. This was a time of tragic spiritual and physical decline for Judah and Israel, yet the prophets offered hope in their numerous descriptions of the yet-to-come messianic king and kingdom. So the Messiah was prophesied; but, in my understanding, he also *appeared* at sundry times and places, mainly before the time of David, but on a few occasions after that. These appearances of the "Angel of YHWH," will also be considered, but not so much because they add to the Messiah "forensic picture" that the Scripture builds, but because they add validity to the idea that God can appear on earth in human form. This, of course, makes the idea of a divine Messiah less implausible.

Now before we commence the study, I thought it might be helpful at the start to do a brief stratospheric flyover of the Old Covenant Bible story so as to give readers some context. As I already mentioned, strong evidence that the Bible is from God is the fact that it answers life's most pressing questions. The Bible tells us that we are created by God, that God is our Father in heaven, that we are his children, but that we have erred and rebelled against him. Nevertheless, God has set in motion a grand plan to restore us back to him so that we might be with him forever and escape the horrors of eternal separation from God. This story is told (the story being told, ultimately, by God) in the context of a single bloodline that begins with Adam and Eve and ends, according to the New Testament, with Jesus of Nazareth. As this bloodline is tracked in the Tanakh (passing through, among others, Noah, Shem, Abraham, Isaac, Jacob, Judah, Boaz, David) we learn that God is deadly serious about sin, that God's plan is to bless all nations, that God works out this plan to bless all nations first through blessing the nation of Israel, and that Israel, sadly, fails for a time in its mission to honor YHWH and be a light to the world. But through that failure and subsequent exile, the knowledge of the one true God is spread among the nations—a dissemination of knowledge that makes many people ready for the coming of the Messiah and the permanent restoration of Israel.[15]

All of this, of course, is not myth, but occurred in real history to real people whom God touched. About 1,600 years after Adam and Eve fell from grace, men and women (who multiplied greatly) became so wicked that God exterminated the whole race in a worldwide flood, except for Noah and his immediate family. About 400 years after that, Abram of Ur (the ruins of this extinct city are near present day Baghdad) "believed in the LORD; and He reckoned it to him as righteousness" (Gen 15:6). Starting with this one man who was a "friend" of God (Isa 41:8), God built up a group of people who knew God and (more or less) obeyed him. "Israel," as they were called, spent 430 years in Egypt, but then God led them out of their bondage to Mount Sinai where they were given God's law through the mediation of Moses. The blessings promised to Abraham began to find fulfillment in the new nation of Israel—a nation that at Sinai became a theocracy that numbered over a million people (Exod 12:37).

The Israelites were people who were all (with a few exceptions) "seed" (descendants) of Abraham and his wife Sarah, whether they were truly God-fearing in their hearts or not. But in a higher, spiritual sense, the men and women of Israel were only truly of Israel if they were "seed" of Abraham's *faith*. In other words, to partake of God's blessings promised to Abraham and his seed, Israel had to be faithful, as Abraham had been, before God. Before continuing on with the biblical history, it would be good to ponder this a little further.

For a holy book that is God's Word to mankind, the Tanakh is perplexingly quiet—or at least it seems to be—regarding the subject of human

---

[15] Regarding Israel's permanent restoration, see the author's book *Kindness Towards Israel.*

afterlife.[16] But there are sufficient mentions of it for Tanakh students to learn that it does exist and that a blessed afterlife is reserved for the righteous only.[17] Where the text *clearly* refers to the blessed afterlife, there is no limitation stated based on nationality: it appears that Israelites are welcome as well as any others, but only if they are righteous.[18] That being said, it is the case that most of the Tanakh is occupied (on the face of it) with Israel and its earthly matters. When we read the Tanakh literally, we see that God made promises to Abraham, and restated them to Isaac and Jacob as well as to the nation of Israel centuries later. The most often mentioned promises had to do with the increase of Abraham's "seed" and the "Promised Land" that they would occupy. Also, God promised at various times and in many ways his general protection and blessings. Because the Tanakh speaks *directly* about the blessed afterlife so infrequently, many over the eons have understood God's promises made to Israel both literally *and* metaphorically: God promised many physical descendants, meaning that there will be many who have the faith of Abraham; God promised a certain piece of land, meaning that all Israel will achieve someday the blessed afterlife. If these promises do indeed have literal *and* metaphorical (many would say "spiritual") fulfillments, then the following needs to be considered.[19]

The Tanakh's history of the Israelites shows that many, maybe most, of the people were not righteous. Moses said to the "stiff-necked" people just before he turned the reins over to Joshua (who then commenced the conquest of the peoples of the land of Canaan):

> It is not for your righteousness or for the uprightness of your heart that you are going to possess their land, but it is because of the wickedness of these nations that the LORD your God is driving them out before you, in order to confirm the oath which the LORD swore to your fathers, to Abraham, Isaac and Jacob.[20]

Now while to some degree even unrighteous people were blessed (for God sends "rain on the righteous and the unrighteous"), and many of them entered the Promised Land, nevertheless, the history shows that, in general, the unrighteous in time were "cursed" in many ways, including being prevented from entering

---

[16] The clearest statements are in Isa 25:7-8; 26:19; Hos 13:14; Dan 12:1-3. Not a few of the Psalms indicate blessed life after death: 16:10; 22:29; 23:6; 30:3; 49:15. Ezekiel, in chapter 37, prophesies that dead bones will rise and that people will come out of the graves. But this may be figurative of the final return from exile. In Exod 32:32 a "book" belonging to God is mentioned (see also Dan 12:1) that probably records those destined for eternal blessed life.

[17] Dan 12:1-3 bluntly and clearly mentions the final judgment and the different eternal destinies of the righteous and wicked.

[18] See especially Isa 25:6-9 and Dan 12:1-3.

[19] Regarding Abraham's "seed" and the land promised to him, see Gen 12:7; 13:15; 15:18.

[20] Deut 9:5

the land, or, later, being killed or ejected from the land. Not all Israel was able to fully partake of the blessings promised to the patriarchs: they were "cut off" in various ways.[21] If history (and the general Tanakh teaching about the sinful nature of all men) is our guide, then we must admit that even if the patriarchal promises have a spiritual fulfillment, not all Israel partakes of that fulfillment: Abraham was probably promised not just physical seed, but seed that would have his faith; but the history after him shows that many were not faithful. Abraham was probably promised not only physical land, but a "better country, that is, a heavenly one"—for Abraham, who lived as a nomad in tents, looked "for the city which has foundations, whose architect and builder is God";[22] but in the earthly *type*, many failed to enter the land, and of those who did enter, many were forced out. When all this is considered, it can be reasonably concluded that only righteous men and women will "inherit the kingdom of God."[23] In any case, how one views the tension between the literal and spiritual fulfillments of the patriarchal promises will affect his or her view of Israelite (Jewish) "salvation." Are all of them saved to eternal blessed life, or are some "cut off" from God and God's people forever? This question existed in Jesus' day (which brought him into much conflict with the political and religious leaders), and it still exists today.

Now let us continue on with the brief biblical overflight. This political-religious people group called Israel, consisting of both "friends" and enemies of God, was brought by God, through his servant Joshua, into the land that God had previously promised to the descendants of Abraham. In general, the job of purging the land of the idolatrous natives was done only half-heartedly. Thus for the rest of Israel's history they regularly had problems with these idolaters and were led into idolatry by them. After obtaining much of the Promised Land, Israel spent about 400 years under the authority of judges. At the end of that time, the people begged for a king to rule over them so that they could be more like the surrounding nations who had their kings and large standing armies.[24] But this demand reflected a deep distrust in God and his judges and prophets—for up till that time, whether the people knew it or not, YHWH had been their "king." God acquiesced to their demand (calling the demand "evil"),

---

[21] Regarding being "cut off," see Exod 12:15; 31:14; Lev 7:27; 23:29; etc. Concerning Israelites not being allowed to enter the Promised Land, see Num 14:26-35. Expulsion out of the land is mentioned in Deut 28:63 and 29:28, and the progressive ejection of the people out of Israel and Judah (during the divided monarchy) is described in 2 Kings and 2 Chronicles.

[22] Heb 11:16 and Heb 11:10

[23] *Sheol*, like the Greek *Hades*, is the netherworld place of the dead. Psalms that indicate that the righteous avoid *Sheol*: Ps 16:10; 30:3; 49:15; 86:13; 116:3, 8. Psalms that indicate that the unrighteous inhabit *Sheol*: Ps 9:17; 31:17; 49:14; 55:15.

[24] See 1 Sam 8 and 12. The prophet and judge Samuel said to the people in response to their demand for a king (1 Sam 12:17): "You will know and see that your wickedness is great which you have done in the sight of the LORD by asking for yourselves a king."

and gave them their first king, Saul of the tribe of Benjamin. But Saul turned out to be unfaithful, so God replaced him with David. This worked out much better because David was a man "after [God's] own heart," and he was of the tribe of Judah, the kingly (and messianic) tribe.[25] The royal era of David and his son Solomon (ca 1000 BC)[26] was the apex of Israel politically and religiously. Through the centuries and many hardships, Israel had been slowly weaned off of the worship of false gods, and had been brought into the knowledge and worship of the one true God, YHWH. Solomon, who was the wisest man on earth, unfortunately turned away from God in his later years. So upon his death the kingdom was divided in two, with "Israel" in the north and "Judah" in the south. The next several centuries were a time of political and religious decline for both kingdoms, and both were eventually destroyed (Israel by Assyria in the 8th century BC, Judah by Babylon a century and a half later). But while God punished Israel and Judah, he blessed them during this time with prophets who pleaded with them to repent, warned them of the coming judgment, but encouraged them with the news that, although their nations would be destroyed and the people either killed or deported, there would one day be a restoration in which God would make the Messiah the ruler of the whole world. This super-human king and YHWH would establish edenic conditions upon earth: "The wolf will dwell with the lamb ... and the lion will eat straw like the ox."[27]

In fact there was a restoration, as recorded in the Tanakh, of "Jews" (i.e., descendants of Judah) after seventy years of Babylonian exile, but it was a trickle and nothing like the restoration foretold by the prophets.[28] Only a small percentage of the Jews returned: The great majority probably numbering in the millions chose to remain where they had now been for several generations.[29] Under the leadership of the High Priest Joshua and the Persian-appointed governor Zerubbabel, the Jews managed to rebuild a temple (and later returning exiles rebuilt the city and walls of Jerusalem), but it was all enough to make a grown man cry, for all was pathetically poor and small compared to the glory

---

[25] 1 Sam 13:14; 1 Chron 28:4

[26] The biblical-era dating used in this book is generally according to E. R. Thiele, "The Chronology of the Kings of Judah and Israel," *Journal of Near Eastern Studies*, 3, no. 3 (Jul 1944): 137-186.

[27] Isa 11:6-7

[28] See Ezra, Nehemiah, Haggai and Zechariah.

[29] "In general, it is of the greatest importance to remember in regard to this Eastern dispersion, that only a minority of the Jews, consisting in all of about 50,000, originally returned from Babylon, first under Zerubbabel and afterwards under Ezra. Nor was their inferiority confined to numbers. The wealthiest and most influential of the Jews remained behind. According to Josephus, with whom Philo substantially agrees, vast numbers, estimated at millions, inhabited the Trans-Euphratic provinces." (Edersheim, *Life and Times of Jesus*, 8.)

days before.[30] As the inspired Tanakh historical account closes, there is a modest temple and temple rites reestablished (under the leadership of Joshua and Zerubbabel), but the Mercy Seat (which was the "throne" of God) and the Ark of the Covenant, upon which the Mercy Seat rested, were long gone. The Spirit of God, according to the prophet Ezekiel, had long since departed,[31] and the Tanakh's post-exilic record does not show the Spirit returning. The core of the entire system of cult devotion and law established by God, through Moses at Sinai, was now neutralized: no Mercy Seat, no place for God; no God, no basis for the Temple and its expiatory rites; and, finally, if none of that, no basis for "Israel." But all this was not entirely unforeseen, for the prophet Jeremiah had said that the day would come when the Ark of the (first) Covenant would no longer exist or be remembered, and when the state of the human heart would be more important than the Temple that housed the Ark.[32] Instead, God would establish a "New Covenant," different than the old one, whereby God would put the knowledge of him and the knowledge of his laws into the hearts of men and women such that all would joyfully serve YHWH.[33] The nations would then know that YHWH is God, and they would then bring their offerings to Jerusalem—also called "YHWH is there" (Ezek 48:35)—where his "Anointed One" rules as king.[34] But none of this was accomplished in the final decades that the Tanakh records nor during the time between the testaments. The establishment of the messianic times that the Tanakh foresees began, according to the New Testament, with the sacrifice of the Messiah, Jesus of Nazareth. In his blood, forgiveness of sins and reconciliation to God is offered to everyone, and with this, the mediatory function of priests and animal substitutionary sacrifices are no longer needed. In time, the full flowering of the messianic age will be realized: the wolf will be at peace with the lamb; every man will sit under his own vine and fig tree; and, as YHWH said through Jeremiah:

> "They will not teach again, each man his neighbor and each man his brother, saying, 'Know the LORD,' for they will all know Me, from the least of them to the greatest of them," declares the LORD, "for I will forgive their iniquity, and their sin I will remember no more."[35]

---

[30] Ezra 3:12; Hag 2:3
[31] Ezek 10
[32] Jer 3:16 and Jer 7:4-7
[33] Jer 31:27-34
[34] Zech 14; Ezek 48:35; Ps 2
[35] Jer 31:34

Chapter One

THE MESSIAH CONCEPT FROM THE CREATION TO SOLOMON

THE "GOOD NEWS" IN THE GARDEN

I t is a biblical fact that all men do evil:

> God has looked down from heaven upon the sons of men to see if there is anyone who understands, who seeks after God. Every one of them has turned aside; together they have become corrupt; there is no one who does good, not even one.[1]

The great King Solomon, who also was a great sinner, said this: "Indeed, there is not a righteous man on earth who continually does good and who never sins."[2] Solomon's father David was so aware of his wretchedness before YHWH that he called himself a "worm."[3] Yet the Bible teaches that we are very valuable worms in the eyes of God. It is good for us in this life to be kept humble—to recognize that we are sinful worms—so that we might repent and seek God. Yet at the same time we should increasingly come to know the extent of our value in God's eyes and how much he loves us. To understand who the Messiah is and what he did is to have some understanding of this seemingly paradoxical reality: We are sinners who are hopelessly lost, like sheep gone astray; yet God, in what he has accomplished through the Messiah, demonstrates his vast love for us.

When some people think of the creation story, they think of a titanically powerful, yet mostly inscrutable, God making a decision, among countless other decisions, to create the "heavens and earth" as well as a new product that is given a name—Adam—that sounds very much like the "soil" (*adamah*) from

---

[1] Psalm 53:2-3
[2] Eccl 7:20
[3] Psalm 22:6

which he was made.[4] But it isn't long till the new product goes bad, so God in exasperation commences a "plan B" that, although it will take lots of time away from his countless other tasks in countless other universes, will put things back in order.

Right from the beginning, however, the Bible appears to portray a very different picture. "In the beginning God created the heavens and the earth."[5] There is no mention here of other universes existing at that time, or at any other time before or after (although angels of various kinds already existed in heaven). Then God said, "Let Us make man in Our image, according to Our likeness."[6] There is no mention of any other living beings being made in his image and likeness, or already existing, elsewhere in this universe or in any other universe. So it appears to be the case that man is absolutely unique, and that there exists no other creatures—anywhere—made in the image and likeness of God. Yes, there could be other universes containing such amazing creatures, but that would be to argue from silence. As far as what God has revealed to us, the human race is an absolutely unique, wonderful, and—in God's eyes—precious product of his infinite love and wisdom. But we are much more than a created "product" in God's eyes. The first page of the Bible shows that we are *royal children* of God who, being made in his image and likeness, have royal responsibilities and royal prerogatives. God *ex nihilo* ("from nothing") created his first and (as far as we know) *only* family. We were made to worship him as our God and Father,[7] to obey him as his children, and to walk with him as his "friend."[8] The intense Divine-human bond intended by God from the beginning is indicated later in the Tanakh by the fact that God will one day be the "inheritance" of his faithful children, and, even more amazing, his faithful children will one day be the inheritance of God.[9]

In the Garden of Eden there were few laws. The first man and woman were commanded to exercise dominion over the earth, to be fruitful and to multiply, and to not eat from the tree of the knowledge of good and evil. Although it is not stated, it is surely the case that Adam and Eve were from the start expected to love God and to love each other. They were under great moral obligation, being as they were children of God made in his image and likeness. They were expected to mirror God's holiness and righteousness, and thereby

---

[4] Gen 2:7
[5] Gen 1:1
[6] Gen 1:26
[7] From time to time in the Tanakh, God is said or indicated to be the "Father" of human beings (see e.g., Deut 32:6; Ps 68:5; Isa 9:6; 63:16; 64:8; Mal 2:10).
[8] Abraham is called God's "friend" in 2 Chron 20:7 and Isa 41:8.
[9] YHWH will be the inheritance/portion of faithful men (Pss 16:5; 73:26; Lam 3:24); faithful men will be YHWH's inheritance/portion (Deut 32:9; Pss 33:12; 94:14; Isa 19:25; Jer 10:16; 51:19; Zech 2:12).

avoid bringing dishonor upon their Creator. Understanding the preciousness of Adam and Eve as well as their high culpability helps us to better understand their fall from grace and God's actions after that. It is bad enough for any living entity to disobey the King of kings, but it is particularly evil when God's royal children disobey him and, thinking they are better and smarter than God, try to usurp his authority. When Eve did this by eating the fruit that God had forbidden, we cannot perceive the enormity of the crime unless we know something about the infinite omnipotence, eternality, and holiness of God, and have at least some understanding of the truth that God made man to be in close fellowship with him forever. Because of this relationship, and in consideration of the fact that man is made in God's image and likeness, we should know that God and man are not altogether dissimilar. With all this in view, we should not be entirely surprised when God, after man's fall, judges him harshly, but then immediately takes an intense interest in his restoration. Also we should not be surprised that in the process of this restoration God stoops down, so to speak, into man's world—to the point that from time to time, according to the Tanakh, he dons human flesh—so that men and women might be elevated once more into fellowship with him.[10]

That the hope of restoration is intimately bound up with the hope of the Messiah is made evident in what God says immediately after the fall; and here the messianic story of redemption begins. After cursing the serpent, who is the devil and who represents all that is evil, God says:

$$\text{וְאֵיבָה אָשִׁית בֵּינְךָ וּבֵין הָאִשָּׁה וּבֵין}$$
$$\text{זַרְעֲךָ וּבֵין זַרְעָהּ הוּא יְשׁוּפְךָ רֹאשׁ}$$
$$\text{וְאַתָּה תְּשׁוּפֶנּוּ עָקֵב}$$

> And I will put enmity between thee and the woman, and between thy seed and her seed; they shall bruise thy head, and thou shalt bruise their heel. (JPS '17)

> And I will put enmity between you and the woman, And between your seed and her seed; He shall bruise you on the head, And you shall bruise him on the heel. (NASB)

The JPS here in the first part agrees with Christian bibles: literally understood, there will be antipathy between snakes and the first human couple, including their descendants. And, of course, this symbolizes the antipathy that will be felt by godly people toward ungodly people (followers of Satan), and vice-versa. In

---

[10] As the book proceeds, we will consider several OT theophanies.

the second half Jewish and Christian versions differ. Who has the better translation in this case? The JPS assumes that the entity bruising the head of the devil (a fatal blow) will be the collective seed just mentioned, that is, the many descendants of Eve; the entity being bruised in the heel by the devil (a non-fatal blow) will likewise be the collective seed. Thus, "they shall bruise thy head, and thou shalt bruise their heel." A problem with this, however, is that the Hebrew does not say "they" and "their," but "he" and "his"—and the "he" is emphatic in that the pronoun (הוא) is used.[11] Now, given this fact, a possible translation could be, "it shall bruise you on the head, and you shall bruise it on the heel"—i.e., "it" being the collective "seed" (descendants) of Eve; but this sounds awkward.[12] I suppose that הוא could be translated "it" or "he" and in any case refer to the collective seed; but then we wonder why God just didn't use the Hebrew for "they" and "their" so as to avoid confusion.[13] A couple of things appear to further support the NASB and other Christian translations. First, it is probable that an individual "he" in the second half of the verse struggles with the individual "you," who is Satan. A collective "they" struggling with the individual "you" would not provide good symmetry with the first half of the verse in which a collective seed of Eve opposes the collective seed of Satan. Second, the Bible, from Adam and Eve onward in time, tracks a bloodline that flows towards the Messiah. "He" will be, from a Jewish standpoint, an amazingly powerful and wise king who will usher in heaven on earth and rule in perfection forever. Perhaps this is the individual who will deal a death blow to the devil and all that is wicked. If so, then Gen 3:15 is our first glimpse of messianic prophecy: The human seed of the woman will one day conquer Satan and evil, and then "death is swallowed up in victory."[14] Yet we must wonder how a mere man could do all this (or, if the JPS is right, how "they"—i.e., men and women—could deal a death blow to Satan).

Implied in the JPS translation of Gen 3:15 is the thought that the godly descendants of Eve (best represented later by Israel) will someday destroy Satan—and overcome sin and separation from God in the process—and thereby reestablish the edenic order. But who can bring men back to perfection once they have been cursed and corrupted? Again, to quote the Scripture, "there

---

[11] The Hebrew word for "seed," *zerah*, is masculine, so "he" could refer to the seed. In the case of the Septuagint translation (the Greek translation of the Tanakh, ca. 200 BC), the Greek word for "seed," *sperma*, is neuter; but masculine "he" and "his" (instead of neuter "it" and "its") is used in Gen 3:15b.

[12] The Koren Jerusalem Bible has: "it shall bruise thy head, and thou shalt bruise his heel." The Judaica Press Tanakh: "He will crush your head, and you will bite his heel."

[13] "Seed" is used individually in Gen 4:25 as well as Gen 21:13, and collectively in many cases. The collective meaning (without precluding the possibility of a single individual within the collective) is far more plentiful.

[14] 1 Cor 15:54 quoting Isa 25:8

is not a righteous man on earth who continually does good and who never sins."[15] Once the masterpiece painting is terribly defaced, who can restore it? Can the painting restore itself?[16] Events after the fall only verify the folly of the idea that mankind can redeem itself: First, God made reentry into the Garden impossible by the stationing of "cherubim" and a "flaming sword."[17] Second, after the flood, God foiled the plans of men to build a tower from earth to heaven.[18] Third, the Scripture testifies that men do not have the means to pay what God demands in order that they might escape God's condemnation of death:

> No man can by any means redeem his brother or give to God a ransom for him—For the redemption of his soul is costly, and he should cease trying forever—that he should live on eternally, that he should not undergo decay.[19]

This must be considered in view of what is said a few verses later: "But God will redeem my soul from the power of *Sheol*, for He will receive me."[20] A man cannot redeem a man, but God can. With God being the highest lawgiver, there must be justice, otherwise injustice and chaos would be universal. There must be a payment for evil committed against God. But to sin against the infinite holy God is to bring upon a man a judicial sentence that he in no way can pay or work off. A man on earth who commits a capital crime cannot diminish the sentence by "good behavior," but is hopelessly destined to be executed or, depending on the state, destined to remain in prison until he dies—"life, without parole." For these reasons and more, the "he" or "it" or "they" that will mortally wound the devil cannot be only human: "With people this is impossible, but with God all things are possible."[21]

Let us now proceed on in biblical time. This book is not a Bible survey, so we will only make a few remarks on our way to the next significant messianic marker. For our purposes the most important thing to observe is the ubiquitousness of sin: Adam and Eve are banished from the Garden and have two sons, Cain and Abel. Cain kills Abel then goes as far away from God as he can.[22] Ten generations later the world is "filled with violence,"[23] so God kills

---

[15] Eccl 7:20

[16] I get the metaphor of a defaced painting from Athanasius' "The Incarnation of the Word," section 14 (Athanasius, *Select Works and Letters* [NPNF 2/4:43-44], www.ccel.org.).

[17] Gen 3:24

[18] Gen 11:1-9

[19] Ps 49:7-9

[20] Ps 49:15

[21] Matt 19:26

[22] Gen 4:16

[23] Gen 6:13

them all, save righteous Noah and his family; but Noah gets drunk as soon as he gets off the Ark and one of his sons, Ham, makes sport of his nakedness and is cursed as a result.[24] Once the race re-multiplies, their pride prompts them to make a name for themselves by building a titanic tower that reaches to the heavens. But God foils the plan, confounds their language, and in the confusion, the race spreads out over the earth and (it is probably the case) has little or nothing to do with God.[25] But, beginning in Gen 12, we are introduced to Abraham (at that point, his name is still Abram) whom God will use, along with his descendants, to reestablish the knowledge of God in the world as well as to initially prepare the way for the Messiah. The Tanakh's brief record from the deception at the tree of the knowledge of good and evil to Abraham (whom the record also reveals as a sinner) verifies that the world is hopelessly enmeshed in wickedness, cannot make its own way back to God, and therefore desperately needs a Savior. We also see that up to Genesis chapter twelve (and beyond) the Bible carefully tracks a bloodline that goes from Adam to Noah to Abraham. What God will promise Abraham will have much to do with the bloodline that descends from this great patriarch.

THE PROMISE GIVEN TO ABRAHAM

It can be justly said that the nation of Israel (the Jewish race) has its beginning in the person of Abraham (who lived about 2000 BC). He grew up in "Ur of the Chaldeans" (near present-day Baghdad, Iraq), but his father Terah took Abraham and his wife Sarah, and Abraham's nephew Lot, to Haran (northwestern Iraq).[26] After some time there,[27] God gave a very special message to Abraham (Gen 12:1-3):

> Now the LORD said to Abram, "Go forth from your country, and from your relatives and from your father's house, to the land which I will show you; and I will make you a great nation, and I will bless you, and make your name great; and so you shall be a blessing; and I will bless those who bless you, and the one who curses you I will curse. And in you all the families of the earth will be blessed."

It appears that Abraham was not initially informed about his destination. Nevertheless, he obeyed and believed that God would lead him and one day make him into "a great nation." But this really took faith, because at that time—

---

[24] Gen 9:20-25
[25] Gen 11:1-9
[26] Gen 11:31-32
[27] Stephan, Acts 7:2-3, indicates that Abraham was in Ur when the Gen 12:1-3 message was given.

and for another two decades—Abraham and Sarah had no children. Before discussing the messianic import of this promise, we should first think some about why God gave it in the first place.

Abraham's father, Terah, was an idolater when he was in Ur and probably also after he and his family moved to Haran.[28] Abraham most likely participated in his father's polytheism. When God told Abraham to leave Haran, it is unclear what Abraham's spiritual state was then, although he did listen to YHWH and departed. A little later in the Genesis narrative, however, it is evident that he acknowledged the one true God, for when he arrived in Shechem, he built an altar to YHWH, and upon arrival at Bethel some time later, built another altar to YHWH *and* "there called upon the name of the LORD."[29] Was God's initial call to Abraham and the initial promise (Gen 12:2-3) based upon the patriarch's faith, upon his obedience, or based simply upon God's sovereign choice and bestowal of unmerited grace? We can't know for sure, although the NT does show that once Abraham did believe, God considered him righteous and began to bless him accordingly.[30] But when the original promise was given, there is no evidence from the narrative that Abraham had done any good works for God, and it is even questionable if he really believed at that point. In any case, the original promise given to the patriarch was given before he performed the "work" of moving to Canaan, and, most importantly, the promise was stated with no conditions: it was an *unconditional* promise given before (from what we know from the biblical narrative) Abraham performed any good works for God, and perhaps even before Abraham truly believed in God.

As the narrative continues, and before God commands Abraham and his sons to be circumcised (Gen 17), it is clear that God protected and blessed Abraham because, as the Genesis 15:6 text testifies, "he believed in the LORD; and He reckoned it to him as righteousness." For the purposes of explaining what follows, the critical question here is this: Did Abraham earn his God-bestowed blessings, or were they ultimately given as an unearned gift? Especially in view of the fact that the original promise and its several restatements in Gen 12-15 are unconditional,[31] and in view of the fact that the blessings were promised and began to be fulfilled before God commanded circumcision, it strongly appears to be the case that we can only say that, at most, the patriarch of the Jews was blessed by God simply because he believed. This question about the basis of Abraham's blessings bears upon the question about the basis of his

---

[28] In Joshua's day, God testified that Abraham's father, Terah, while "beyond the river" … "served other gods" (Josh 24:2).
[29] Gen 12:6-8
[30] Gen 15:6; Rom 4
[31] Gen 12:7; 13:14-17; 14:19-20. Also, all of Gen 15.

descendants' blessings, for the original promise was not just for the patriarch, but for his children as well.

Before going on, let it be said that this original promise given by God to Abraham (Gen 12:2-3), as well as the original promise to give Abraham the Land of Canaan (v. 7), have literal *and* spiritual meanings. God's purpose from the beginning is to reverse the death curse incurred when Adam and Eve sinned. Everything that follows Gen 1-3 must be understood in view of this. Yes, Abraham is promised offspring and land, and God has fulfilled this, and will continue to fulfill this. At the same time, the promise must have much to do with the undoing of the death curse and the elimination of that which now separates men and women from God. The promise here is clearly an extremely significant event, and so, when we read that through the "seed" of Abraham, "all nations of the earth shall be blessed" (Gen 12:2; 22:18), we can rightly suspect that this "seed" has much to do with reinstituting eternal life and reconciling man back to God.

In order to make a right translation of the Hebrew of God's original promise to Abraham, it may be helpful to understand a couple more things regarding translation biases of Christian and Jewish translators of Gen 3:15. Christian versions translate Gen 3:15 so as to show that a future "he"—i.e., the Messiah—will one day destroy Satan and thereby bless the world. Believing from the start that Jesus is divine, they are glad to translate so that the Messiah owns the mission of doing what it seems that only God can do. On the other hand, the Jewish versions by and large translate so as to show that a future "they"—i.e., godly Jews—will one day neutralize Satan by their righteousness and thereby bless the world. This reflects the differing understandings of salvation among Christians and Jews: for Christians, salvation (the destruction of Satan and the reversal of the death curse) is mainly a "work" of the Messiah, whom they perceive as divine. For Jews, only God, of course, can provide blessed life after death; but this is enabled, so to speak, by the fidelity and good works of his chosen people. But there is more to the story here. In the eyes of those making the various Jewish versions of the Tanakh, there is the feeling that if an individual "he" is acknowledged to be the "seed" that defeats and kills Satan, then he accomplishes a task on behalf of mankind that only God can do. If this person is the Messiah—which, given the testimony of the rest of Scripture, he probably is—then it may be the case that the Messiah is divine; but that appears to contradict God's testimony elsewhere in the Tanakh regarding his absolute singularity. So, as a result of all this, there is a strong tendency for the Jewish versions to emphasize personal and collective good works, and to avoid any interpretation and translation that appears to put the Messiah in a divine light.

Now let's look a little closer at the initial Abrahamic promise. Jewish and Christian versions in general agree on all of Gen 12:2-3 except the last line, so we will concentrate on that.

Like with Gen 3:15, Jewish and Christian translations of this verse differ similarly: the former translate in some cases so as to emphasize the saving works of men, the latter, so as to emphasize the saving work of the Messiah.

וְנִבְרְכוּ בְךָ כֹּל מִשְׁפְּחֹת הָאֲדָמָה

And all the families of the earth Shall bless themselves by you. (JPS '85)

And in you all the families of the earth will be blessed. (NASB)

In the JPS '85, the "families of the earth" bless themselves (reflexive); in the NASB, the families are blessed by an outside source (passive). The JPS '85 here emphasizes the group: as the seed of the woman group of Gen 3:15 destroys the devil, by their doing so they bring blessings upon themselves. In other words, the collective seed of Abraham (the "by you" or "in you") are blessed in that they will one day destroy the devil, sin, and death.[32] We know, by the way, that the "by you"/"in you" speaks of Abraham's descendants because when the same promise is repeated in Gen 22:18, it says that the nations will be blessed "in [Abraham's] seed."[33] Now what can we say about this?

There is here an ambiguity that allows either translation. The verb וְנִבְרְכוּ is in the Niphal form, which normally indicates the passive voice ("and they will be blessed"), but can sometimes have a reflexive meaning ("and they will bless themselves"). Christian translators go with the former passive meaning (with the thought that the families of the earth are blessed by an outside force, i.e., the Messiah who provides salvation), and some Jewish translators favor the reflexive meaning (with the thought that salvation does not come from without, but is earned by men and women as they strive toward holiness). Which translation is right? Perhaps the Lord has intended some purposeful level of ambiguity in this verse as well as in Gen 3:15, for even if the Messiah in both verses is in view, it is still the case that the Messiah is one of the members of the seed of Eve and Abraham. Understood as an individual, he truly does bless Israel and the other families of the earth; as representative of Israel and humanity in

---

[32] Some Jewish translations favor the passive here. The Koren Jerusalem Bible and the JPS '17 version are the same: "in thee shall all the families of the earth be blessed." The Judaica Press Bible has "all the families of the earth shall be blessed in you." The Artscroll Tanakh, like the JPS '85, uses the reflexive translation: "and all the families of the earth shall bless themselves by you."

[33] The same promise regarding "seed" is also given to Isaac (Gen 26:4) and Jacob (Gen 28:14).

general, in a manner of speaking it could be said that the earth's families by his wonderful work bless themselves. It just seems, however, that if the import of these two obviously significant verses extends to a reversal of the death curse, then one way or another, God must provide the primary means to bring this about. In any case, as we proceed on in time—especially once we get to the time of David and the prophets at his time and after—we will see that the figure of the Messiah looms larger and larger. And this will give increasing credence to the view that the "seed" that bruises Satan's head and that blesses the whole world should be understood more as an individual and less as the collective descendants of Eve/Adam and Abraham.

The promise given to Abraham that we have just covered is the only promise/prophecy given during the patriarch's lifetime that, in the Christian view, plainly has to do with the Messiah. But there is much else in the patriarch's life that portends and/or typifies the Messiah and events in his life. I should briefly mention four examples here (admittedly, employing some hindsight). First, consider the events of Gen 15: Abraham (before he and Sarah were blessed with a child) doubted God's promise regarding future descendants, so God swore to him that he would indeed have many descendants and that they would possess the Promised Land. Then God sealed the oath, in ancient near-eastern fashion, by passing between the pieces of freshly-killed animals. Thus, YHWH put himself under a decree of death should he fail to bring Abraham's descendants into the land and keep them there. In view of later history, one could argue that because his descendants never occupied the land *permanently*, God, at some point, had to submit to the solemnized oath that he had made—something that he perhaps accomplished through the suffering and death of the Messiah. Second, when the promised son did come, it may be that the *miraculous* birth of Isaac portended something for the distant future "seed" of Abraham and Sarah.[34] Third, we know from Ps 110 that Abraham's meeting with Melchizedek (Gen 14), the king of Salem, portended something messianic: David's son and "Lord," who sits at YHWH's right hand, is decreed by YHWH, via solemn oath, to be "a priest forever according to the order of Melchizedek." Because the priesthood of Melchizedek preceded the Aaronic priesthood (and all "Israel," including the Levites, submitted as it were to Melchizedek whilst they were in the loins of Abraham),[35] one could say that the reinstitution of the Melchizedekian priesthood upon the advent of the Messiah would render the Aaronic priesthood of secondary or even of no importance (the latter would likely be the case if the Messiah did indeed provide, in himself, an offering sufficient to save all mankind). Finally, we cannot forget the awe-

---

[34] Gen 21:1-7
[35] Something suggested in the NT, in Hebrews chapter seven.

full and dread-full events of Gen 22 in which Abraham was commanded by God to sacrifice his "only son" Isaac. An ocean of ink could not fully record all that happened here (including what Abraham had to deal with intellectually and emotionally) and all that it meant.[36] But surely there must be something wonderful in the fact that the "Father of Nations" went up Moriah to sacrifice his "only son," yet this earthly father (Abraham) knew for certain that his heavenly "Father" would provide a "lamb" in Isaac's place.[37] Is it too much at this point to mention that Isaiah, more than a millennia later, prophesied of a "He" who would be "like a lamb that is led to slaughter," and that YHWH would cause "the iniquity of us all to fall on him"?[38]

So far I have suggested that we should view the crushing of the devil's head in Gen 3:15 and the blessing of all nations of the world as best being accomplished by some-ONE of the "seed" of the woman and, nineteen generations later, of the "seed" of Abraham. As we move along, we will increasingly see that this "He" has attributes that one would think could only belong to God. As I said in the Introduction, a divine Messiah should not be considered impossible, for the Tanakh has many occurrences of God appearing in the flesh or at least in visible form. Two of the more enigmatic occur during the first epoch: In the garden God walked within earshot of Adam and Eve "in the cool of the day" (Gen 3:8), and later when Noah and his family, and all the animals, were safely embarked on the ark, the text says that "the LORD shut him in" (Gen 7:16, JPS '85). One could say that these instances really don't prove God's physical presence, and perhaps that is so; but when God visited Abraham and Sarah one day by the trees of Mamre (Gen 18), it is very difficult to see this as anything else than a theophany in which God appears in human form.

It seems more than a coincidence that the first time God shows up obviously in the flesh, his mission has to do with the continuance of the "seed" that we have been considering—the seed that will bless all the families of the earth. Could it be that YHWH was trying to show at the very start of "Israel"

---

[36] Calvin wrote: "Yet not only is the death of [Abraham's] son announced to him, but he is commanded with his own hand to slay him, as if he were required, not only to throw aside, but to cut in pieces, or cast into the fire, the charter of his salvation, and to have nothing left for himself, but death and hell.... But he was unwilling to measure, by his own understanding, the method of fulfilling the promise, which he knew depended on the incomprehensible power of God." (John Calvin, *The Penteteuch*, vol. 1 of *Calvin's Commentaries* [Grand Rapids: Associated Publishers], 216-217.)

[37] On the climb up the mountain, Isaac had asked, "Behold, the fire and the wood, but where is the lamb for the burnt offering?" Abraham replied, "God will provide for Himself the lamb for the burnt offering, my son." Some Jewish translations also use "lamb" here. Perhaps the "lamb" spoken of here in a prophetic sense points beyond the "ram" that ended up being Isaac's sacrificial substitute on Moriah.

[38] Isa 53:7, 6

that God can appear and dwell with men as a man? The narrative of Gen 18 says that "three men" came to Abraham and the yet-childless Sarah during, not the "cool of the day," but the "heat of the day." Abraham rushed to meet them and "bowed himself to the earth" before them, then had Sarah hastily prepare a meal, which they then ate. It seems that one of the men was YHWH, and the other two were angels (who show up in Sodom in the next chapter). YHWH then said this: "I will surely return to you at this time next year; and behold, Sarah your wife will have a son."[39] It had been over twenty years since God promised to make Abraham a "great nation." When Sarah, who was well past childbearing age, heard YHWH say this, she doubted, scoffed, and laughed— a response that lapped over to the naming of her miracle son when he did indeed come a year later: "Isaac" (*laughter*). But the Lord gently admonished: "Is anything too difficult for YHWH?"[40] And so, as the LORD promised, he "visited" Sarah the following year, and the "impossible" was accomplished.[41] It seems the LORD wanted to personally superintend—"face to face"—the successful continuance of the Holy Seed by encouraging the great patriarch and his skeptical wife to "hang in there." Beginning with Abraham, God's people— that is, his "kingdom"—would be built up. And one of those people would one day be the ONE who would destroy the devil, evil, and death. YHWH was surely intensely interested in getting that kingdom, and the Messiah of that kingdom, off to a successful genetic start.[42]

JACOB'S BLESSING (GEN 49:10)

As the NT says, "they are not all Israel who are descended from Israel."[43] Because most Jews understand their primary patriarch to be Abraham, we should note here that God's highest blessings did not extend to all of his descendants. Of Abraham's sons, Isaac was favored and Ishmael sent away.[44] Of Isaac's sons, Jacob was favored far more than Esau, so much so that YHWH much later said of him: "I have loved Jacob; but I have hated Esau."[45] It appears that neither Ishmael nor Esau were faithful to YHWH. In the biblical narrative Ishmael and Esau, and their descendants, slowly fade from the scene; but Isaac

---

[39] Gen 18:10

[40] Gen 18:14, my translation.

[41] Gen 21:1-3

[42] What YHWH did (Gen 19) after he left Abraham is symbolic of what the Messiah will do in the future. YHWH got Lot and his family out of Sodom and then destroyed the city completely.

[43] Rom 9:6

[44] Gen 21

[45] Mal 1:2-3

and Jacob and their descendants flourish, and through their loins are passed the seed of the Messiah.[46]

As YHWH was intensely interested in the maintenance of Abraham's faith and in the successful passing along of the Holy Seed, so was he interested in Abraham's grandson Jacob. Long before Jacob gave a very special deathbed messianic blessing to his son Judah (which we will soon discuss in some detail— Gen 48:10), God spoke to Jacob several times to encourage him to keep walking in faith and to know that he was never without divine protection. In one of these communications (Gen 32), YHWH came to Jacob in the form of a "man" and wrestled with him through the night. Long before this, Jacob (through his mother's cunning) stole his older brother's birthright.[47] Fearing retaliation from Esau, Jacob fled to Haran—with nothing but his shepherd's staff—where some of his relatives still remained. On the way there, he had the dream of a ladder reaching from earth to heaven upon which the angels of God went up and down. YHWH, who was above the ladder, repeated the promises already made to Abraham and Isaac, and then assured Jacob that he would be protected from all harm.[48] In Haran Jacob flourished, obtaining wives, concubines, and a sizable retinue of livestock.[49] But his uncle became jealous and, once again, Jacob had to flee—this time at the LORD's command, but as a relatively wealthy man. But as he approached the Promised Land, Jacob received news that his brother Esau was coming with four hundred (probably armed) men. He assumed that Esau was bent on destroying him and his family. So near the river Jabbok,[50] Jacob prayed that the LORD would fulfill his promise and protect him from his brother.[51] Then that night, Jacob wrestled with the "man" already mentioned. It had been twenty years since YHWH, in the ladder dream, had promised to protect and bless him.

The Hebrew text of Gen 32:25-31 says that this mystery man wrestled with Jacob through the night until daybreak. Even though the man injured Jacob's thigh, Jacob insisted that the man bless him, and would not let him go until he did. As dawn broke, the man at last blessed Jacob and changed his name to "Israel," "for," as the man said, "you have striven with God and with men and have prevailed" (v. 28).[52] When Jacob asked for the man's name, he replied, "Why is it that you ask my name?" (v. 29)—a counter question that seems to imply that Jacob should have already known it. After the sun was up

---

[46] Gen 21:12; 26:2-5; 28:13-15

[47] Gen 27

[48] Gen 28

[49] Gen 29-30

[50] The Jabbok is a modest-sized stream that flows out of ancient Gilead (modern-day Jordan) and joins the River Jordan about halfway between the Sea of Galilee and the Dead Sea.

[51] Gen 32

[52] See also Gen 35:9-10.

and the man was gone, the Tanakh records (Gen 32:30 [v. 31 in Judaica Tanakh]):

$$\text{וַיִּקְרָא יַעֲקֹב שֵׁם הַמָּקוֹם פְּנִיאֵל כִּי־רָאִיתִי}$$
$$\text{אֱלֹהִים פָּנִים אֶל־פָּנִים וַתִּנָּצֵל נַפְשִׁי}$$

> So Jacob named the place Peniel, for he said, "I have seen God face to face, yet my life has been preserved." (NASB)

> And Jacob named the place Peniel, for (he said,) "I saw an angel face to face, and my soul was saved." (Judaica)

The text here is clear: Jacob believed that he had wrestled with God—in Hebrew, with *elohim*. It does not say that he wrestled with an "angel" as the Judaica Tanakh has it. Several elements confirm what the text plainly says. First, the "man" had the authority to change Jacob's name from "deceiver" to "struggles [with] God," an authority in this case that appears divine. The new name surely was meant to recall what transpired that night (as well as Jacob's struggles with God generally), that he had "struggled [with] God" and not only survived, but "prevailed." Jewish translators think that Jacob struggled with an angel or with a mysterious "divine being,"[53] options that are possible in that he struggled with *elohim*, a term that on a few occasions is used of angels and mighty men.[54] But the new name *israel* excludes this possibility, because the *el* component of it (*isra-el*, "struggles-God")—which is the singular of *elohim* (but not used as often as *elohim*)—is seldom if ever (as a word that means "God," not just "mighty one") used for angels or men in the Tanakh.[55] Finally, in one vein of Old Covenant thinking, one necessarily died when one saw God.[56] Jacob was amazed that he survived the encounter, not because he had seen a *created* angel face to face, but because he had seen *God* face to face.[57] Not a few ancient Jewish commentators, and even some Christian ones, understand *israel* to consist of *ish* ("man"), *raah* ("to see"), and *el* ("God" or "Mighty One"),

---

[53] Michael Fishbane says regarding Gen 32:25: "Jacob's mysterious adversary is surely supernatural, and most traditional Jewish commentators have taken him to be angelic." (Adele Berlin, Marc Zvi Brettler, and Michael A. Fishbane, *The Jewish Study Bible* [New York: Oxford Univ. Press, 2004].)

[54] E.g., see Exod 21:6; 22:8-9 (MT 7-8), 28 (MT 27); Ps 82:1, 6; 97:7; 138:1.

[55] See the lexicons. The same thought also applies to the name that Jacob gave to the place: *Peni-el*, "face of God."

[56] See Exod 33:20; Judg 6:22-23; 13:22; Isa 6:5.

[57] Gideon and Manoah (Judg 6, 13) felt the same way when they were visited by the *uncreated* Angel of the LORD. Just before Jacob died, in blessing the sons of Joseph, Jacob called God "The angel who has redeemed me from all evil" (Gen 48:16). This helps us understand that the Angel of YHWH is the same essence as YHWH.

rendering a meaning of "man who sees God/a Mighty One."[58] This idea is iffy just from the fact that it tries to pack too much into a short name; but it is rendered extremely unlikely by the simple fact that Jacob is given his new name "Israel" to memorialize what he had just done all night long, i.e., "striven with God". In the Hebrew, "striven" is based on the verb root *sara*; without there being an amazing, but meaningless, coincidence, it must be the case that the *sra* part of *israel* is based on the same root and means the same thing.[59]

Jewish Bible versions, based on rabbinical interpretations, are very hesitant in general to depict God in biblical narrative as being able to break into time and space in human form. Part of this hesitancy is based upon biases that have accumulated since the beginning of the Christian era. But the plain text of Scripture shows in this case, as well as in several others, that God can, and has, come in the flesh in order to help weak men and women accomplish his will.[60]

The Tanakh's "forensic picture" of the Messiah is built up within the genetic line that, as I have said before (given that this is Holy Scripture), is going somewhere, and going somewhere very important. So far we've seen that someone will destroy the devil, sin, and death, and that through this person (who is descended from Abraham) all nations and their peoples will be blessed. Now Jacob, through a deathbed blessing, will add a little more to the messianic picture. But first, we should note the remarkable circumstances that brought him down to Egypt where he gave that blessing.

The Tanakh records the births of twelve children (including one daughter, Dinah) to Jacob and his wives Rachel and Leah, and his concubines Bilhah and Zilpah, while he was in Haran.[61] After Jacob returned to the land of Canaan, Benjamin was born to Rachel, but she died during the delivery.[62] Because Jacob had loved Rachel more than Leah and his concubines, he greatly favored Benjamin and Rachel's only other son, Joseph. When Benjamin was still a toddler, the other sons became jealous of Joseph (who was probably a

---

[58] For Rabbinical and early Christian commentators using this rendering, see James L. Kugel, *The Bible as it was* (Cambridge: Harvard Univ. Press, 2001), 226-29.

[59] The *i* preceding *sra* in *israel* is simply the imperfective aspect marker of the verb: Jacob's (and Israel's) struggle is not a one-time event, but is ongoing.

[60] Hosea 12:3-5 says that Jacob in his adulthood "contended with God," and then says: "Yes, he wrestled with the angel and prevailed; he wept and sought His favor. He found Him at Bethel and there He spoke with us, even the LORD, the God of hosts, the LORD is His name." As with the "Angel of the LORD" events that we will consider in due course, we have here what seems to be some identity between the "angel" with whom Jacob wrestled and "the LORD" whom he had previously seen at Bethel. Jacob testified to this identity at the end of his life when he said in the course of blessing the sons of Joseph: "The God before whom my fathers Abraham and Isaac walked, the God who has been my shepherd all my life to this day, the angel who has redeemed me from all evil, bless the lads" (Gen 48:15-16).

[61] Gen 29-30

[62] Gen 35

teenager at that time) because their father favored him in special ways, including the bestowal upon him of an "ornate" coat. After Joseph had two dreams that indicated symbolically that his brothers would one day bow down to him, his brothers' jealousy and distain became so intense that they conspired to kill him; but Reuben and Judah interceded, so he was sold into slavery instead.[63] In the minds of many Christians, Joseph's life was remarkably *typical* of the Messiah: he was handed over to the gentiles (Ishmaelite traders ≈ Romans) who put him in the "heart of the earth" (in Pharaoh's dungeon ≈ tomb), but by and by he was exalted to Pharaoh's (≈ God's) right hand.[64] Because of Joseph's suffering and exaltation, "all the earth" prostrated themselves at his feet ("all the earth" ≈ "at the name of Jesus every knee will bow").[65] In fulfillment of Joseph's dreams, and according to God's sovereign providence, the brothers twenty years later in the midst of a terrible famine prostrated themselves before Joseph, begging for bread and for their lives. But Joseph, understanding the mysterious ways of God, forgave them and made provision for them to bring their father to him and then to dwell with him, for the famine was only just beginning.[66] After their father Jacob died and was buried with great ceremony and lamentation in the Promised Land, Joseph's brothers, fearing retribution, again groveled at Joseph's feet, begging forgiveness.[67] Joseph's reply is forever a memorial to God's sovereignty and love:

> "Do not be afraid, for am I in God's place? As for you, you meant evil against me, but God meant it for good in order to bring about this present result, to preserve many people alive. So therefore, do not be afraid; I will provide for you and your little ones." So he comforted them and spoke kindly to them.[68]

Joseph's messianic typology is a fitting context within which his Father's messianic blessing was given (Gen 49:8-12)—not to Joseph and his two boys, but to Judah, the son who had kept his other brothers from killing Joseph many years before (Judah, once in Egypt, also offered to enslave himself to Joseph so Benjamin could go free). As the great patriarch lay upon his deathbed, he pronounced a "blessing" upon Judah, which was also a prophecy of what would happen to his descendants "at the end of days."[69] Jacob said that Judah would be like a lion who would rule over his brothers as well as his enemies, and his

---

[63] Gen 37
[64] Gen 37, 39-41
[65] Gen 41:57
[66] Gen 42-45
[67] Gen 50
[68] Gen 50:19-21
[69] "At the end of days," see Gen 49:1, Judaica Tanakh.

robe and garments would be soaked with the blood ("wine") of his enemies. In the midst of this, Jacob said (v. 10):

$$\text{לֹא־יָסוּר שֵׁבֶט מִיהוּדָה וּמְחֹקֵק מִבֵּין רַגְלָיו}$$
$$\text{עַד כִּי־יָבֹא שִׁילֹה וְלוֹ יִקְּהַת עַמִּים}$$

> The scepter shall not depart from Judah, nor the ruler's staff from between his feet, until Shiloh comes, and to him shall be the obedience of the peoples. (NASB)

> The scepter shall not depart from Judah, nor the ruler's staff from between his feet; so that tribute shall come to him and the homage of peoples be his. (JPS '85)

If the "He" who will destroy the devil and be a blessing to the whole world will be a *king*, then this blessing/prophecy tells us that he must be of the tribe of Judah (Jacob's fourth son). Judah's descendants will be the future kings of Israel. From these a mighty king will come who is identified (if the NASB is correct) as "Shiloh," whom the peoples of the world will honor and obey. The Septuagint[70] has a rendering similar to the JPS above (the original translators perhaps had שֶׁלוֹ [lit., "who to him"] instead of שִׁילֹה in the [now lost] Hebrew text that they had before them): "until there come the things stored up for him."[71] I lean towards understanding this as a name or an appellation indicating what he will do and/or be.[72] "Shiloh" appears to be related to the word for "peace" (*shalom*), which is something that the Messiah will one day bless the nations with. And it must be more than a coincidence that the city where the Tabernacle and Ark of the Covenant (which supported the Mercy Seat, the "throne" of YHWH) ended up after the Exodus was named "Shiloh."[73] In any case, the blessing/prophecy clearly bestows royal leadership upon the tribe of Judah, and strongly indicates that someone from that tribe "at the end of days" will rule "the peoples" of the world.

So let us take stock. If we had been on the earth at the time of Jacob, and somehow knew about the promises that were much later gathered into the Bible

---

[70] Ancient Greek translation of the Tanakh ca. 200 BC.

[71] L. C. L. Brenton, *The Septuagint Version of the Old Testament: English Translation* (London: S. Bagster and Sons, 1870), Gen 49:10.

[72] Gesenius suggests that שִׁילֹה is based upon שָׁלֵי (which means something like "quietness" or "privacy"). Thus, perhaps Shiloh means "the peaceable one" or "peace-maker." (Wilhelm Gesenius and Samuel P. Tregelles, *Gesenius' Hebrew and Chaldee Lexicon to the Old Testament Scriptures* [Bellingham: Logos Bible Software, 2003].) This might remind us of Solomon, whose name is based on *shalom* (Solomon being a *type* of the Messiah). Also worthy of note is that the Messiah described in Isa 9:6 is called the "Prince of Peace."

[73] Josh 18:1

(and assuming that we believed in God and trusted that he would work hard to somehow rescue us out of this wretched world), then we would perceive that God would one day work through a king who would bless the world with eternal peace through his conquering of the devil, evil, and death. We would think about the "He" who would bruise Satan's head; we would ponder the fact that God had told Abraham that "in you" (singular) all nations would be blessed; and we would note with much interest that some future descendent of Abraham, Isaac, Jacob, and Judah would be some-ONE named "Shiloh," whose glory and power would bring about the submission of the whole world; yet this "lion" (Gen 49:9) would be humble enough to ride the foal of a donkey (Gen 49:11).[74] Finally, we would wonder if future events and/or prophecies would tell us more about this special man.

Of course, we know now that later events did do much to fill in the messianic "forensic picture." But substantial prophetic additions to this picture were not forthcoming until the time of David, about 800 years later. We will soon consider these additions; but first, we should learn a little about the intervening time—of Moses and the Exodus, the conquest and the time of "the judges"—when God made regular appearances in physical form in order to guide, instruct, and protect the young nation of Israel.

THE ANGEL OF THE LORD GUARDS THE GODLY SEED

One of the names of the Messiah is "God with us" (*immanuel*—Isa 7:14). Certainly God was with his chosen people right from the start, with Abraham, Isaac, Jacob, and with the Israelites in Egypt. What happened during the 430 years that Israel spent in Egypt is not recorded in the Tanakh (other than they multiplied rapidly and were enslaved by the Egyptians—Exod 1), but as the Tanakh picks up the story at the end of that period, we see that God is definitely with his people as he leads them out of Egypt into the Sinai wilderness and finally into the Promised Land. And he remains with his people during the era of the judges (another 400 years) and beyond. On many occasions during this time, God appears and speaks, but in most cases we don't know *how* he spoke or appeared. But there are several exceptions, and the details are sometimes vivid. YHWH appears as fire, smoke, and nonspecific human-appearing form; but the preeminent physical manifestation of YHWH is in the form of "the Angel of the LORD." As we briefly consider the activity of this Angel, we

---

[74] Compare with Zech 9:9: "Rejoice greatly, O daughter of Zion! Shout in triumph, O daughter of Jerusalem! Behold, your king is coming to you; He is just and endowed with salvation, humble, and mounted on a donkey, even on a colt, the foal of a donkey." Jesus made his final entry into Jerusalem on a young donkey (Matt 21:1-10; Mark 11:1-10; Luke 19:28-38; John 12:12-16).

should keep in mind what Jacob said, just before he died, in blessing the sons of Joseph (Gen 48:15-16):

> The God before whom my fathers Abraham and Isaac walked, the God who has been my shepherd all my life to this day, the angel who has redeemed me from all evil, bless the lads.[75]

In Jacob's view, God and the Angel were the same. This God-Angel had shepherded Jacob and had "redeemed" him—but one only redeems another at one's own personal cost.

I'm sure Moses would have agreed with Jacob's view, for Moses (also a shepherd) was led mightily by YHWH and protected from "all evil." Moses came close to not surviving infancy, for Pharaoh had decreed the death of all Israelite baby boys. They were to be thrown alive into the Nile.[76] But Moses' mother and sister craftily engineered his "salvation": they cast off Moses into the Nile in a little boat knowing that Pharaoh's daughter was bathing just downstream. Their long-shot hope was fulfilled when Pharaoh's daughter, out of compassion, fetched Moses out of the river.[77] So Moses' pattern of life was analogous to Joseph: sold down the river, so to speak, then elevated to the court of Pharaoh. But Moses' royal status wasn't to last long: when he became a young man, he killed a fellow Egyptian, and as a result had to flee the wrath of Pharaoh. His flight took him to the eastern edge of the Sinai Peninsula where he was taken in by a Midianite family.[78] One day while he tended the family's flock near "Horeb," that is, Mount Sinai, the Tanakh records the following:

> The angel of the LORD appeared to him in a blazing fire from the midst of a bush; and he looked, and behold, the bush was burning with fire, yet the bush was not consumed. So Moses said, "I must turn aside now and see this marvelous sight, why the bush is not burned up." When the LORD saw that he turned aside to look, God called to him from the midst of the bush and said, "Moses, Moses!" And he said, "Here I am." Then He said, "Do not come near here; remove your sandals from your feet, for the place on which you are

---

[75] הַמַּלְאָךְ הַגֹּאֵל אֹתִי מִכָּל־רָע ("the angel who has redeemed me from all evil"). The Hebrew says here that this God-Angel is "the one who redeems" (ha-goel), meaning that the help given is given sacrificially. Under the Mosaic Law the "kinsman-redeemer" (goel) was called such because he gave of himself in order to save his deceased brother's name from extinction (Deut 25:5-10; Ruth 3:9). The general principle applies to the situation between God and man: In order to save man from the penalty incurred by his sins, God must act as "the one who redeems" (ha-goel), that is, he must pay in some satisfactory substitutionary manner the penalty due for man's sins (Job 19:25; Ps 49:7; Isa 59:20).

[76] Exod 1:22
[77] Exod 2:1-10
[78] Exod 2:11-22

standing is holy ground." He said also, "I am the God of your father, the God of Abraham, the God of Isaac, and the God of Jacob." Then Moses hid his face, for he was afraid to look at God.[79]

So much could be said about this, but for our purposes, we need only take note of the remarkable equivalence between the Angel of YHWH and YHWH. Later in Scripture, the Angel of YHWH will appear as a man, but here, he appears as fire in the midst of the bush. At this point, Moses had been shepherding on behalf of his adopted Midianite family for forty years,[80] so he had a lot of time to think about God and about his own situation and the impossibility of ever seeing his own people again. But nothing is impossible with God: "Certainly I will be with you, and this shall be the sign to you that it is I who have sent you: when you have brought the people out of Egypt, you shall worship God at this mountain."[81] Thus said YHWH who, the text says, was in the fire; the same YHWH who called to Moses out of the fire as the Angel of YHWH. For it says that "The angel of the LORD appeared to him in a blazing fire from the midst of a bush," then says that "God called to him from the midst of the bush."[82] The Angel of YHWH "appeared" and, after telling Moses to remove his sandals, testified, "I am the God of your father, the God of Abraham, the God of Isaac, and the God of Jacob." The text is straightforward: the Angel of God is in the fire, and God is in the fire, and this God-Angel is the God of the patriarchs and of Israel.

As in the past, God appears out of concern for his people, Israel, and more specifically, for the maintenance of the special bloodline that will one day produce the Messiah. God commissioned the reluctant Moses to lead his people out of Egypt so that they would not be consumed by that "iron furnace"[83] and the royal seed lost (and, thus, the crusher of Satan's head lost, and mankind thereby doomed to perpetual separation from God).

When Moses led Israel out of Egypt, God was made manifest in the form of a pillar of cloud which led the million-plus people by day, and a pillar of fire that led them at night.[84] When they came to Mount Sinai (where God had

---

[79] Exod 3:2-6

[80] Acts 7:23, 30; Exod 7:7

[81] Exod 3:12

[82] This feature of God speaking of himself in the first person and in the third person is reflected in the revealing of his name. God first identifies himself to Moses (Exod 3:14) as "I AM" and a few moments later (3:15) as YHWH, which most commentators understand to mean "HE IS." Here, God identifies himself to Moses as "I AM who I AM," and forty years later God says to the Israelites through Moses, "I, I AM HE" (Deut 32:39). See Isaac A. Dorner, *A System of Christian Doctrine* (Edinburgh: T & T Clark, 1883), 346.

[83] Deut 4:20

[84] In Exod 13:21-22, God goes before Israel in the pillar of cloud/fire. In Exod 14:19, the "Angel of God" is said to go before Israel, and then the Angel and the pillar of cloud move to behind the people when they are threatened by Pharaoh and his army.

given Moses the original commission), God appeared as (or in) fire, smoke, lighting, thunder, and cacophonous noise around the top of the mountain.[85] But when Moses went up on the mountain, and when Moses went to the "tent of meeting" (where he met with God before the Tabernacle was built), it seems to be the case that he met with God "face to face," as "a man speaks with his friend."[86] Even the seventy elders and Aaron and his sons who went up on Sinai with Moses saw a human-like manifestation of God:

> [T]hey saw the God of Israel; and under His feet there appeared to be a pavement of sapphire, as clear as the sky itself. Yet He did not stretch out His hand against the nobles of the sons of Israel; and they saw God, and they ate and drank.[87]

One wonders if these men "ate and drank" *with* "the God of Israel." Be that as it may, "they saw God" and he did not "stretch out his hand" against them (i.e., God did not kill them). These cases of seeing God in human form seem to go somewhat against the grain of what YHWH told Moses (after he and Israel had spent some months at Mt. Sinai) when Moses asked to see YHWH's full glory:

> "You cannot see My face, for no man can see Me and live!" Then the LORD said, "Behold, there is a place by Me, and you shall stand there on the rock; and it will come about, while My glory is passing by, that I will put you in the cleft of the rock and cover you with My hand until I have passed by. Then I will take My hand away and you shall see My back, but My face shall not be seen."[88]

So in this case, Moses did not see God's face; and yet, Moses did meet with God "face to face" on many occasions.

As the story of Moses continues through the forty years of wilderness wanderings, the narrative of the proceedings of Israel does not mention the "Angel of the LORD"; although it is clear that God remains with them until the death of Moses and after. If at the burning bush, YHWH and the Angel of YHWH were the same God speaking out of the fire, then it follows that as God was subsequently with the nation, so was the Angel of YHWH. What God said while Israel was still at Sinai seems to verify this:

> Behold, I am going to send an angel before you to guard you along the way and to bring you into the place which I have prepared. Be on your guard before him and obey his voice; do not be rebellious

---

[85] Exod 19-20
[86] Exod 33:11; Num 12:8; Deut 34:10
[87] Exod 24:10-11
[88] Exod 33:20-23

toward him, for he will not pardon your transgression, since My name is in him.[89]

This Angel, according to the LORD, has great power and authority: he has the power to preserve the whole nation such that they arrive intact at the threshold of Canaan, and he has the authority to forgive or not to forgive sins. It would seem that only God can do these things.[90]

The Angel of the LORD reappears at the end of the wilderness era, not directly to Moses or the people of Israel, who had just arrived on the "plains of Moab" just short of the Promised Land, but to an enigmatic Aramean named Balaam.[91] Why did the Angel appear to Balaam and not to his own people? Not because he wanted to help Balaam, but because he wanted to protect his people from Balaam.[92] As always, God and the Angel of YHWH work for the protection of Israel and its Holy Seed. Balaam was apparently an internationally known diviner and prophet, and so Barak, the king of Moab who greatly feared the Israelites, desperately wanted Balaam to come and magically curse the "horde" which had invaded his land. Again, much could be said about this disturbing (and sometimes humorous) story, but we will stick to the pertinent facts.

King Balak sent envoys to bring Balaam to Moab.[93] They offered him a handsome "fee for divination," but YHWH said to Balaam after Balaam sought his counsel: "Do not go with them; you shall not curse the people, for they are blessed."[94] King Balak wouldn't take no for an answer, so he sweetened the deal

---

[89] Exod 23:20-23. In several places in the Tanakh, God's "name" is said to occupy the place where YHWH is, e.g., the tabernacle at Shiloh (Jer 7:12), Jerusalem (1 Kings 11:36), and the Temple (1 Kings 9:3). For YHWH's name to be there is the same as saying YHWH is there. As YHWH's name dwells in the temple, so YHWH's name dwells in the Angel that goes before Israel. The Angel of YHWH whom YHWH sends ahead of Israel in Exod 23, and the "Presence" (lit. "Face") of YHWH who will go up with Israel to the Promised Land (Exod 33:14), are equivalent (this confirmed by Isa 63:9). The angel mentioned by God in Exod 33:2 is not the Angel of YHWH, but a created angel (see Ernst Hengstenberg, *Christology of the Old Testament*, trans. Theodore Meyer [London: T. & T. Clark, 1868], 1:126-128). Among *living* beings, only the Angel of Exod 23 is said to have God's name within him.

[90] Regarding God's command to "obey his voice," it is interesting that at the end of his mission, Moses said: "The LORD your God will raise up for you a prophet like me from among you, from your countrymen, you shall listen to him" (Deut 18:18), which is the same as saying, "you shall obey him." At the time of John the Baptist, the Pharisees were aware of "the Prophet" like Moses who was to come (see John 1). In Jesus' high priestly prayer—prayed just before his death—he twice said that the name of the Father had been given to him (Luke 17:11-12). Moses and Jesus were similar in several remarkable ways: Both came out of Egypt; both interceded for their wicked countrymen; both were rejected by their people; although neither was of the house of Aaron, both functioned as priests; and both were great prophets. See Rachmiel Frydland, *What the Rabbis Know about the Messiah* (Messianic Publishing Co., 1991), chap. 7.

[91] Num 22

[92] Josh 24:9-10

[93] Num 22

[94] Num 22:12

and sent envoys again, more distinguished than the first, who essentially offered Balaam a blank check, if he would just come. Now Balaam had already heard from God—"Do not go"—but Balaam, apparently craving the notoriety and fabulous reward, sought God's counsel again, perhaps thinking that God might change his mind. It seems that Balaam was going to figure out a way to go one way or the other, so God "changed" his mind, and gave him the green light: "That night God came to Balaam and said, 'if the men have come to call you, rise up and go with them; but only the word which I speak to you shall you do.'"[95] But the LORD was not happy with Balaam. Note here that it is God who gives him the command to only speak God's words. So Balaam saddled up his donkey and headed south with Balak's embassy. While he was on his way to Moab, the Angel of YHWH, with his sword drawn, met Balaam with the intention of killing him. Balaam's donkey saw the Angel first, indicating that the spiritual state of the donkey was superior to her master's. The narrative shows that both the Angel and Balaam were well aware of the diviner's duplicitous motives: He acted like he wanted to honor God, but deep within he lusted after the reward promised by the king, even if that meant doing harm to a million or more of God's people.

> Balaam said to the angel of the LORD, "I have sinned, for I did not know that you were standing in the way against me. Now then, if it is displeasing to you, I will turn back." But the angel of the LORD said to Balaam, "Go with the men, but you shall speak only the word which I tell you." So Balaam went along with the leaders of Balak.[96]

God knew that Balaam's motives were not right, but with his perfect foreknowledge, he also knew that whatever evil Balaam might do, he would work it all out for the good of his people. What we should especially notice here is that when God first permitted him to go, God told him to only speak his (God's) words. But later when the Angel of YHWH—who appears in human-like form, with sword drawn—opposes the diviner, the Angel commands him to speak only his (the Angel's) words. And we should also notice that when Balaam finally met King Balak at the border of Moab, he said: "Behold, I have come now to you! Am I able to speak anything at all? The word that God puts in my mouth, that I shall speak."[97] Balaam went on to speak the words that YHWH put in his mouth, and reiterated several times to Balak that this was the only thing that he could do. This story makes it clear that YHWH's words were also the Angel of YHWH's words. And both YHWH and the Angel of

---

[95] Num 22:20
[96] Num 22:34-35
[97] Num 22:38

YHWH were not fooled by Balaam's seeming obedience in pronouncing blessings over Israel instead of curses.

Not long after this incident, the army of Israel defeated Sihon, king of the Amorites (and the Midianite kings associated with him), and took his land.[98] In the process of this, Balaam, who had apparently sojourned in Midian after he fulfilled his contract with King Balak, was killed with the sword.[99] The reason why was this: Balaam did not curse Israel, and thus greatly disappointed King Balak; but according to what Moses said after the Amorites and Midianites were defeated, Balaam did advise the Midianite women (and because the Moabites were allies, the Moabite women) to lead the Israelite men into fornication and idolatry.[100] And this is what happened in the "affair of Peor": thousands of the men of Israel were led into idol worship by women of Midian and Moab while Israel dwelt upon the plains of Moab, and, as a consequence, God punished Israel with a plague that killed 24,000.[101] And because Midian had so conspired against Israel, God, through the army of Israel, killed all their men and most of their women. All this because Balaam spoke words that YHWH/the Angel of YHWH had not commanded him to speak. Words that harmed God's people. So the LORD slew him.

When Joshua first led the Israelites over the Jordan River into the Promised Land, he met "the Commander of YHWH's army."[102] This Commander, like the Angel of YHWH who opposed Balaam, had his sword drawn; and this Commander told Joshua to remove his sandals, just like the Angel of YHWH in the burning bush commanded the same of Moses, for in both cases the ground upon which they stood was "holy ground."[103] It is surely the case that this Commander of YHWH's army was the Angel of YHWH. As this Commander-Angel commissioned Moses at the start of his ministry, so he commissioned Joshua at the start of his. And as to the life of Moses, the Angel of YHWH appears as bookends that enclose a life well lived: God personally gave Moses his commission, and God personally buried Moses when he died after observing the Promised Land from the top of Mount Nebo—the Land that the LORD did not allow him to enter during his earthly life.[104]

---

[98] See Num 22:4; Num 31; Josh 13:21-22

[99] Josh 13:21-22

[100] Num 31:16

[101] Num 25

[102] Josh 5:14 (my translation)

[103] Joshua bowed before the Commander of YHWH's army and called him "Lord." When YHWH visited Abraham at the trees of Mamre (Gen 18), the patriarch bowed down before him and called him "Lord." David much later in his vision of heaven called the Messiah sitting at the right hand of YHWH "Lord" (Ps 110:1).

[104] Deut 34

The Angel of YHWH appears three times in the book of Judges—that is, three times during the 350 or so years (when judges ruled the land) between the conquest and King Saul—and is not seen again until David's sinful census.[105] The first appearance in Judges occurs soon after Joshua's death. The "Commander of YHWH's army" had obviously been with Israel all along, for they nearly always had success in killing or driving out the Canaanites, Amorites, and other pagan peoples of the Promised Land. The effort, however, was overall not executed with a whole heart, for the various campaigns did not take them very far north, and even in regions where the enemy was attacked and defeated, pockets of resistance remained. God knew that these remaining idolaters would be a "snare" to the Israelites.[106] In consequence of this, the Tanakh records:

> Now the angel of the LORD came up from Gilgal to Bochim. And he said, "I brought you up out of Egypt and led you into the land which I have sworn to your fathers; and I said, 'I will never break My covenant with you, and as for you, you shall make no covenant with the inhabitants of this land; you shall tear down their altars.' But you have not obeyed Me; what is this you have done? Therefore I also said, 'I will not drive them out before you; but they will become as thorns in your sides and their gods will be a snare to you.'"[107]

The Angel here clearly speaks as YHWH in the first person: "I brought you up," "I … led you," "I have sworn." It is this Angel who made the initial promises to the patriarchs, and it was the Angel who got Israel out of Egypt and got them successfully into the Promised Land. The Angel testifies of what he had previously commanded: "*I* said … 'you shall make no covenant with the inhabitants of this land; you shall tear down their altars.'" Yet Exod 34:12-13 records that YHWH said this, not an angel: "Watch yourself that you make no covenant with the inhabitants of the land …. But *rather*, you are to tear down their altars …." The Angel here furthermore says: "Therefore *I* also said, 'I will not drive them out before you; but they will become as thorns in your sides and their gods will be a snare to you." But Joshua indicated not long before that it would be YHWH who would cease from driving out the nations before Israel if the Israelites got too cozy with the peoples they had failed to destroy:

> Know with certainty that the LORD your God will not continue to drive these nations out from before you; but they will be a snare and a trap to you, and a whip on your sides and thorns in your eyes, until

---

[105] Judg 2:1-5; 6:11-24; 13; 2 Sam 24
[106] Josh 11; Judg 1:27-36; 2:20-23; 3:1-6
[107] Judg 2:1-3

you perish from off this good land which the LORD your God has given you.[108]

There can be no doubt that the Angel of YHWH (once he arrived in Bochim) speaks in the first person as God, and with all the authority of God. Did he appear here in human form? The text doesn't say, although the fact that he "came up from Gilgal (near Jericho) to Bokim" (somewhere up on the ridge west of Jericho) gives the appearance of a human being making the physically demanding uphill journey. Be that as it may, the next two appearances of the Angel of YHWH in the book of Judges are clearly in human form, as we shall now see.

The LORD's watch-care over his people is evident through the book of Judges, despite their cycles of great sin. Ignoring the warnings of Moses and Joshua, the people not long after the death of the latter turned away from YHWH and went a-whoring after the gods of the indigenous Canaanites.[109] So God, out of love, chastised them by sending various marauding foreign kings and their armies. And because of his compassion and grace, he would raise up capable men—and a woman—to lead them in overcoming their oppressors. And after the victory, Israel would serve YHWH for a season before turning again to their baser instincts, and the cycle of oppression followed by deliverance through a new judge would begin again.

The first oppressor was Cushan-rishathaim, king of "Aram of the two rivers," a region somewhere in ancient Mesopotamia. He put Israel under his feet for eight years; but Othniel became infused with the Spirit of YHWH and threw off this yoke.[110] After some time, the people again "did evil in the sight of the LORD," so the LORD empowered Eglon, king of Moab, along with the Ammonites and Amalekites, to fight against and defeat the men of Israel. But God took compassion on his people and raised up the left-handed warrior Ehud to assassinate the Moabite king and lead his people to overthrow the Moabite domination.[111] Again, the land found rest for a season, but Israel must have sinned yet again for they came under the control of the Philistines, whose cities were mainly on the coast. Again the people were in misery, so God used "Shamgar the son of Anath, who struck down six hundred Philistines with an oxgoad," and Israel was saved yet again.[112] In the next depressing cycle, Israel

---

[108] Josh 23:13
[109] Deut 28; Josh 23-24
[110] Judg 3:7-10. Othniel was the nephew of Caleb. Joshua and Caleb were the only spies who brought back a good report (Num 13:30; 14:6-9). Because of that, the LORD decreed that, of all the adult men at that time, they would be the only ones to survive the forty years of wilderness wonderings and enter the Promised Land (Num 14:24, 30; Deut 1:34-38).
[111] Judg 3:12-30
[112] Judg 3:31

came under the control of Jabin, king of the Canaanites in Hazor, and his army commander Sisera. The prophetess Deborah was judge at the time. At the command of the LORD, she commissioned Barak to muster an army which soon thereafter defeated Sisera and his army by the river Kishon in the Jezreel Valley. At the end of the battle, a gentile woman named Jael, who was sympathetic towards Israel, killed General Sisera who had fled the battlefield. Whilst he slept, exhausted, in her tent, she drove a tent peg through his temple. Thus, the honor of victory went to a woman and not to Barak.[113] While the battle between Barak and Sisera raged, the men of Maroz, an Israelite town in the vicinity of the battle, held back from helping their brothers. As a result, the Angel of YHWH, who had always been intensely concerned about Israel and the preservation of its Holy Seed, condemned the town for its cowardice and unfaithfulness:

> "Curse Meroz," said the angel of the LORD, "Utterly curse its inhabitants; because they did not come to the help of the LORD, to the help of the LORD against the warriors."[114]

Israel went on to defeat and kill King Jabin which ended the Canaanite oppression and ushered in forty years of peace. But, true to form, Israel again "did what was evil in the sight of the LORD," so "the LORD gave them into the hands of Midian seven years."[115] It was during this time that the Angel of the LORD commissioned a man named Gideon to save his people (Judg 6).

The Midianites, along with their allies the Amalekites and other "sons of the east," invaded Israel like a swarm of "locusts."[116] Being nomadic peoples of the eastern desert, they brought their livestock and camels, which, being "innumerable," decimated the crops of the Israelites.[117] Things got so bad that the chosen people took to living in caves. Sadly, this was a family conflict, for the Midianites (whom Israel had already come close to annihilating just before their entry into the Promised Land) were the descendants of Midian who was one of the sons of Keturah, whom Abraham took as a concubine about the time that Sarah died.[118] Keturah had six sons by Abraham. The extent that they partook of the promises that God made to their father (regarding seed, blessing, blessing to all nations, land) is revealed in Gen 25:5-6:

---

[113] Judg 4
[114] Judg 5:23. We typically understand that God helps us in our battles. We learn here that the missions of God and his faithful followers are mysteriously mutually supportive.
[115] Judg 4:24; 6:1
[116] Judg 6:5
[117] Judg 6:5
[118] Gen 25:1-2

> Now Abraham gave all that he had to Isaac; but to the sons of his concubines, Abraham gave gifts while he was still living, and sent them away from his son Isaac eastward, to the land of the east.

In other words, while the sons of Keturah (and, earlier, Hagar), as sons of Abraham, obtained benefits, they were not to be heirs; for only through the miracle son of Abraham's wife Sarah, that is, Isaac, were his descendants (lit. "seed") to be reckoned.[119] In the half-millennium between Abraham and the Exodus, the descendants of Midian, who took the name of their forefather, became numerous in the steppe and desert areas east and south of the Promised Land. Jethro, the man who took in the fugitive Moses and gave him his daughter, Zipporah, to wife, was a Midianite and "priest of Midian."[120] But eighty years later when Moses and Israel arrived at the plains of Moab, just short of their goal, Midian did not help them, but sought their harm.[121] Maybe this was partly due to a long-simmering brotherly jealousy. And perhaps because of this jealousy and because Israel nearly annihilated Midian as a result of the "sin of Peor" on the eve of the conquest, the Midianites at the time of Gideon (about 200 years after the conquest) were eager to wreak havoc on Israel.

God chose the "valiant warrior" Gideon to lead his people in overcoming the Midian invasion,[122] so that an illegitimate line of Abrahamic descendants would not annihilate the legitimate line—for the bloodline of the Holy Seed had to be preserved. The Angel of YHWH, according to the Tanakh, came to Gideon while he was threshing wheat in a wine press; that is, threshing wheat not on a hilltop where the wind could blow the chaff away, but in a lower more concealed place that would not be easily seen by the Midianites. The Angel of YHWH came to Gideon and sat under an Oak tree, and—calling him not so much what he was then, but what he would be—said: "The LORD is with you, O valiant warrior."[123] Gideon immediately seemed to recognize that his surprise visitor was a messenger from God. So he took the opportunity to express his doubts about God's care for him and his people, for they were wasting away under the marauding Midianites. Despite his lack of faith, Gideon was given a very special mission by the Angel: "The LORD looked at him and said, 'Go in this your strength and deliver Israel from the hand of Midian. Have I not sent

---

[119] Gen 21:12; Heb 11:18. The quasi-illegitimacy of the children of Abraham's concubines is not what ultimately excludes from being full heirs. Of Isaac's children, one became the full heir, Jacob, and the other, even though a legitimate child of Isaac and Rebecca, was marginalized. As God says in Mal 1:2-3, "I have loved Jacob; but I have hated Esau." Full heirs are those who are chosen by God and righteous in his eyes. This is especially true regarding the *spiritual* meaning of heirship, i.e., salvation.

[120] Num 10:29; Exod 2:16

[121] Num 31:15-16

[122] Judg 6

[123] Judg 6:12

you?'"[124] Gideon (like Moses), however, expressed doubt about his ability to carry out such a mission. "But the LORD said to him, 'Surely I will be with you, and you shall defeat Midian as one man.'"[125] Still skeptical, Gideon doubted that YHWH was really in the angel who spoke to him—this angel who apparently looked like a man, for he "*sat*" under the Oak tree, had a "staff … in *his hand*," and spoke with Gideon "*face to face*."[126] So he asked for a "sign" of confirmation.[127] After Gideon had brought an offering of goat meat, unleavened bread, and broth to the Angel, the Angel satisfied Gideon's desire for a confirming sign: with a touch of the tip of his staff, the Angel incinerated the offering and then vanished from sight. With this, Gideon, with amazed relief, was convinced: "O my, O Lord YHWH! For I have seen the angel of YHWH face to face."[128] The *thought* here is certainly the same as that expressed by Jacob (and Manoah, see just below) after he survived the night of wrestling with the mystery man: "I have seen God face to face, yet my life has been preserved."[129] Most important for us to note in the Gideon story is that the Angel spoke in the first person ("I") as YHWH: "The LORD looked at him and said …. 'Have I not sent you?'" Did he appear as a man? The description is quite anthropomorphic, but we can't know for sure. But some time later, in another turn of the wheel, the Angel of YHWH did appear again (Judg 13) to facilitate the preservation of the Holy Seed, and there is much evidence to show that he appeared as a human being.

Gideon indeed led Israel to defeat the Midianites and push them out of the Promised Land. But about a century later we find Israel again, because of apostasy and idolatry, under the thumb of a heathen nation—this time the coast-dwelling Philistines.[130] In concern over the preservation of Israel and the Holy Seed who would one day crush the head of Satan, God again intervened by sending his Angel, but on this occasion, to the parents of the one who would begin to deliver Israel (i.e., Samson) from the Philistines. The Angel of YHWH first appeared to the future mother (who remains unnamed through the story) of Israel's savior, and then a little later to both the mother and her husband Manoah. They had been unable to have children, but the Angel—stamping his testimony with the miraculous and the divine—told the woman that she would

---

[124] Judg 6:14
[125] Judg 6:16
[126] Judg 6:11, 21-22
[127] Judg 6:16
[128] Judg 6:22, my translation
[129] Gen 32:30. When Sarah chased away the pregnant Hagar out of the camp (Gen 16), Hagar was visited by the Angel of YHWH. The Angel spoke as God in the first person ("I will greatly multiply your descendants" v. 10). After the appearance, Hagar expressed surprise that she survived the encounter (v. 13): "Then she called the name of the LORD who spoke to her, 'You are a God who sees'; for she said, 'Have I even remained alive here after seeing Him?'"
[130] Judg 13:1

soon conceive and have a son. The Angel decreed that the son would be a *Nazarite* from birth (the woman understood this to be from birth until death), that is, a man totally consecrated to the service of God (which meant, among other things, that he should never cut his hair).[131] And the woman was told that her son would "begin to deliver Israel out of the hands of the Philistines." When the Angel of YHWH appeared a little later to both Manoah and his wife, the Angel basically repeated what he had already said to the woman alone. In response, Manoah offered to prepare a meal—a "young goat"—for the visitor, but the Angel told him to offer it up instead as a burnt offering to the LORD.[132] Manoah complied, and as the fire and smoke rose up from the altar, the Angel arose with it and disappeared. "When Manoah and his wife saw this, they fell on their faces to the ground," and realized at that point that they had been visited by God: "And Manoah said to his wife, 'We shall surely die, because we have seen God!'"[133] But Manoah's wife reasoned thus:

> If the LORD had desired to kill us, He would not have accepted a burnt offering and a grain offering from our hands, nor would He have shown us all these things, nor would He have let us hear things like this at this time.[134]

Note here that the antecedent of the three uses of "He" in this text is "the LORD." In the story, it was the Angel of YHWH who accepted the offering and who gave the wonderful news regarding things happening then and things to come. And it was a divine miracle in their eyes for the Angel to arise and disappear in the flames that went heavenward from Manoah's altar.

The narrative makes plain that, while the Angel was with them, neither Manoah nor his wife recognized him as an angel or as YHWH. After the woman first saw the Angel and spoke with him, she told her husband that she had seen a "man of God" and that he appeared "like the appearance of the angel of God, very awesome."[135] In other words, she perceived him as a man who looked like an angel. When the Angel later appeared to both Manoah and his wife, Manoah asked him, "Are You the Man who spoke to the woman?" The Angel answered, "I am."[136] Further evidence that they perceived that the Angel was a man was the desire of Manoah to "prepare a young goat" for the strange visitor—whom they apparently believed to be a prophet (indicated by the

---

[131] The law of the Nazarite, laid down in Num 6:1-21, stipulated that the man voluntarily taking this vow of consecration to God should not cut his hair, drink wine, nor become defiled by coming into contact with a human corpse.

[132] Judg 13:15-16

[133] Judg 13:20, 22

[134] Judg 13:23

[135] Judg 13:6

[136] Judg 13:11

woman calling him a "man of God," which here and there in the Tanakh refers to a prophet of God). Their incomplete perception of "the man" began to change, perhaps, when they heard the Angel's response to Manoah's query about his name: "The angel of the LORD said to him, 'Why do you ask my name, seeing it is wonderful?'"[137] This answer is enigmatic; but there is something appropriate about it, given what the Angel said and did, and something supernatural. One cannot help comparing this answer with a portion of the name given to the Messiah about four centuries later by the prophet Isaiah: "And his name will be ... wonderful."[138] The Hebrew word that Isaiah uses, *pele*, is closely related to that used by the Angel, both denoting something stupendously and miraculously wonderful, yet to some extent, incomprehensible.[139]

So the "man of God" was "wonderful," something Manoah and his wife no doubt realized when the Angel went up in the fire and when they perceived that they had seen God and yet their lives were spared. And the "wonderful" nature of the Angel was especially understood when the prophecy was fulfilled through the miraculous birth of Samson—who, indeed, "[began] to deliver Israel from the hands of the Philistines."[140] God appeared to Manoah and his wife as a man, albeit one that looked, in Manoah's wife's view, like an "angel of God, very awesome."[141]

There is one more appearance of the Angel of YHWH (before the time of Solomon) that seems like the bookend enclosing the period of the conquest and the judges: Upon entering the Promised Land, Joshua was met by the "Commander of YHWH's army" who had his sword drawn and who declared that Joshua was standing upon holy ground; four centuries later the Angel of YHWH appeared to David, with his sword drawn ready to destroy Jerusalem.[142] After David repented of his vainglory that prompted his ordering of a nationwide census, and after God sent a plague as punishment, the king was instructed by God to build an altar atop the rocky ridge upon which the avenging Angel stood, a place called "Mount Moriah" where the Temple would one day be built—that is, a place of "holy ground." One detail in this appearance of the Angel is interesting: as the Angel is killing thousands of the people, "from Dan to Beersheba," and is just about to annihilate Jerusalem, the

[137] Judg 13:18
[138] Isa 9:6
[139] Isaiah calls the Messiah פֶּלֶא, and the Angel calls himself פִּלְאִי. According to Strong's Lexicon, both nouns are based upon פָּלָא (Strongs # 6381), a verb meaning, according to BDB, "be surpassing, extraordinary." The Judaica Bible translates *pele* in Judg 13:18 as "hidden"; JPS '85, "unknowable."
[140] Judg 13:5
[141] Judg 13:6
[142] 2 Sam 24; 1 Chron 21

Tanakh records: "the LORD relented from the calamity and said to the angel who destroyed the people, 'It is enough! Now relax your hand!'"[143] The Angel here seems to be a different person than YHWH. When the Angel of YHWH visited and spoke to Gideon, the narrative says that YHWH spoke; when the Angel of YHWH visited Manoah and his wife, the narrative says that the Angel of YHWH spoke; when the Angel of YHWH appeared to David after the census, YHWH spoke to the Angel, ordering him to stay his slaying hand. Yet the command given to David (through the prophet Gad) to build the altar at the threshing floor of Araunah the Jebusite (on Mt. Moriah, where the Angel of YHWH stood) is at one point said to have been given by YHWH (2 Sam 24:19; 1 Chron 21:19) and at another point said to have been given by the Angel of YHWH (1 Chron 21:18).

The appearances of the Angel of YHWH in general reveal an ambiguity regarding the question about whether the Angel of YHWH is the same person as YHWH or a different person. As we have already seen, the Angel of YHWH who spoke to Moses out of the burning bush spoke in the first person as YHWH; yet later YHWH spoke about his Angel, in the third person, who he planned to send ahead of Israel on their way to the Promised Land.[144] All of the cases that have been cited so far involve physical-appearing manifestations of YHWH or the Angel of YHWH (e.g., "fire," "smoke," "hand," "feet," "man"). Most of these cases feature the physio-audible voice of YHWH or the Angel of YHWH. And in three of the events, the Angel of YHWH has his sword drawn.[145] These appearances of God prove, by the authority of Scripture, that God can manifest himself in time and space in what appears to human beings as material substance. Also strongly indicated by these historical narratives is a mysterious identity between the Angel of YHWH and YHWH that exists alongside what appears to be non-identity. "The Angel of YHWH appeared" to Moses in the fire of a desert bush, and out of that fire the Angel said, "I am the God of your father, the God of Abraham."[146] The Angel of YHWH appeared to David on Mount Moriah, and YHWH commanded the Angel to cease his destruction of the Israelites and their capital city.[147] YHWH is One; yet there is mysterious composition within this unity that comprises the One God.

Does the Angel of the LORD resemble the Messiah in some ways? A few interesting observations can briefly be made. In nearly all of his physical appearances so far, God in one way or another protects people who believe in

---

[143] 2 Sam 24:16
[144] Exod 3, 23
[145] Num 22:23; Josh 5:13; 1 Chron 21:16
[146] Exod 3:2, 6
[147] 2 Sam 24:15-17

and honor God, and through this, God protects the Holy Seed that will one day destroy Satan, sin, and death. Of course, much of this protection is given to the sons of Abraham, Isaac, and Jacob—that is, to the people of *Israel*, who, though far from perfect, believe in and honor God. The LORD, who walked in the Garden with Adam and Eve, covered the guilty pair with animal skins; the LORD locked Noah and his family safely in the Ark when the rain began; the LORD provided a miraculous son for Abraham through whom would come one who would bless the whole world; the LORD protected Jacob from Esau and changed his name to the name of the new godly nation; the LORD preserved Israel by commissioning Moses to bring them out of Egypt; the LORD went before Israel for forty years in the desert; the LORD kept Balaam from cursing Israel; the LORD fought Israel's battles as Joshua led them into the Promised Land; the LORD raised up Gideon to save Israel from the Midianites; the LORD raised up Samson to save Israel from the Philistines; and finally, the LORD punished David and Israel in order to save them from themselves—that is, to chastise them so that they would in the future rely on the LORD and not on themselves. As this study proceeds, we will see that the Messiah is a man, of the royal Davidic line, who has compassion for his people and thus rules his people—and the rest of the world—with perfect righteousness and justice. God showed up in the person of the Angel of YHWH in order to protect the Holy Seed that led to the Messiah; this study will try to show that then God shows up in the person of the Messiah in order that the rest of mankind might be saved.[148] Admittedly, the fact that the Angel of YHWH saves and that the Messiah saves does not necessarily imply identity. There is one interesting piece of Scripture, however, that probably does show a mysterious identity between the Angel and the Messiah.

If we reach into the biblical future for a moment, we see in the book of Daniel (chap. 3) one more case of God's "angel" appearing at a critical moment to protect God's righteous people. And here we may see something of the Messiah in the angel, who is probably the Angel of YHWH—although as described through the pagan mind of the great Babylonian king who at about that time destroyed Jerusalem and brought Judah to an end. Nebuchadnezzar, as the story goes, had taken from Jerusalem to Babylon in the first deportation (ca. 605 BC) four teenagers (among many others) who were of the royal family.[149] The purpose was to train them in all the ways of the Chaldeans so

---

[148] It is interesting that *the* Angel of the LORD is never mentioned in the New Testament, although in a number of instances *an* angel of the LORD appears in order to inform, to guide, or to help.
[149] Given what Dan 1:3 says, it is probable that Daniel and his friends were of royal blood. This was the opinion of Josephus (NAC Dan 1:3, citing: *Antiquities*, 10. 10. 1.). Nebuchadnezzar's taking away of some of the "royal family and of the nobles" very likely

that they might serve the king's administration. Their names were Daniel, Hananiah, Mishael and Azariah; but the king gave them the Babylonian names of Beltashazzar, Shadrach, Meshach and Abed-nego.[150] A few years later when Nebuchadnezzar ordered that all bow down and worship a gigantic gold image that he had made, Daniel's three friends refused to submit, and as a result were thrown into a fiery furnace at the order of the enraged king. To Nebuchadnezzar's amazement, instead of seeing three bodies burning in the furnace, he saw four men walking about in the furnace, one of whom the king perceived as a "son of the gods," i.e., someone divine.[151] Now we must understand that while Nebuchadnezzar was then clearly no saint and without understanding of monotheism, he was nevertheless then, as well as later when he did have better knowledge and a softer heart, an instrument employed by God to work out his long-range good plans. In other words, he was God's "servant."[152] With this in mind, we can at least be open to the idea that his words recorded in this account are words that really mean something significant. So Nebuchadnezzar called the fourth man in the furnace a "son of the gods," obviously believing that he had something to do with the preservation of Shadrach, Meshach and Abed-nego.

After he called the three out from the fire, and found not even a singe mark on their clothes or hair, the king, utterly amazed, exclaimed: "Blessed be the God of Shadrach, Meshach and Abed-nego, who has sent His angel and delivered His servants who put their trust in Him!"[153] Note that Nebuchadnezzar calls the fourth man in the fire a divine "son" as well as an "angel" sent by the Hebrew God. Here, it may well be the case that the Angel of YHWH came to help people of the Holy Seed at a critical moment, just like he had previously come to help those mentioned earlier. The "House of David" in this case may have been indirectly protected in that this gave Nebuchadnezzar and his royal heirs respect for the God of Judah and for the royal Davidic line that God had chosen to lead Judah.

It should be remembered that Nebuchadnezzar's heir to the Babylonian throne, Evil-Merdoch, released King Jehoiachin out of his Babylonian prison, and treated him (and presumably his family) kindly. Jesus, according to the NT, was a legal descendant of Jehoiachin.[154] That this was the Messiah helping the three uncompromising young Jewish men in the fiery furnace is indicated

---

fulfilled the prophecy given by Isaiah to King Hezekiah that descendants of his would become "officials in the palace of the king of Babylon" (Isa 39:7).

[150] Dan 1:6-7
[151] Dan 3:25
[152] Jer 25:9; 27:6
[153] Dan 3:28
[154] 2 Kings 25:27-30; Jer 52:31-34; Matt 1:11 (Matthew calls Jehoiachin "Jechoniah").

by the angel being called a "son of the gods":[155] in addition to being a son of man, the Messiah, as we will soon see, is also declared by God (2 Sam 7:14; Ps 2:7) to be the Son of God. That this was YHWH in the form of the Angel of YHWH, is indicated by Nebuchadnezzar calling him God's "angel." Yet, at the same time, the king gave credit to the Hebrew God for the deliverance of the three young men from the fires of the furnace. One can call the furnace scene messianic, for a fourth appears among the "men" who is called a divine "son" and is called God's "angel" who saves Shadrach, Meshach and Abed-nego—yet the king gives credit to the Hebrew God for the deliverance of the young men.

Be that as it may, the messianic Tanakh texts that we will soon investigate will present to us several indications of identity between YHWH and the Messiah. This, of course, will be difficult for some to seriously consider. It will be less of a challenge to show that the Messiah is, for example, God's "Anointed" and "Servant" and "Shepherd" who will fight on Israel's behalf—"heaping up the dead"[156]—before ruling forever as the "King of kings" of Israel and all other nations. In other words, the Messiah, like YHWH, will deeply care for and ensure the survival of Israel.

THE MESSIANIC CONCEPT BLOSSOMS WITH DAVID AND THE PSALMS

As said before, the Tanakh, being God's written revelation to man, is going somewhere critically important. From Genesis' "He shall bruise you on the head" to Zechariah's "Behold, your king is coming to you … humble, and mounted on a donkey,"[157] God, it can safely be assumed, is laying out a history of, and plan for, mankind which seeks to do what is of intense interest to God and of eternal life-and-death importance to man: that is, to reconcile man back to God so that he might not perish forever.[158] As we've seen, God obviously works this history/plan out bilaterally, that is to say, in partnership with man, for from the beginning, the Holy Scripture teaches that the "seed" of Eve will one day destroy the devil, sin, and death (Gen 3:15)—which is something that reason tells us that only God can do. If we can imagine ourselves living at the time of each step of the progressive unfolding of the "forensic picture" of the Messiah that we've discussed so far, we would learn that this seed of Eve (not a "they" but a "He") would, as was told to Abraham, bless the whole world.[159]

---

[155] The Aramaic word here (*elah*) can be translated as either "gods" or "God."
[156] Ps 110:6
[157] Gen 3:15; Zech 9:9
[158] See John 3:16.
[159] Gen 12:3; 18:18; 22:18

The messianic bloodline would pass through Isaac and Jacob,[160] and the latter would reveal, through the Holy Spirit, that the bloodline would descend in the future from his son Judah: Jacob said in his blessing to Judah that he would be, of all his brothers, the royal tribe.[161] The Bible story from Judah's time onward orbits around the tribe of Judah, and this is especially so at the time of David and after. Whatever bloodline the Scripture intensely follows through the course of its historical narrative (and is the focus of prophecy) necessarily must be the bloodline of the Messiah who, in partnership with God, will bring about a reconciliation between man and God.

Meanwhile, in the biblical narrative, as God appears physically and intervenes on behalf of his people, we can be sure—because this is recorded in *Holy Scripture*—that God is superintending the maintenance and the survival of the messianic bloodline. And this is what we have seen with the appearances of the Angel of YHWH and other manifestations of God: God's angel(s) protected Jacob from Laban and Esau;[162] the Angel commissioned Moses to save Israel from the corruption of Egypt;[163] the Angel went before Israel for forty years in the wilderness and was their guardian;[164] the Angel, as "commander of YHWH's army," went before Israel into the Promised Land and fought on their behalf;[165] the Angel commissioned Gideon to save Israel from the Midianites;[166] and the Angel commissioned Samson (through his parents) to begin to save Israel from the Philistines.[167]

Before we look at the blossoming of the messianic concept with David and his psalms, a few interesting items should be considered. First, the prophecies that concern the messianic bloodline that we have looked at so far do not say anything about the Law that God gave to Moses and Israel at Mount Sinai. This, of course, could easily be explained by the fact that the prophecies (that the "seed" of Eve would bruise Satan's head, that the "seed" of Abraham would bless all nations, and that a descendant of Judah named "Shiloh" would rule "the peoples") were given long before the giving of the Law. But the appearances of the "Angel of YHWH" that occurred after the institution of the Law (to Balaam, Gideon, Manoah and his wife, and David) do not involve any discussion of the Law either. In comparison to the preservation of believing people in Israel and the Holy Seed, the ethical and ritual features of the Mosaic

---

[160] Gen 26:4; 28:14
[161] Gen 49:8-12
[162] Gen 31-32
[163] Exod 3-4
[164] Exod 23:20-23
[165] Exod 23:23; Deut 3:22; Josh 5:13-15; 10:14; 23:3
[166] Judg 6:11-24
[167] Judg 13

Law appear to be of lesser concern.[168] A couple of elements of the Angel's appearances to Gideon and Manoah seem to add legitimacy to this thought: In both cases, God, through the Angel, visited them directly, that is, without the mediation required under the Law. In other words, no Aaronic (Levitical) priest mediated. There was also no effort to have their burnt offerings presented at the Tabernacle (which was at Shiloh in those days). Offerings of meat were offered to the Angel of YHWH in each case, and in both cases the Angel, acting in priestly function, consumed the offerings by fire. Not only did the offerors not die when they had seen God, but they likewise did not die when they made offerings apart from the required mediation of an Aaronic priest. In Manoah's case, not only did the Angel mediate (between Manoah/his wife and God), but he appeared to have merged with the offering when he "ascended in the flame of the altar."[169] This last curiosity will make more sense in light of what the Psalms and the latter prophets will say later on about the Messiah.

The mother of the prophet Samuel (the prophet who anointed David as king) was the first in Scripture to call the Messiah the "Messiah" (*mashiach*)—that word, we should recall, meaning literally "anointed one." Now before her time, the Tabernacle, sacred items within the Tabernacle, and the priests who served there, had been anointed according to the Mosaic Law;[170] but as yet there had been no mention of a very special king called the "anointed one." Hannah, one of two wives of Elkanah, as the story begins in 1 Sam 1, had been unable to have children. But Hannah, while at the Tabernacle in Shiloh one day, made a deal with YHWH: if he would give her a son, she would offer him up to lifelong service to God. YHWH heard, and not long after, she conceived and had a son, and named him Samuel—"God hears." After the boy was weaned, as per her vow, she took him to Shiloh where he would remain under the supervision of the High Priest, and in the service of YHWH at the Tabernacle, from that time on. In response to these events, Hannah prayed a prayer of profound thankfulness to God. At the end of this prayer—after what may be the first literal declaration in the Tanakh of God's ability to provide blessed life

---

[168] In the Christian view, the Mosaic Law is of lesser importance because it is fulfilled by the Holy Seed, who is the Messiah. The Mosaic Law does not claim to make a man utterly righteous before God, for the purpose of obtaining blessed eternal life after earthly death, through the expiatory sacrifices mandated by the Law. The Law has no clear (literal) teaching on how to achieve "salvation" after one dies. All is applied to earthly temporal life. Therefore, the expiatory rituals in the Law must be figurative of greater realities that involve man's eternal restoration to God. The probable reason why the messianic "forensic picture" and the appearances of the Angel of YHWH do not involve the Law, but do involve the Holy Seed, is because the sacrifices mandated by the Law are not sufficient to save a man eternally, whereas the sacrifice of the Messiah is sufficient to make a (believing) man utterly righteous before God and thereby eliminate the barrier that would otherwise preclude his eternal restoration to God.

[169] Judg 13:20

[170] See Exod 30:22-33.

after death ("The LORD kills and makes alive; He brings down to Sheol and raises up"[171])—Hannah said:

> Those who contend with the LORD will be shattered; against them He will thunder in the heavens, the LORD will judge the ends of the earth; and He will give strength to His king, and will exalt the horn of His anointed.[172]

Here are intersected several key messianic factors: "Sheol," i.e., the grave, is potentially not the end of the story; God judges all and destroys his enemies; and a great king called "His anointed"—the Messiah—is in the midst of these events and in the process being strengthened and exalted by God. Hannah's son, Samuel, would go on to be a great prophet and the last judge of Israel. He also anointed the first two kings of Israel, Saul and David, and thus they became the first *messiah* ("anointed one") kings in Israel. Before going on to consider the effect that David and his psalms had on the growing "forensic picture" of the Messiah, let us consider one more thing that occurred just before Saul was made king that is of critical importance to the concept of the Messiah.

Through the nine hundred or so years between the time when Israel first went down to Egypt and when Samuel ruled as prophet and judge, the nation had no human king, for God was their king. Samuel was a capable and godly judge who did nothing but good for his people. But Samuel's sons, who helped their father judge the people, were not so good.[173] So when King Nahash of the Ammonites threatened to attack Israel, the elders decided that they wanted a king, like other nations, who could lead them and fight their battles on their behalf.[174] Israel's elders informed Samuel of this, and Samuel laid it before the LORD, who then replied:

> Listen to the voice of the people in regard to all that they say to you, for they have not rejected you, but they have rejected Me from being king over them. Like all the deeds which they have done since the day that I brought them up from Egypt even to this day—in that they have forsaken Me and served other gods—so they are doing to you also.[175]

After Samuel anointed Saul as king, the Tanakh records:

---

[171] 1 Sam 2:6. Job's declaration of life after death (Job 19:25-27) is probably older. Life after death is perhaps implied by the mention of God's "book" in Exod 32:32-33. After Hannah, David spoke about the rescue from Sheol (Ps 16:10).
[172] 1 Sam 2:10
[173] 1 Sam 8:3
[174] 1 Sam 8, 10, 12
[175] 1 Sam 8:7-8

> Thereafter Samuel called the people together to the LORD at Mizpah; and he said to the sons of Israel, "Thus says the LORD, the God of Israel, 'I brought Israel up from Egypt, and I delivered you from the hand of the Egyptians and from the power of all the kingdoms that were oppressing you.' [Samuel then said] But you have today rejected your God, who delivers you from all your calamities and your distresses; yet you have said, 'No, but set a king over us!'"[176]

The above reveals the universal and eternal standard: YHWH alone should be the king of his people. Some years later, when Samuel was "old and grey," he reminded the people of YHWH's goodness and provision long before they had a king, and told them of their great "wickedness" and "evil" in craving after one. Then, as a sign of YHWH's displeasure with Israel, Samuel prayed for YHWH to send severe thunder and rain, which in short order came, and the wheat crop that was just being harvested was destroyed.[177]

In view of our messianic subject matter, the moral of this story is this: the Messiah must be God, if he is to be the permanent king of people who love and obey God; for if his essence consists of the human nature alone, then according to the clear standard revealed in First Samuel chapters 8-12, his kingdom must in some significant measure be seen as "evil" in God's eyes.[178] If it was evil for Israel to desire a *temporary* human king, how much more evil would it be for Israel to desire an *eternal* human king—and thereby reject God as their king forever? As we consider David and his psalms, as well as the prophets after him, we must keep this standard solidly in mind. This will help in the interpretation of the many challenging Tanakh texts to come which indicate that the Messiah is divine.

The first king of Israel, Saul of Gibeah, was a handsome, brave, and capable man, but he did not fully trust God. He, on more than one occasion, took matters into his own hands, just like kings are apt to do.[179] So YHWH

---

[176] 1 Sam 10:17-19

[177] 1 Sam 12

[178] The patriarchs Abraham, Isaac, and Jacob were not said to be kings, although, in the case of Abraham, he was powerful enough to be called a "prince" by the Hittites (Gen 23:6) and to go to war against kings and defeat them (Gen 14). Moses was not considered a king, although he presided over a well-structured government that in general was successful in warfare against foreign kings. Joshua and the judges were not kings, although they warred against foreign kings and were mostly victorious (leading men offered to make Gideon king, but he refused). Any future king was to remain humble, so that "his heart [might] not be lifted up above his countrymen" (Deut 17:20). Kings tend to usurp God's authority, and people ruled by kings tend to revere and trust the king more than God (compare 1 Sam 8:20 with Deut 1:30). Kingdoms ruled by human kings are, in the eyes of the infinitely holy and omnipotent God, *inherently* evil, whether the kingdom contains God-fearing people or not. YHWH is a "jealous God" (Exod 20:5) who will not give his "glory to another" (Isa 42:8).

[179] 1 Sam 13:8-14; 1 Sam 15

rejected Saul (who continued on like he wasn't rejected) and chose a better man, one after God's own heart, David, son of Jesse the Bethlehemite, of the tribe of Judah. The process of finding and anointing David was dangerous for Samuel (who had already notified Saul of his rejection),[180] for Saul's royal self-identity had already, so to speak, gone to his head (as is commonly the case with kings), and thus he was not willing to abdicate and was jealous of any rivals. Based on God's instructions, Samuel did not initially know the exact identity of the new king, only that he was a son of a man named Jesse who lived in Bethlehem. When Samuel met Jesse and his sons (under the pretense of coming to offer a sacrifice to YHWH at Bethlehem, so as to not raise the suspicion of Saul or his spies), YHWH told Samuel that none of the seven young men present were the chosen one. So Samuel asked Jesse if he had brought all his sons, to which Jesse replied: "There remains yet the youngest, and behold, he is tending the sheep."[181] Samuel then commanded that the young shepherd be quickly fetched.

> So [Jesse] sent and brought him in. Now he was ruddy, with beautiful eyes and a handsome appearance. And the LORD said, "Arise, anoint him; for this is he." Then Samuel took the horn of oil and anointed him in the midst of his brothers; and the Spirit of the LORD came mightily upon David from that day forward.[182]

Through a series of providential circumstances, David, not long after, became Saul's personal musician (for he composed songs and played the harp) and armor bearer. But it wasn't long till Saul became aware of David's anointing, and so, for several years, David was a fugitive on the run from Saul who wanted to kill him. By and by, Saul died, and all Israel eventually submitted to David and accepted him as their king.

Up to the time of Samuel's anointing of David, the "forensic picture" of the Messiah did not consist of much, although what was there was significant: The Tanakh taught that there will be a male descendant of Eve, who will in turn be a descendant of Abraham, Isaac, Jacob, and Judah, who will put an end to the devil, will bless all nations, and will be a great king who will have worldwide dominion. The Tanakh also revealed that God has no problem with showing up from time to time in what appears to be human flesh—sometimes as the Angel of YHWH, or simply as a "man" (who, for example, ate the meal prepared by Sarah and Abraham, and who wrestled through the night with Jacob). There is some evidence from David's psalms that he had some conception of the messianic bloodline that he participated in: Several of his

---

[180] 1 Sam 16:2
[181] 1 Sam 16:11
[182] 1 Sam 16:12-13

psalms (that we will consider a little later) indicate in various ways that the great king who would come from his own loins would eventually bring great blessings and peace to the whole world. David certainly knew from Jacob's blessing of Judah (Gen 49:10) that the legitimate kingly line had to be of the tribe of Judah.[183] In any case, with David and the Psalms—especially his own psalms—the "forensic picture" will blossom. This blossoming begins with the expansion of the "Messiah," that is, "the Anointed One," concept.

Samuel "anointed" David with oil, the basic Hebrew verb being מָשַׁח, *mashach*, meaning to "smear, anoint."[184] In view of this event, David, in several places, is called (to translate the Hebrew literally) "the one who is anointed" (i.e., with oil)—that participle (which in time becomes a proper noun-title) being מָשִׁיחַ, or to transliterate, *mashiach*, which has come down to us as the title, "Messiah."[185] As *mashiach* is applied to David, it does not take on the flavor of the eschatological king who will destroy Satan once and for all, but it does take on this flavor in several psalms that depict characteristics and abilities of a future Davidic king that can only be fully fulfilled by *The* Messiah.[186] One interesting thing to note here, before proceeding on to the amazing 2 Samuel 7 prophecy, is this: Ps 89, which is about *The* Messiah, says that David—the first Judean "anointed one"—was anointed with God's "holy oil." This most likely refers to the "holy oil" that, according to the Mosaic Law, was produced (from various spices and from olive oil) for the purpose of anointing the Tabernacle, its equipment, and the priests who served there.[187] The Law demanded that it was to be used for no other purpose. But David, who was not a priest, was anointed by Samuel, who was a Levite, but not of the Aaronic (priestly) branch. On the face of it, this appears illegal; but God allowed it, even commanded it. This certainly did not make David an Aaronic priest in addition to a king;[188] but it does probably foreshadow the priestly function that David's descendant, the Messiah, would one day have (this being directly prophesied in Psalm 110, a psalm of David).

The Messiah concept first mentioned by Hannah now blossoms with David: not just in the prophecies that were made in regard to him, and not just in several of the psalms written by him, but in his person as well. David is a

---

[183] Regarding David's awareness that Judah was the royal tribe, see 1 Chron 28:4. Also see Ps 60:7 and Ps 108:8.

[184] BDB, מָשַׁח

[185] 2 Sam 19:22; 22:51; 23:1

[186] Pss 2; 45; 89; 132

[187] Exod 30:22-33

[188] Although it is interesting that David ate the consecrated bread that was reserved for the priests (1 Sam 21:1-6), directly consulted the Urim and Thummim on the priestly ephod (1 Sam 30:7-8), and donned the priestly ephod and danced before the LORD when he brought the Ark to Jerusalem (2 Sam 6:14).

"type" of Messiah: He is not *The* Messiah, but one whose life and character prefigure the Messiah. Not everything in his life typifies the Messiah, of course, but there are many aspects of his life that remarkably point to what the prophets would later say about the Messiah: David was a shepherd, filled with God's Spirit, who loved the LORD; he was persecuted and he suffered terribly, but was raised up to be king, and acted as a priest on behalf of his people. As we will see in chapter two, much of the Messiah concept has to do not only with his exaltation, but with his suffering—the former coming only upon the completion of the latter. David's entry into the public world, upon the event of his anointing, was not all glorious. Things went well for the first few years of David's service to Saul, but not long after David's miraculous exploit of killing Goliath, Saul, in intense jealously, turned against him and tried to kill him. David was not expelled from Saul's house all at once, but the day soon came when he never ceased being on Saul's most wanted list, fleeing the king as long as the king lived.[189] But David had the great advantage of trusting God, and of knowing that God would one day fulfill what he had promised when the young shepherd boy was anointed: that one day he would be king over Israel.[190] Even after Saul died in battle with the Philistines about fifteen years after Samuel anointed David, only Judah came over to him initially. For the next several years, he had to fight his way to mastery over all of Israel. And even then, the gentile nations, that occupied the rest of the land that God had given to the sons of Abraham, still had to be attacked and overcome—a process that took up most of the rest of David's life. And there were internal struggles in which close friends, advisors, priests, and even sons, turned against him, threatening his life and kingdom.[191] But in all this, David stayed faithful to YHWH, and YHWH gave him the victory, such that at the end of his life, he could say, "Is not my house established before God?"[192] David's path from shepherd boy to king might have gone much quicker if Israel (including Saul) had better honored and submitted to God's word given through Samuel—that is, that revealed that Saul had been replaced by David. But David's path was apparently intended to prefigure the path that the Messiah himself would one day take.

Nathan's Amazing Prophecy for David (2 Sam 7; 1 Chron 17)

Soon after David had finally overcome the opposition of those loyal to Saul's house, and after he had established his throne in Jerusalem and brought the Ark of the Covenant there, David had it in his heart to build a temple for

---

[189] 1 Sam 18-30
[190] 2 Sam 5:2
[191] 2 Sam 13-20
[192] 2 Sam 23:5 (JPS '85)

the Ark and for YHWH whose throne was the mercy seat that covered the Ark. Nathan, the prophet of God who would serve David from that time on, told the king to go ahead with his plan, assuming that YHWH would surely be for such a noble enterprise.[193] But Nathan spoke too quickly: God spoke to him that night and told him to return to the king with a different plan. This plan would disappoint David a little, but also bless him profoundly.[194] In the first part of Nathan's message, YHWH informed David that he would not be the one to build God a "house" to live in. What YHWH said in this first part is important to understand, so that what is said in the second part makes long-term sense. YHWH, through Nathan, said to David:

> Are you the one who should build Me a house to dwell in? For I have not dwelt in a house since the day I brought up the sons of Israel from Egypt, even to this day; but I have been moving about in a tent, even in a tabernacle. Wherever I have gone with all the sons of Israel, did I speak a word with one of the tribes of Israel, which I commanded to shepherd My people Israel, saying, "Why have you not built Me a house of cedar?"[195]

Here, YHWH gives David a mild rebuke. For God had been with his people all along, even long before the desert Tabernacle: God was with Abraham, Isaac, and Jacob, and had visited the former and the latter in the flesh. God was with his people during their four centuries in Egypt, and he was with them when he brought them out of that "iron furnace." During the forty years of wilderness wanderings, God was pleased to dwell with his people in a "tent," and as they conquered the Promised Land, the "Commander of YHWH's army" went before them. Even during the period of the judges, when "everyone did what was right in his own eyes,"[196] God was with them, twice appearing bodily in the form of the Angel of YHWH.[197] But now that David was king—and the people had a king like the kings of the nations surrounding them—it is probably the case that David slipped a little bit into thinking like those other kings: kings must have glorious temples in which to house their gods, so that the gods are kept close by and at the immediate service of the king when needed. The Philistines had a temple for Dagon, the Arameans had a temple for Hadad, the Ammonites had a temple for Molech, and Israel must have a temple for YHWH. But YHWH's message through Nathan enlightened David on this subject: YHWH had never asked for a temple, for YHWH's first priority all

---

[193] 2 Sam 7:1-3
[194] 2 Sam 7:4-16
[195] 2 Sam 7:5-7
[196] Judg 21:25
[197] Judg 6, 13

along had been to *be* with his people—something he had done quite well enough without a temple or even a tabernacle-tent.

For the purposes of the most discerning and right interpretation of Nathan's prophecy, the *principle* established in this first part must first be understood, a principle that fits in with the overarching principle that we have seen from the start, that is, that God's Word to man is given to man so that he might do his part in bringing to pass God's earnest desire to save men from eternal separation from him. The Bible is the only authorized instruction manual that tells men and women about God and about how they—from their fallen state—can be reconciled to God. So the principle set forth in the first part of Nathan's prophecy is a truth expressed that is in accordance with this overarching principle: God is willing and able to be with his people, and he doesn't need a temple—a "house"—in order to do this. In fact, God had been very close to David because of David's love for God. David had worshipped God "in Spirit and in truth," with a "circumcised heart." But building YHWH a temple could have the effect of keeping him at arm's length. YHWH, however, being compassionate, gracious, and forgiving, knew David's heart well, and knew that David meant well, and knew as well that having a temple, however imperfect, would work toward the long-range good of the nation. So YHWH honored David's "desire of [his] heart"; although with the condition that it would not be David who would build the Temple, but his son.

We must keep in mind not only this "God with us" principle, but also the principle learned when Israel first asked for a king: *it is best when God, alone, is our king.* These two principles (as well as the "over-arching" principle: God's Word is meant to *save*) affect our interpretation of *core* biblical prophecies: one way or the other, these core prophecies must deal with how mankind can come to recognize God as king and be reconciled to him, and thereby avoid eternal condemnation. When I say "core biblical prophecies," I mean prophecies that have to do with the messianic "Holy Seed" subject matter of the Bible. Especially meant here are prophecies that have to do with David's royal descendants, and the preservation of that royal Seed which culminates in that promised one who will destroy the devil and usher in blessings for all nations, i.e., the Messiah. Because God's Holy Scripture "is going somewhere, and somewhere very important," we should be open to more profound eschatological interpretations of prophecies that appear at first glance to be prophecies that only concern temporal/earthly people, places, and events related to David's descendants. The 2 Sam 7 prophecy before us speaks of an earthly Davidic kingdom and an earthly temple; but based upon the principles just mentioned, these earthly things must have figurative/symbolic meaning of far greater things.

I know that this might seem somewhat question-begging, that I'm trying to theologically "stack the deck" before going on to consider this prophecy that has been interpreted in many ways. But, honestly, that's not the case. I'm simply trying to set an interpretive basis that is itself based on love and reason. If you, dear reader, were walking through the mountains with your son, and suddenly you saw that he was unknowingly just about to walk over a high cliff, would you yell to him some information about how he can best enjoy the smells and sights of the forest, or yell some pleasant nature poetry to him from Thoreau or Emerson, or perhaps inform him of your plans to give him a special gift? No, I'm sure you would do what any father or mother would do: out of love and preservation of what you've poured so much of your life into, you would cry out for him to stop so that you would not lose him forever. Likewise, the Bible is God's "cry" to us so that we might avoid eternal death and instead come into a reality that is infinitely perfect and appropriate: eternal fellowship with, and submission to, the God who made us, in whom "we live and move and have our being," and who rightfully should be our only king. Let us keep in mind these principles as we consider this prophecy that was given by God to David through Nathan the prophet.

So YHWH told David that he had got on just fine long before any consideration of a temple, and that he had been with David all along, raising him from being shepherd of sheep to being shepherd over all Israel (a miracle that depended not at all on a temple). With that, YHWH asked the following rhetorical question: "Are you the one who should build Me a house to dwell in?" Before David could answer, Nathan said this:

> The LORD also declares to you that the LORD will make a house for you. "When your days are complete and you lie down with your fathers, I will raise up your descendant after you, who will come forth from you, and I will establish his kingdom. He shall build a house for My name, and I will establish the throne of his kingdom forever. I will be a father to him and he will be a son to Me; when he commits iniquity, I will correct him with the rod of men and the strokes of the sons of men, but My lovingkindness shall not depart from him, as I took it away from Saul, whom I removed from before you. Your house and your kingdom shall endure before Me forever; your throne shall be established forever."[198]

At the first, David had it in his heart to build a "house" for YHWH. But God effectively, through the rhetorical question, says "no" (a blunt "not" is given in 1 Chron 22:7-8). But God, in an ironic twist, here tells the king that he

---

[198] 2 Sam 7:11b-16

(YHWH) instead will build a house for him (David), in essence saying, "you won't build a house for me, but I will build a house for you." The literal meaning of this is clear enough: David will not be the man to build a temple for YHWH—surely a disappointment for David—but YHWH will greatly honor and bless David by building a lasting dynasty ("house") for him. As the prophecy proceeds, whatever disappointment David might have felt for being denied the temple construction rights is quickly melted away by the news that a temple for YHWH will indeed be built, not by David, but by his "descendant," literally (as we've seen before), "seed." This descendant, who will build God's temple ("house"), and who will sin, will possess a throne that YHWH will cause to last "forever." And YHWH will be like a father to this son of David, and this son will be like a son to YHWH. In the course of this, David's "throne [i.e., his dynasty] shall be established forever." Let us now consider the short-term fulfillments of all this, as well as the long-term fulfillments that can be discerned in the context of the principles spoken of above.

In consideration of this prophecy and God's refusal to allow him to build the temple (for YHWH said to David: "you shall not build a house to My name, because you have shed so much blood on the earth before Me" [1 Chron 22:8]), David accumulated everything that was needed for the Temple's construction and furnishing, and shortly before his death commanded his son Solomon to build God's "house."[199] When YHWH said to David, "I will raise up your descendant after you .... He shall build a house for my name," David some years later understood this to apply (based on a revelation from YHWH) to his son Solomon.[200] Solomon was successful in this mission, the temple was built, and YHWH took up his abode there.[201] When YHWH said, "I will establish the throne of his kingdom forever," this, in the short-term prophetic fulfillment view, is best understood as saying that Solomon's dynasty (the same as David's dynasty) would last a very long time (the Hebrew word, עוֹלָם, olam, can indicate a very long time or forever—the latter often being the case). This interpretation seems reasonable enough, but it leaves us with several pressing questions. First, the kingdom of David's son was prophesied to last olam, but Solomon's kingdom lasted only forty years and his dynasty (succession of Davidic/Solomonic kings) after him endured less than four centuries: In 586 BC Jerusalem (along with its temple) was destroyed, and Zedekiah, the last Davidic King (of Judah) was captured by the Babylonians. Upon King Nebuchadnezzar's order, they killed all of Zedekiah's sons as the defeated king

---

[199] 1 Chron 22, 28
[200] 1 Chron 22:9
[201] 1 Kings 5-8

watched, then put out his eyes and led him away to imprisonment and eventual death in Babylon.[202] Since then, till this day, there has been no Davidic king that has sat upon the throne of Israel.[203] In regards to the temple that David's son would build, in the context of this prophecy, it is not unreasonable to assume that God intended it to endure as long as David's dynasty endured, that is, for a very long time, or even forever. But the Temple was destroyed at the time of the kingdom's downfall (586 BC). According to the prophet Ezekiel, the Spirit of YHWH exited the Temple shortly before its destruction,[204] and then when the shadow of the former temple was built when a remnant of Jews returned from the Babylonian/Persian exile, there is nothing said in the Tanakh regarding the Spirit's return at that time.[205] It appears to be the case that the Spirit was absent through the intertestamental period, on through to the time of the post-exilic temple's destruction by the Roman General Titus in AD 70. In any case, after that time, there has been no "house" for YHWH.

For one who is deeply concerned about his or her eternal destiny, and who searches the Scriptures to find answers, this prophecy, if taken in this short-term sense, would leave such a one thinking, "where are we going with all this? Whether some king's dynasty lasts three hundred or four hundred years, what does that have to do with me and my desperate need for salvation from eternal death?" In view of our human situation and in view of what necessarily must be the purpose of Holy Scripture, this question is completely justified. Considering the Scriptural context, this prophecy must point to realities that far transcend in importance and consequence the mere historical fact of an earthly dynasty that flowered for a relatively long time, but then disappeared.

This, of course, is the "over-arching principle" mentioned previously, that is, that principle stated from the beginning which insists that the "Holy Seed," as it flows along in Bible history, is going somewhere very important—so important that man's eternal destiny is intimately bound up with who the "He" will eventually be.[206] As we consider the "long-range" meaning of this prophecy, let us also keep in mind the principles that have been recently considered, viz., that for the long run, only God should be our king, and for the long run, God's

---

[202] 2 Kings 25; Jer 52
[203] The Hasmonian rulers of Judah, 2nd-1st centuries BC, were not descendants of David.
[204] Ezek 10
[205] The books that involve the time of the return from exile and not long after—Ezra, Nehemiah, Haggai, Zechariah, and Malachi—present no clear indication that the Spirit of God returned at this time. Ezekiel 43 prophesies the return of the Spirit, but the temple in his vision is obviously an eschatological one that has a high probability of being symbolic of higher realities. There is no historical evidence (biblical or otherwise) that the second temple was modeled after the temple of Ezekiel's vision.
[206] By the way, in Hebrew "he" is *hoo*, and "she" is *hee*.

desire and ability is to be close to his people—he does not need a temple for this.

When the LORD said, "When your days are complete and you lie down with your fathers, I will raise up your descendant after you, who will come forth from you," the use of "descendant"—in Hebrew, *zerah*, "seed"—is similar to that in Gen 3:15 and 22:18: the far future is in view as well as something wonderful.[207] The "something wonderful" in Gen 3:15 is this: "[Eve's seed] will [eventually] bruise [Satan's] head." In Gen 22:18: "In your seed all the nations of the earth shall be blessed." Now in the prophecy before us, "seed" in verse 12 could be taken as collective; but the context certainly precludes this, for YHWH says: "I will establish *his* kingdom" (v. 12), and "*He* shall build a house for my name" (v. 13). Just like in Gen 3:15's "*He* will bruise [Satan's] head," the text here employs the third person masculine pronoun הוא, *hoo*, before the verb so that there is no doubt who will be doing the building of God's house: not a "she" or a "they," but a very special "He" will build God's house and have a "throne" and "kingdom" that will last *olam*. Finally, not only will he be David's son, but he will be YHWH's "son" as well.

Let us now apply the principle that says that only God can be king in the long run. In "the long run" is certainly intended in this prophecy, for YHWH says three times that the throne and kingdom that descends from David will last *olam*. By this repetition, it strongly seems to be the case that this Davidic kingdom will indeed go on without end, or, at very least, for a very, very long time.[208] If so, if this king is merely a man, then an "evil" situation will obtain for as long as the kingdom endures.[209] So we should at least consider the possibility that the person referred to here is someone who—somewhat like the Angel of YHWH—can be so profoundly close to God that he can speak the words of God, and God does not see him as a usurper of his throne. In other words, we should consider the possibility that he is divine: like God has come to the world, as we have seen, in the form of a man-angel, God comes to us in the form of a man-king. What has preceded so far in this study does not preclude this possibility: this man will slay Satan, bless all nations, and be a Judean king who will have the obedience and worship of all nations.

---

[207] Gen 22:18 is parallel to Gen 12:3. The former has "in your seed," the latter, "in you." If 2 Sam 7:12's "seed" only referred to Solomon, YHWH would have simply said, "Your son will build a house for my name." But the language employed here is similar to other places where distant descendants are meant (which may prophetically refer as well to a particular distant descendant). For example, see Gen 13:15-16; 28:13-14; Deut 1:8.

[208] Jeremiah indicates that Davidic kings will reign until the natural order is broken (33:19-21). See also Ps 89:29, 36-37.

[209] After God destroyed their wheat harvest, the people confessed that their desire to have a human king was "evil" (1 Sam 12:19).

In support of this possibility is this surprising declaration, concerning David's "seed," spoken by YHWH through the mouth of Nathan:

$$\text{אֲנִי אֶהְיֶה־לּוֹ לְאָב וְהוּא יִהְיֶה־לִּי לְבֵן}$$

Literally, "I will be as a father to him and he will be like a son to me."[210] The words here could be figuratively taken to mean that this descendant of David is a "son" only in the fact that he is dearly loved by God; but Psalm 2—which is about God's "Anointed" who will be given universal rule—shows that the Messiah will truly be the Son of God. At the beginning of this psalm, the kings of the earth are said to be in league "against the LORD and against his Anointed." But YHWH scoffs at this opposition and in spite of it installs the Messiah as king at Zion. The Messiah then speaks and tells us what YHWH said concerning him:

> I will surely tell of the decree of the LORD: He said to Me, "You are My Son, today I have begotten You. Ask of Me, and I will surely give the nations as Your inheritance, and the very ends of the earth as Your possession."[211]

It is clear in this psalm that the Messiah is an individual and that he is an individual Son of God. The Son here cannot be the entire nation of Israel because the Son is spoken of (and speaks of himself in v. 7) throughout the psalm in the singular—whether "Anointed [One]" or "Son" or "King" or the several pronouns used (in the first, second, and third person).[212] That the Messiah is solidly identified as "Son"—specifically God's Son as verse seven shows us—is revealed in the final verse: "Kiss the Son, lest he be angry, and you perish in the way, for his wrath is quickly kindled."[213] This shows that "Son" is another title for "Messiah," a title earned not because he is a son of man, but because he is a Son of God. Could all this refer to *any* king in David's dynasty, perhaps referring first to David (whom the NT says wrote this psalm)? Perhaps; but from what we have considered so far in the book, and in view of the supernatural aura of this "Son" in Psalm 2 (and in view of what is yet to come), it is most likely the case that a certain descendant of David is in view here who

---

[210] My translation.

[211] Ps 2:7-8

[212] God refers to Israel as his "son" in Exod 4:22-23 and Hos 11:1. YHWH is called Israel's "Father" (Deut 32:6), yet those in Israel who act "corruptly" toward God are considered (according to Moses) "not his children" (Deut 32:5). See Rom 9:6-7; Luke 3:8.

[213] Ps 2:12 (ESV). Jewish versions take Ps 2:12 differently. E.g., JPS '85, "Pay homage in good faith, lest he be angered," and Judaica Press, "Arm yourselves with purity lest He become angry." At such a critical point, given the context, it seems like the use of the Aramaic *bar* is too much of a coincidence for it not to mean "son."

will far eclipse the glory and power and righteousness of all other Davidic kings. If YHWH truly has a son, then it is probably the case that the Son shares in his nature, like a human son shares in the human nature of his father.

Also in support of the possibility of the Son's divinity is the end of Nathan's prophecy as recorded in the parallel text found in 1 Chron 17. The end of the 2 Sam 7 version says (YHWH's words to David): "Your house and your kingdom shall endure before Me forever; your throne shall be established forever." The 1 Chron 17 prophecy is overall much the same as 2 Sam 7, although there is no mention of the son's sin or God's punishment of him. And the prophecy's last verse is different: "But I will settle him in My house and in My kingdom forever, and his throne shall be established forever."[214] The subject of the 2 Sam 7 version is David's "house" (i.e., his dynasty); the subject of the 1 Chron 17 version is God's "house." This is very interesting: Just before the prophecy, David expresses the desire to build God a house. YHWH does not go along with this desire, but tells him that he (YHWH) will build him (David) a house. Then YHWH tells David that his "seed," a "He," will build YHWH a house, and, according to the 2 Sam 7 version, the house that YHWH will build for David will last forever. Finally, the 1 Chron 17 version of the final verse tells us that the "seed" of David—who will build YHWH's house—will live in the same house that he built for YHWH! To summarize both versions, David will have a kingdom that lasts forever, David's "seed" will have a kingdom that lasts forever (an extension of David's dynasty/kingdom), YHWH will have a kingdom that lasts forever, and David's "seed" will be "in" YHWH's house and kingdom forever. The son of David is in David's house, i.e., in his dynasty; but, according to 1 Chron 17:13-14, he is as well a Son of YHWH who is in YHWH's house. When God says that he will "settle" David's son in the "house" that that son will make for God, what house is he referring to? Solomon did indeed build a house for God (the Temple), but Solomon never lived there (he had his own glorious palace). At this point there is no way to really know the answer to this question; but it does seem like something "wonderful" is meant. Just the fact that YHWH and the future human Davidic king will dwell in the same house is jaw-dropping, for Israel was then under the Law decreed by God (through Moses) at Sinai that permitted only the High Priest to enter the Most Holy Place of the Tabernacle, and that only once a year in order to atone for the people. So something beyond the Mosaic Law seems to be in view here. Especially in view that this house, in which God and the Son live, will endure *forever*, it must be the case that this house is established and endures in the context of the principles already stated: viz., God is reconciling men back to himself, only God should be man's king, and God's great desire is

---

[214] 1 Chron 17:14

to be with his people. In any case, God gives us here a great addition in the "forensic picture" of the Messiah, a picture that contains a mysterious blurring of the "seed" of David and of the Son of God.

"When he commits iniquity" (2 Sam 7:14) could be seen as running against this possibility of the son's divinity, for God necessarily does not sin. This appears mainly to be an element of the *short-term* fulfillment of the prophecy, referring specifically to Solomon who sinned greatly; yet he was *Jedediah*, "beloved of YH," through his life.[215] But Solomon, as far as we know, was never punished "with the rod of men and the strokes of the sons of men." It is also difficult to think of the Messiah as a sinner, for everything that the Tanakh shows us about him only indicates his righteousness and perfect justice.[216] In due course, however, we will consider several prophecies that testify that the Messiah indeed suffers for sin—not for his own sins, but for the sins of all other men.

Messianic Psalms

So far the "forensic picture" of the Messiah, which slowly develops through time, consists of the following: he will be a descendant of (Adam and) Eve, Abraham, Isaac, Jacob, Judah, and David. He will bless all nations, and as "Shiloh," the obedience of the nations will be his. His kingdom and throne will last forever, and the relationship between him and God will be so close that he will consider YHWH his father, and YHWH will look on him as his Son. Finally, he will build God a "house" in which he will also dwell.

Now before we look at these psalms which emphasize and expand upon what we've already learned, let us first consider the main messianic names/titles by which the Messiah will be identified from this point forward. We've already introduced his greatest title (although in the Tanakh only used of him a few times), that is, "the Messiah," which is the current English way of saying *ha-mashiach*, "the-anointed one." Up till this point, this title comes from the mention of the Messiah by Hannah, and the fact that David was anointed by Samuel, and was thus considered as God's *mashiach*. Another important messianic title is "Servant." In the Tanakh, a man who was especially close and obedient to God (e.g., Abraham) was called "God's servant." Beginning with David, the term takes on messianic flavor. In the context of Nathan's prophecy, YHWH twice instructs Nathan, "Say to my *servant* David." In David's great prayer of thanksgiving just after hearing Nathan's prophecy, he calls himself

---

[215] 2 Sam 12:25
[216] See Isa 53:6.

God's "servant" ten times.[217] Later, we will see that the "servant" of God serves God by suffering for God and his fellow men.[218] Because the Messiah will be of ． the "seed" of David, several titles will be based upon this bloodline: he will be called "David," the "Branch" coming from David, and the "Root" and "Branch" of Jesse (David's father).[219] The importance of these titles will become evident a little later.

As we proceed into the messianic psalms, it needs to be mentioned that the Psalms in general bring to the Tanakh a noticeable concern about what happens after death. This development comes at a time when, as we have seen, the prophecies about the Messiah have begun to multiply. The two themes are inextricably linked: the Messiah will be a royal Son of God who will bless all nations by his work of defeating and killing the devil; as a result, the curse of death and separation from God will be overcome, and mankind's intense dread of soul extinction, or some kind of post-mortem horrible afterlife, is permanently relieved. So as the theme of Messiah develops in the Tanakh, the doctrine of *salvation* develops also. Prior to David, as we have seen, the question of the afterlife hardly arises—although the reality and awareness of it can be implied from several texts: As soon as the curse of death fell upon Adam and Eve, they obviously remembered the paradise that they had lost, and agonized over how to get it back; Enoch, the seventh from Adam, appears to have been excepted from the death event, for he "walked with God," and "God took him";[220] Moses referred to God's "book" which most likely contained the names of righteous men and women slated for blessed immortality;[221] and the witch of Endor, on behalf of King Saul, "brought up" Samuel, who appeared to be very much alive, aware of past and present events, and still able to predict the future.[222] Now with the Psalms, and especially with those of David, we have some of the first biblical consideration of the subject as such. A brief look at some of the highlights may be helpful at this point in this way: the intensification of the concern about what happens after death will naturally lead to one wondering if the Messiah has something to do with the solution to this concern.

---

[217] The superscriptions of Pss 18 and 36 say this: "A Psalm of David the servant of the LORD." David calls himself God's "servant" three times in Ps 86 (vv. 2, 4, 16). In Ps 89 God twice calls David "my servant" (vv. 3, 20), and in Ps 143, David, in speaking to YHWH, twice calls himself "your servant" (vv. 2, 12).

[218] Preeminently in Isa 53.

[219] E.g., Ezek 37:24-25 ("David"); Jer 23:5 ("Branch"); Isa 11:1, 10 ("Branch," "Root").

[220] Gen 5:24

[221] Exod 32:32-33. David's Ps 69 also speaks of God's book that will lack the names of the unrighteous (v. 28). See as well Dan 7:10; 12:1; Mal 3:16; Luke 10:20; Phil 4:3; Heb 12:23; Rev 3:5; 13:8; 17:8; 20:12, 15; 21:27.

[222] 1 Sam 28

David and other writers of the Psalms here and there agonized over the difficulty of life, which included universally the punishment of God which led eventually to death. They wondered if "Sheol"—the netherworld place of the dead—would catch them and keep them, just like it had the Levites Korah, Dathan, and Abiram who opposed Moses' authority and demanded priestly rights that God had bestowed only upon Aaron and his sons.[223] The dread over the specter of Sheol is bitterly expressed by Heman the Ezrahite (Ps 88:3-7):

> For my soul has had enough troubles, and my life has drawn near to Sheol. I am reckoned among those who go down to the pit; I have become like a man without strength, forsaken among the dead, like the slain who lie in the grave, whom You remember no more, and they are cut off from Your hand. You have put me in the lowest pit, in dark places, in the depths. Your wrath has rested upon me, and You have afflicted me with all Your waves. Selah.

Several psalms complain that Sheol is a place where no one offers praise to God because those there are dead.[224] At the same time, these psalms appear to use this fact to question God's wisdom for allowing it: it seems that Sheol serves no purpose, and is of no benefit to God, because no thankfulness or praise to God emanates from there. Heman, after making the above lament, implies that God will suffer loss because there is no one in Sheol to declare the love of God. David makes the point that the "dust" of Sheol has no capability to praise God or declare his faithfulness. Fortunately, the Psalms do not leave us on this depressing note.

David is the first in biblical time (with the probable exception of Job—Job 19:23-27) to *plainly* testify, through the authority of God's Spirit, that the horror of Sheol is not the end for those who love God:

> I have set the LORD continually before me; because He is at my right hand, I will not be shaken. Therefore my heart is glad and my glory rejoices; my flesh also will dwell securely. For You will not abandon my soul to Sheol; nor will You allow Your Holy One to undergo decay. You will make known to me the path of life; in Your presence is fullness of joy; in Your right hand there are pleasures forever.[225]

Pardon me if I interject a "Hallelujah!" here! After three millennia, here is at last an inspired testimony of the fact of a blessed afterlife. And, quite interesting for

---

[223] Num 16

[224] E.g., Ps 6:5 (David): "For there is no mention of You in death; in Sheol who will give You thanks?" Ps 30:9 (David): "What profit is there in my blood, if I go down to the pit? Will the dust praise You? Will it declare Your faithfulness?" Ps 88:11 (Heman): "Will Your lovingkindness be declared in the grave, Your faithfulness in Abaddon?"

[225] Ps 16:8-11. See also Pss 30:3; 56:13; 86:13.

our overall subject, this testimony is given by the one who was a type of the Messiah to come, David, and by whose name the Messiah would forever be associated. One wonders why it took so long. Why wouldn't this be the subject right from the start of the Bible (much like it is right from the start of the NT)? God's ways are mysterious, and we'll probably never know this side of the final judgment. It may have something to do with the fact that not long after Adam and Eve were ejected out of the Garden of Eden, humanity became far more corrupt than we realize.[226] And so, the knowledge of God and concern about the afterlife were overcome by wickedness and the cares of this world, so much so, that even inspired men of old were wont to mention it, and, in any case, if they had, they would have then been "throwing pearls before swine." Men like Enoch, Noah, Shem, Abraham, Isaac, and Jacob believed, but few if any others. And when Moses brought Israel out of Egypt, there was little true faith in them, judging by their rebellion and YHWH's decision to leave nearly all of them as carcasses in the desert. They continued to be idolaters who ignored the true God and obsessed about the things and pleasures of temporal life. "Everyone did what was right in his own eyes" during the time of the judges, but with the coming of David and his kingdom, there came an increase of the knowledge of God and, correspondingly, the knowledge that God can save men and women from sin and death. This is exactly what David and others say in the Psalms: that God will not abandon righteous souls in Sheol (also known as "the pit"), but will "redeem" them by paying for their iniquities, and as a result, bring them up "from the depths of the earth."[227]

Unrighteous men and women, on the other hand, will not be found recorded in God's book along with the righteous. "The wicked," says David, "will return to Sheol, even all the nations who forget God."[228] Despite all the pain and injustice of this world, God, in the long run, will bring evildoers to justice, and the righteous will be vindicated: "salvation" will be provided for all who, like David, love the LORD and gladly carry out his will.[229] Then righteous

---

[226] Evidence of this is the human condition that prompted God to flood the world: "Then the LORD saw that the wickedness of man was great on the earth, and that every intent of the thoughts of his heart was only evil continually" (Gen 6:5).

[227] See Pss 16:10; 30:3, 9, 12; 34:22; 49:15; 56:13; 71:20; 86:13; 116; 118:17-18; 103:3-4; 130:8.

[228] Ps 9:17

[229] See Ps 37:39 (David: "the salvation of the righteous is from the LORD"); Ps 40:16 (David: the righteous love God's salvation); Ps 50:23 (Asaph: Sacrifice of thanksgiving and righteousness brings salvation); Ps 51:12 (David: "restore unto me the joy of your salvation"); Ps 53:6 (David: "that the salvation of Israel would come out of Zion!"); Ps 62:1-2, 6-7 (David: from God is salvation); Ps 71:23 (David: God redeems his soul); Ps 77:15 (Asaph: God redeems his people by his power); Ps 98:3 ("All the ends of the earth have seen the salvation of our God"); Ps 103:3-4 (David: God pardons all iniquity, redeems David's life "from the pit"); Ps 118:14, 15, 21 (YHWH is our salvation); Ps 119:174 ("I long for your salvation"); Ps 130:8 (God will "redeem Israel from all [its] iniquities"); Ps 132:16 (God will clothe his priests and holy ones

men and women will be with God forever and praise him for all eternity. The writers of the Psalms many times say that they look forward to God's salvation, or that those who honor and obey God will eventually receive salvation. As with the few pre-Davidic mentions of "salvation," it is generally the case that its use in the Psalms is not completely clear: do the writers mean *temporary* salvation (often translated "deliverance") from earthly problems, or do they, at least in some cases, mean *eternal* salvation from endless death in Sheol? In most cases, there is no way to tell. But one psalm, Ps 116 (no author given, but possibly David), may indicate that *eternal* salvation is meant (vv. 3-4, 12-13):

> The cords of death encompassed me and the terrors of Sheol came upon me; I found distress and sorrow. Then I called upon the name of the LORD: "O LORD, I beseech You, save my life!" What shall I render to the LORD for all His benefits toward me? I shall lift up the cup of salvation and call upon the name of the LORD.

Here, *rescue* from "the terrors of Sheol" is clearly what the writer means by "save my life!" and "the cup of salvation." But this might be a cry to "save" his life at some point in his life before old age and the inevitable death of the body that comes with it. In other words, it is unclear (as in other instances) whether he means salvation from eternal death—never to be threatened by it again—or simply deliverance from *premature* death. Right after this, the psalmist says, "Precious in the sight of the LORD is the death of his godly ones."[230] It is hard to understand how this could be so if death (for the righteous) were *not* the portal to reunion with God and wonderful everlasting fellowship with him. If eternal death were the reality, the death of the saints would be staggeringly tragic, not "precious." In any case, there are many cases of the mention of "salvation" in the Psalms and after that in the major and minor prophets. Given the principle that we began with—which says that the subject matter of the Tanakh must deal primarily with God and his plan to restore mankind—it is probably the case that "salvation" often means salvation from eternal separation from God. If we for a moment may reach three centuries (from David's time) into the future to judge this question, the prophet Isaiah, in one of the clearest statements about the afterlife, showed that "salvation" *is* the overcoming of death *forever*:

> The LORD of hosts will prepare a lavish banquet for all peoples on this mountain; a banquet of aged wine, choice pieces with marrow, and refined, aged wine. And on this mountain He will swallow up

---

with salvation and joy); Ps 145:19 (David: God "will fulfill the desire of those who fear Him, He will also hear their cry and will save them.").

[230] Ps 116:15

the covering which is over all peoples, even the veil which is stretched over all nations. He will swallow up death for all time, and the Lord GOD will wipe tears away from all faces, and He will remove the reproach of His people from all the earth; for the LORD has spoken. And it will be said in that day, "Behold, this is our God for whom we have waited that He might save us. This is the LORD for whom we have waited; let us rejoice and be glad in His salvation."[231]

"Salvation" is the noun, and "save" the verb, denoting rescue from death; but here, it is perfectly clear that this rescue results in ongoing blessed life with no further threat of death, for death itself is subject to death, and is no more.[232]

So along with the filling in of the "forensic picture" of the Messiah at the time of David, there is a blossoming of the awareness and knowledge of the afterlife. "Salvation" becomes the favorite word to denote the rescue from death from the netherworld that they called "Sheol." And in the Psalms, YHWH is time and again said to be the "Redeemer," in that he is the "Savior," of all who call upon his name.[233] So as we now consider several messianic psalms, let us know that the inspired writers of these psalms were most likely very concerned about the question of "salvation" and that the Messiah had something to do with the achievement of it.

We left off at Nathan's prophecy to David recorded in 2 Samuel 7 (parallel 1 Chronicles 17). Up till that point, God gave us only a few bits of messianic information, but what was there was eye opening: a man would come who would deal the devil a death blow, he would bless the whole world, and he would be a mighty king—descended from Jacob's son Judah—who would rule the whole world. God's Word given through Nathan added some very special details to the picture: the Messiah would be a descendant of David who would build a "house" for God, live with God in that house, be "like a son" to God, and possess a throne and a kingdom that would last forever. From the beginning, I said that it is inconceivable that a mere man could be all that the Scripture says that the Messiah is, and do all that the prophecies say that he will do. And this thought comes up right at the start: how could a mere man destroy the devil and in the process restore man back to God (and through this, bless the whole world)? Man is but a speck of dust, yet he alone will save mankind and the universe from eternal corruption? I don't think so. So from the start, I allowed the possibility of divine influence—even divine substance—in this man, and showed that the possibility of it is biblically not impossible: The

---

[231] Isa 25:6-9

[232] See 1 Cor 15:26; Rev 20:14.

[233] YHWH as "Redeemer" see Pss 19:14; 31:5; 34:22; 49:15; 55:18; 69:18; 71:23; 77:15; 103:4; 119:154; 130:8. YHWH as "Savior" see Pss 17:7; 106:21. Compare with Isa 49:26 and 60:16.

Tanakh many times (mainly in the Pentateuch) presents historical cases of the Almighty showing up in finite-appearing physical manifestations—especially, as we have seen, in the person of the Angel of YHWH.

Now we'll look at several psalms that are in general understood by both Jews and Christians to be messianic—Psalms (according to recent Jewish and Christian translations) 2, 72, 89, and 110. As we look at each of these, I will first point out the elements in each that are elements of the "forensic picture" that we have already drawn. If a psalm, for example, speaks of a future king who will rule the whole world, then just by that alone we can be quite sure that the psalm has the Messiah as its subject matter. Once we identify these already-known messianic elements, and thereby can assure ourselves that the psalm is messianic, then we can look further in the psalm to see if there is anything new that the psalm brings that will add to our concept of the Messiah.

PSALM 2—THE MESSIAH IS GOD'S "ANOINTED ONE"

There can be no doubt that Ps 2 (along with Ps 110) speaks of the eschatological Messiah. The content and tone of the psalm is eschatological and otherworldly, and, as such, it is very difficult to see in it any of the Davidic kings of the Tanakh history: they all fall far short of what this psalm envisions for God's "Anointed One." Psalm 2 consists of three main themes: first, that YHWH and his Messiah are opposed by the nations and their kings; second, that notwithstanding this opposition, YHWH makes his Messiah king over the world (enthroned at Zion) and pronounces him his "Son"; third, that YHWH will give the Messiah the power and authority to conquer the nations and rule absolutely over them. In the MT (Masoretic Text) there is no superscription for this psalm, although it is identified as Davidic in the NT.[234]

Is there anything in Ps 2 that is already contained in the "forensic picture"? Indeed there is: The king is installed on "Zion," which indicates that he is a Davidic king. Also, harkening back to Nathan's prophecy, YHWH here calls this king his "Son," a son whom YHWH will give dominion over all the world, just as was said of "Shiloh" in Gen 49:10. Obviously, Ps 2 speaks of *the* Messiah.

Now what can be learned in addition to what we already know? First, despite my repeated use of the appellation "Messiah" thus far, other than Hannah's mysterious reference to a future king called God's "anointed" (and, of course, several references to King Saul and King David as the same), there has been no clear signal that the Messiah would be called "the Messiah." Calling him such right from the start of this book is a significant anachronism, but one

---

[234] Acts 4:25-26

that had to be employed so that we knew from the start what or who we were talking about. But with Ps 2:2, there can be no doubt that another name for the One who is the subject of this book is the "Messiah," which is the current English way of saying the Hebrew word *mashiach*, the literal meaning being, "anointed one." And it will turn out in time to be the preeminent name, even while its use later on in the Tanakh will be surprisingly infrequent.

At the beginning, we learned that there would be ongoing "enmity" between the "seed" of Satan and the "seed" of Eve, and that in time, the heal of the "He" of the seed of the woman would be "bruised" by the devil. In other words, the One who would finally kill Satan would in the process be wounded by him.[235] The thought of the Messiah being "bruised" is expanded upon in Ps 2:1-3: In fact, all the nations of the earth and their kings and rulers—i.e., the "seed" of Satan—are seen here in league against YHWH and against his Messiah. The scope of rightful theocratic authority supposed here is absolute and universal, and the scope of rebellion is worldwide. This far transcends the extent of Israel's/Judah's historical theocracy and the extent of the periodic rebellions of the nations surrounding Israel/Judah during the time of David, Solomon, and the divided monarchy. The opposition to YHWH and the Messiah in vv. 1-3 is universal and intense: The nations and their leaders do not at all desire to be under the authority of God and his earthly regent. Will this opposition prove deadly for the Messiah? Ps 89 will indicate that it will, and the prophets that will be considered in chapter 2 will positively confirm it. Be that as it may, Ps 2 goes on to show (vv. 8-12) that YHWH and his Messiah will overcome all enemies and at last bring all the earth under their supreme authority.

So we learn here that God's Anointed One will be greatly opposed and that it will take some time for him to overcome his enemies (in that it will take some time to "break them" and "shatter them like earthenware"). The last three verses of the psalm certainly show that one's relation to YHWH is intimately related to one's relation to the Son. The "Now, therefore" of v. 10 indicates that kings and judges of the earth, in view of the facts about King Messiah that have already been stated, should act accordingly and in the fear and reverence of YHWH. In other words, allegiance and obedience to the Son is parallel with worship of YHWH. To be pleasing to the Son is to be pleasing to God. Verse 12 seems to emphasize this, although there is disagreement on its translation today mainly along the lines of Christian and Jewish interpretation:

---

[235] Gen 3:15

> Kiss the Son, lest He be angry, and you perish in the way, when His wrath is kindled but a little. Blessed are all those who put their trust in Him. (NKJV)

> Pay homage in good faith, lest He be angered, and your way be doomed in the mere flash of His anger. Happy are all who take refuge in Him. (JPS '85)

The disagreement is mainly over the imperative right at the start: נַשְּׁקוּ־בַר. The verb *nashak* just about everywhere literally means "to kiss," a meaning that can be interpreted figuratively: for example, "to honor" or, as the JPS has it above, "to pay homage." But what do we make of the next word, *bar*? It could be taken in the little-used sense of "pure" or "chosen,"[236] a translation preferred by Jewish versions to some extent based on a desire to avoid rendering to the Son that which is due to God alone. But far and away, *bar* in the Tanakh means "son"— although there is the problem that it is, strictly speaking, not Hebrew, but Aramaic, and as such, should not be signifying "son" in a Hebrew psalm long before Aramaic made major inroads into the language and eventually displaced it (after the return from the Babylonian exile).[237] *Bar*, of course, is used in the Aramaic portions of Ezra and Daniel, but this word for "son" occurs in the rest of the Hebrew Tanakh only four times, three of those instances being found in Prov 31:2, and once in our verse in question. Most Christian versions translate *bar* as "son," prompted somewhat by the Christian desire to see the Son honored on par with the Father.

The linguistic and historical realities that pertain to the proper understanding of this text are mostly lost in antiquity. Nevertheless, the following should be considered: In this preeminent messianic psalm that introduces with such solemnity and gravity the Son of God, how could it be that the final critical imperative in the psalm would have a closely related language's word for "son," yet have it stand for a meaning other than "son"? To put this another way, given the fact that Ps 2 is primarily about God's Son, if any word appears in the closing critical imperative that in any way brings to mind "son"—even if the original language word used is from another language—it is most probably the case that God (the inspirer of this psalm) wants us to continue to think in terms of the Son, perhaps at the same time that we are thinking in terms of God. If God did not want us to think that nations and their kings and rulers should "kiss the Son," but rather kiss (pay homage

---

[236] Song 6:9-10

[237] The lexicons are divided on the question of *bar*'s possibility of meaning "son" in pre-exilic era Hebrew. Gesenius, one of the early and most thorough Hebrew lexicographers, believed that Hebrew poetry allowed its use (in Ps 2:12 and Prov 31:2), and thus renders Ps 2:12 "kiss the son."

to) himself, the last word he would have employed here to signify "pure" devotion would have been a word that could easily be taken as meaning "son." Yes, Aramaic influenced Hebrew quite a bit later, but it was also to some extent Hebrew's source language: for Jacob was, as the Scripture testifies, a "wondering Aramean,"[238] and Abraham and his father Terah lived in Paddan-Aram for many years before that. Even at the time of Psalm 2's composition, and certainly after, many would have recognized their Syrian neighbors' word for "son," and thus understood the end of the psalm to mean that one should love and honor the Son greatly, lest the Son be angry and one "perish in the way."[239] If this is so, then the psalm teaches us to love, honor, and obey the Son much like we do his "Father" YHWH.

The question of whether the end of Ps 2 should be rendered "pay homage in good faith [to YHWH]" or "kiss the Son" is arguably, in light of what we already know about the Messiah, a moot point. For we know that God has decreed that "to him shall be the obedience of the peoples" (Gen 49:10), an authority and power given by God, as shown in Ps 2:8-9, that is universal and absolute.

> Ask of Me, and I will surely give the nations as Your inheritance, and the very ends of the earth as Your possession. You shall break them with a rod of iron, You shall shatter them like earthenware.

Even if v. 12 speaks of the homage due to YHWH, there can be no doubt that those who "take refuge in Him" will also honor and obey the Son. To be pleasing to YHWH, the rulers and "kings of the earth" must cease their rebellion "against the LORD and against His Anointed," described in vv. 1-3, repent, and give their allegiance to both God and his anointed regent on earth.[240]

PSALM 72—THE MESSIAH BRINGS WORLDWIDE PEACE AND PROSPERITY

There were several voices in Ps 2: the author, the kings and rulers of the nations, the LORD, and the Messiah, each speaking in turn. In Ps 72, only the author King Solomon speaks. Most of the statements in this psalm can be taken as either prophecy (e.g., "he will judge your people with righteousness"—v. 11)

---

[238] Deut 26:5

[239] This makes me think of the Black Oblisk of the Assyrian king Shalmaneser III that portrays in relief "Jehu son of Omri," king of Israel, performing obeisance before the Assyrian king, with his face on the floor only inches away from Shalmaneser's feet. It may be that Jehu actually kissed the Assyrian king's feet in order to show his total submission and to assuage the anger of Shalmaneser. In any case, the Assyrian kings regularly spoke of sparing the lives of those enemies who surrendered and "seized" their (the Assyrian kings') feet.

[240] See John 5:23.

or as blessing/benediction ("may he judge your people with righteousness") that pertain to Solomon himself and at the same time refer to "the king's son" (v. 1). Most modern versions, including Jewish ones, go with the latter (although the verbs used in each are simple imperfects, and can be translated as the former). Even if the psalm is translated as an extended benediction, each element of what Solomon hopes for should be taken—because this is Holy Scripture—as what *will* happen. This is especially so when this psalm is understood as messianic, and thus has to do with the special One who is a part of the special bloodline that the Scripture has been so interested in, and who will one day bless all nations.

Just like Ps 2 far transcended the person and works of King David, Ps 72 far transcends the person and works of Solomon or any of his dynastic successors. The king of this psalm will rule forever and usher in worldwide peace and prosperity because of his perfect judgment and righteousness. Solomon indeed ruled over Israel at its apex of size and glory, and there was peace through most of his reign; but as time went on, he increasingly sinned (took too many wives/concubines, who then led him into idolatry) and the kingdom collapsed just after his death.[241] In any case, the land over which he ruled was only a small part of the entire world. "All kings" and "all nations" will one day bow down before and serve the king of this psalm, but they did not do such for Solomon or any others in his subsequent dynasty. Could it be that Solomon here only refers to himself and/or his immediate son in the hyperbolic way that the near-eastern kings of those times referred to themselves? The Assyrian king Tiglath-Pileser I (ca. 1100 BC), for example, on an octagonal clay prism recording his life's exploits, called himself "the powerful king, king of hosts, who has no rival, king of the four quarters [of the world], king of all rulers, lord of lords, king of kings."[242] It was typical of ancient kings to boast of their omnipotent power, universal domain, and even divine essence. If this is all that Solomon had in mind—and God was aware of it—then his psalm would not have made it into the canon of Holy Scripture. In view of God's purpose for Holy Scripture that we have already discussed, there would have been little or nothing to gain for God or man by this psalm being there, for it could tell us little or nothing about God and his will for mankind such that they might be saved. Other than the acknowledgments of God in vv. 1 and 5 (vv. 18-20 are not part of Solomon's psalm, but a doxology that closes the second book of Psalms), Ps 72 only glorifies the king, who, if he is not the Messiah, is only a man, and not worthy of the sort of praise which should be offered to God alone. No, given what we know already about God's over-arching purpose for mankind, what we have

---

[241] 1 Kings 11-12
[242] *Assyrian and Babylonian Literature* (New York: D. Appleton and Co., 1901), 12.

learned about the Messiah, and what we will further learn about him, it must be the case that Ps 72 refers ultimately to "the king's son" who will be perpetually righteous and bless the whole world, not just Israel, i.e., the Son who is *the* Messiah.

Ps 72 has two great themes: the worldwide rule of the king and the worldwide blessings that he brings. Thus, from what we already know of the Messiah, the psalm must be about him. The Messiah's rule is without end and universal (vv. 7, 8, 11):

> In his days may the righteous flourish, and abundance of peace till the moon is no more. May he also rule from sea to sea and from the River to the ends of the earth. And let all kings bow down before him, all nations serve him.

The Messiah brings blessings to all (v. 17b):

> In him may all nations be blessed; may they call him blessed. (BSB)

We are already familiar with these messianic themes. The psalm goes on to fill in some color to these themes, helping to beautify our developing "forensic picture."

Regarding the Messiah's reign, we learn from v. 17a that his name will "endure forever" and "increase as long as the sun shines." Nathan's prophecy (2 Sam 7) spoke about a son of David whose throne and kingdom would last forever. Some have taken that to mean simply that David's dynasty would go on for a long, but limited, time. This verse seems to preclude that view: Not only does this king bring peace "until the moon is no more" (i.e., for a very long time, perhaps without end), he is so impressive that his name remains indefinitely and, as time goes on, grows interminably in its fame.[243] "His name" can only apply to a particular man within the Davidic bloodline/dynasty, not to all of the Davidic kings who ruled Judah during the divided monarchy era.

We recall from early in our study that the Messiah is said to bless the whole world (Gen 12:3; 22:18). In Ps 72 we have presented to us a few details that explain how he will bless the world, including one detail that will hint at the Messiah's sacrificial work. First, he blesses the world by being a king and judge who is righteous, and who therefore cares deeply about his people. He cares about all of them, with special attention put on his sheep who are "afflicted," "needy," and "poor" (vv. 2, 4, 12-13). He makes sure that they receive righteous justice, and he supplies their needs because he has

---

[243] The prophet Isaiah (9:7) says this regarding the Messiah: "There will be no end to the increase of His government or of peace, on the throne of David and over his kingdom, to establish it and to uphold it with justice and righteousness from then on and forevermore. The zeal of the LORD of hosts will accomplish this."

"compassion" on them (v. 13). But there is some indication here, in v. 14, that he cares not only about his people's temporal needs, but their eternal needs as well:

> He will rescue their life from oppression and violence, and their blood will be precious in his sight. (NASB)

> He redeems them from fraud and lawlessness; the shedding of their blood weighs heavily upon him. (JPS '85)

The Messiah is deeply concerned about the bodies and, especially, the souls of his people, such that the sight of their blood and their deaths weigh "heavily upon him." Out of this deep concern, he takes protective action on their behalf: he will "rescue" them, or as the JPS better puts it, "He redeems them."[244] This is Mosaic Law language that typically referred to the ransoming or buying back of men or women who had fallen on hard times and enslaved themselves.[245] The Messiah is willing to redeem men and women from the hardships of this world, and perhaps implied here also, from the horrors of death. But notice that it is the Messiah that redeems, that is, gives whatever is necessary in order to secure the release of his people from "fraud and lawlessness," "oppression and violence," and, it is probably the case, death. Notice also that the Messiah's heart and actions are precisely parallel to those of God:

> O Israel, hope in the LORD; for with the LORD there is lovingkindness, and with Him is abundant redemption. And He will redeem Israel from all his iniquities (Ps 130:7-8). Precious in the sight of the LORD is the death of His godly ones (Ps 116:15).[246]

When we think of the Messiah redeeming men and women, the words of Ps 49:7-8 should be kept in mind:

> No man can by any means redeem his brother or give to God a ransom for him—for the redemption of his soul is costly, and he should cease trying forever.

The Messiah redeems, yet a mere man cannot give to God the redemption price for another man, for it is too "costly."[247]

Another way that the Messiah blesses the world, as shown in Ps 72, is through the bestowal of material blessings. During his righteous reign, there will be a super-abundance of grain and fruit growing on the mountains (v. 16).

---

[244] גאל is the usual word for "redeem," and pertains to the redemption of both men and animals.

[245] See Lev 25.

[246] The Hebrew word for "precious" (יקר) is the same in both Ps 72:14 and Ps 116:15.

[247] It seems providential that the Hebrew word here for "costly" is יקר.

No one who comes under his shade will go hungry. And finally, the Messiah blesses the world by bringing lasting peace, in fact an "abundance of peace till the moon is no more"—that is, for forever.[248] With conditions like these under the reign of the Messiah, "the righteous," as v. 7 says, "will flourish." What a promise for those who love God and gladly come under his Messiah's authority!

PSALM 89—THE MESSIAH IS THE SUFFERING SERVANT OF GOD

The mighty King David fought many wars to bring the land (promised by God to Abraham and to Israel) under the control of YHWH's people, the Israelites. As has already been discussed, David wanted to build God a permanent temple to dwell in, but because David was a man of war who had "shed much blood,"[249] God chose Solomon—the king of *shalom*—to build him a house. For as much as YHWH is a judge and a warrior who comes on the Day of the LORD, "heaping up the dead,"[250] he is far more the God of peace— the God who had peace before the creation—who is working out a plan to restore permanent peace to it. David said this just before he died:

> Truly is not my house [full of light] with God? For He has made an everlasting covenant with me, ordered in all things, and secured; for all my salvation and all my desire, will He not indeed make it grow?[251]

David, who had trusted in God since his youth and who had seen time and again his amazing hand of provision, believed with all his heart that God's promises were "yea and amen." God had well-ordered David's life (despite the many hardships and heartbreaks) and well-ordered his dynasty. David testifies here that Nathan's prophecy regarding his posterity had been a "covenant" that God was certain to fulfill.[252] Very interesting to note here is that this covenant— which spoke of the eternal throne and kingdom of his son, the Messiah—well-orders not only his dynasty, but his "salvation" as well; for, as we will discover by and by, *One* in the former is to make the latter possible.

The kingdom of Israel was secure—and its sphere of influence extended over an area approximating the land that God had promised—when Solomon came to the throne. His father was a man of war, but Solomon was a man of peace who ruled over a people who were happy, prosperous, and at peace with their government and with foreign nations. Solomon's wisdom and judgment,

---

[248] V. 7.
[249] 1 Chron 22:8
[250] Ps 110:6
[251] 2 Sam 23:5
[252] As we will soon learn, God made this covenant *with an oath* (Ps 89:3, 35).

and wealth and splendor, became famous in the near-eastern world. Even the Queen of Sheba came several hundreds of miles to see the man and his happy people.[253] After spending some time with the king, she praised him, saying:

> I did not believe their reports until I came and my eyes had seen it.
> And behold, the half of the greatness of your wisdom was not told
> me. You surpass the report that I heard. How blessed are your men,
> how blessed are these your servants who stand before you continually
> and hear your wisdom.[254]

It may have been that some people then (maybe even Solomon himself) might have pondered God's covenant with David (given via Nathan) and wondered if Solomon might be that "He," written about so long ago, who would indeed have an eternal throne, bring the whole world into submission to him, and usher in worldwide everlasting peace. For those who might have thought this way, it wasn't long—two or three decades after Solomon became king—till the truth of things became evident. In violation of God's Law given to Moses, Solomon, like other kings, took many wives and concubines—700 of the former, some from the royal families of the nations surrounding Israel—and they prompted him to accommodate the worship of their gods in Israel.[255] Solomon was then sucked into the worship of those gods. So YHWH brought problems on Solomon, both foreign and domestic: Nations under tribute rebelled; the people grumbled because of burdensome taxes; and an Ephraimite rebel arose, Jeroboam, whom Solomon then tried to capture and kill.[256] Solomon, who had begun so well, who had built the temple in Jerusalem and "in all his glory" had dedicated it to YHWH, eventually showed his natural human colors and, thus, fell away from God. So God ended his earthly life much sooner than might have been the case. God had promised him long life, if he would just continue to trust and obey;[257] but, sadly, that wasn't to be.

When Solomon's son, Rehoboam, took over, the people and their elders had had enough of Solomon, and asked the new king to lighten the various loads imposed upon them by his father's government. But Rehoboam listened to unwise youthful advisors, rebuked the elders of Israel for their negative attitude, and threatened to make things even harder on the people. So ten of the tribes rebelled and then rallied around Jeroboam (mentioned above, of the tribe of Ephraim), and went their own way.[258] Judah, Benjamin, and Simeon

---

[253] She travelled about a thousand miles if she came, as some believe, from the southern part of the Saudi Arabian peninsula, i.e., present day Yemen.

[254] 2 Chron 9:6-7

[255] 1 Kings 11

[256] 1 Kings 11:14-12:15

[257] 1 Kings 3:14

[258] 1 Kings 12:1-17

stayed with Rehoboam.[259] So God's chastising hand came down hard on Rehoboam: He lost most of his kingdom, and then after some time, what remained was attacked and overrun by Pharaoh Shishak and his army—a debacle which left Judah impoverished and Jerusalem and the Temple stripped of much that was valuable.[260] For a while, it seemed like David's "house" (dynasty) might end barely after it began. If so, it could have proved the end of YHWH worship, for YHWH had promised that the Davidic royal "seed" would endure forever and rule forever; but now it looked like YHWH had not told the truth and therefore could not be trusted—let alone, worshipped.

During the reign of Solomon, and possibly extending into that of Rehoboam, lived a man named Ethan who was famously wise (so wise that Solomon was compared to him), and who wrote—through the inspiration of God's Spirit—one of the psalms in the Tanakh which we know today as Psalm 89.[261] Ethan was very familiar with God's covenant made to David, given by the prophet Nathan, regarding the building of God's "house" and about the "seed" of David who would be the builder of it. Ethan probably lived long enough to witness the split of the kingdom under Rehoboam and maybe even was there when Pharaoh Shishak attacked. Or it could have been that the Spirit of God informed him of the disastrous events to come, which, between his own concerns and the concerns of the Spirit, prompted him to express the distress that he felt regarding God's promise to David and what appeared like God's breaking of his promise to David. This great worry is the great question that resonates in the background throughout Ps 89. But there is something greater that also resonates through the psalm: the deeply-held belief that God is good and that because of that, he will in the long run fulfill what he has promised. Even though the psalm appears to question God's goodness—"Where are Your former lovingkindnesses, O Lord, which You swore to David in Your faithfulness?"—it is surely the case, based on what Ethan has already said, that he assumes that God will show his goodness again and fulfill what was promised to David and his seed forever. This is the purpose of the psalm: Even in the face of what appears like God failing to be faithful to his Word—and thus making it appear like the Israelite YHWH religion is false—it is in fact the case that God will be faithful, because God really *is*, he is the creator of everything, and he is absolutely holy and righteous.

And this is where Ethan begins, with exulting in the many ways in which God is good. This is the first of three main themes in the psalm (vv. 1-18). The second section focuses on the Davidic covenant, to some extent repeating what Nathan told David, but here giving yet-unknown details and increased

---

[259] 1 Kings 12:21. Simeon's territory was within that of Judah.
[260] 1 Kings 14:25-26
[261] The superscription says: "A Maskil of Ethan the Ezrahite."

solemnity (vv. 19-37). The last section goes into some detail about the suffering that the Messiah will experience—a suffering that seems to end in death and the extinction of the Davidic royal line (vv. 38-45). At the end (vv. 46-51), as already mentioned, Ethan in so many words asks YHWH how this could be: God's goodness is sure, and the promises made to David and his Messiah are sure; yet now the Messiah is subject to the severe reproaches of his enemies (v. 51). It doesn't seem like the Davidic royal line will continue. But this is not the final conclusion that Ethan wants us to draw: When he says, "Where are your former lovingkindnesses, oh Lord," he expects us to recall the first two sections of the psalm, and know that lovingkindness is necessarily an attribute of the LORD, and that the LORD has vowed that his lovingkindness will always remain with David and his seed, such that his dynasty goes on forever in the person of the Messiah. In short, Ethan in essence says, "I worry now, but I *know* that God will fulfill his promise made to David." Thus, the psalm is intended to prompt readers to maintain faith in God's promises even in times of doubt.

The first eighteen verses are mainly about God's goodness, something that Ethan wants to firmly establish right off, so that when the distressing questions come later, there will be a firm foundation upon which to draw conclusions. Men rightly praise YHWH and rejoice in him and fear him because he is the incomparable and awesome God of truth; because he is the creator of heaven and earth and is therefore their owner and controller; and because he is the strength and the glory of men, and their protector. Ethan presents three qualities of God that establish the unchangeable truth that God will keep his promises. First, he *is* faithfulness: So much is this so that this quality surrounds him and permeates the heavens, that is, everywhere where God is; and this faithfulness extends to all who serve him, and thus they proclaim his faithfulness to an unfaithful world. Second, God *is* lovingkindness: This, as well as "truth," goes before God, and everywhere God goes, and his kingdom grows, the quality of lovingkindness will ever expand; and thus, God's people (like Ethan) "sing of the lovingkindness of the LORD forever."[262] Finally, he *is* righteousness: This quality of perfect holiness (along with justice) is the foundation of his throne (i.e., his government); and thus, those who love him and do his will are exalted and rejoice in his name without ceasing.

Once Ethan establishes the principle of God's absolute goodness, he goes on to remember and expand upon the promises that God gave to David (vv. 19-37), and assure us in the process that those promises will surely be fulfilled. In this psalm the Messiah will twice be called God's "anointed," three times be called God's "servant," and once God's "son"—all titles of the Messiah that we have already learned. And what he says about the promises made to David is

---

[262] Ps 89:1

mostly what we've already learned from Nathan's prophecy: David's throne, through his dynasty (his "seed"), will be established "as the sun" and "like the moon" forever before God. He will be the "highest of all the kings on earth," crushing all of his enemies under his feet. David and his house will endure because God's lovingkindness and faithfulness will always be with him. As God says in v. 33: "I will not break off My lovingkindness from him, nor deal falsely in My faithfulness." That is, the results are guaranteed.

There are some details in this recounting of Nathan's prophecy, however, that intensify the colors that are already there. What are these details? In 2 Sam 7, God, through the mouth of Nathan, told David that certain things would transpire in the future.[263] Here in Ps 89, what God promised to David is called a "covenant," in fact, a covenant that God assures us is "confirmed" (v. 28). Regarding it, God says (v. 34): "My covenant I will not violate, nor will I alter the utterance of My lips." Calling Nathan's prophecy a "covenant" gives it a very high level of solemnity and trustworthiness. But there is even more here: in fact God "*swore* to David" that these things would be so (v. 35): "Once I have sworn by My holiness," says the LORD, "I will not lie to David." That is, the unconditional covenant given to David is absolutely reliable because God's holiness is absolutely a fact. The level of solemnity/gravity on display here is much like that depicted in several other biblical cases of God making a promise. For example, after Abraham had obeyed God and (all but) offered up Isaac as a sacrifice on Mount Moriah, the Angel of YHWH said:

> By Myself I have sworn, declares the LORD, because you have done this thing and have not withheld your son, your only son, indeed I will greatly bless you, and I will greatly multiply your seed as the stars of the heavens and as the sand which is on the seashore; and your seed shall possess the gate of their enemies. In your seed all the nations of the earth shall be blessed, because you have obeyed My voice.[264]

As we see here, God's promise that "all the nations of the earth shall be blessed" through Abraham's "seed" is given with a solemn oath: "By myself I have sworn," declared YHWH.[265] Thus, it is sure to happen. The LORD also swears to the fact that all the living will one day come under his authority:

---

[263] That is, there are several prophecies regarding the future, but there is no mention of this being a "covenant," or of God predicting these events with an oath. That being said, it is obvious enough that this is a covenant; and David later calls it so in his "last words," 2 Sam 23:5.

[264] Gen 22:16-18

[265] YHWH swears by himself because there is no higher authority/person by which he can swear. See Heb 6:13-19.

I have sworn by Myself, the word has gone forth from My mouth in righteousness and will not turn back, that to Me every knee will bow, every tongue will swear allegiance.

And God swore that the rebellious wilderness Israelites would not survive long enough to enter the Promised Land: "Therefore I swore in My anger, truly they shall not enter into My rest."[266] These three examples testify to the seriousness of God when it comes to the core theme of the Bible, that is, how man can be "saved," i.e., reconciled to God. In the first example, he swears that worldwide blessing (salvation) will come to the whole world through Abraham's seed. In the second example, he swears that all will eventually submit to his rule—which is what people do when they repent and are saved. And the last example symbolically shows that it is absolutely certain—because God promised it with an oath—that all who do *not* bow the knee to him (not just outwardly, but inwardly) will be thrust from his presence and die an eternal death in the "wilderness." In view of all this, it is clear that God wants readers of this psalm to know for certain that what he prophesied to David, through Nathan, *will* come to pass—because God is "not wishing for any to perish."[267] And so, he will in due time reveal his Messiah so that the devil and death are destroyed, and the whole world is blessed with salvation.[268]

Another detail of Psalm 89's reiteration of Nathan's prophecy is worth noting. In the original prophecy, YHWH said that the Messiah would be "*like* a son" to him, and that YHWH would be "*like* a father" to the Messiah.[269] This left room for interpreters to see the relationship between the two as being at most analogous to a father-son relationship, but not really one. Ps 89:26-27 appears to make that interpretation unlikely, for God says here of the Messiah,

He will cry to Me, "You are my Father, my God, and the rock of my salvation." I also shall make him My firstborn, the highest of the kings of the earth.

Here, God's servant David (i.e., the Messiah—recall that David was already dead by this time) cries out to YHWH, "You are my Father!" This is a testimony of a true father-son relationship. And YHWH's designation of the Messiah as his "firstborn" testifies to his preeminence.[270]

Let us look at one more detail of this Ps 89 section that remembers Nathan's prophecy. This detail doesn't just add color intensity to our picture of the Messiah, but is a new and specific detail that hints at something very

---

[266] Ps 95:11
[267] 2 Pet 3:9
[268] That God can be trusted to do what he says, see Num 23:19 and Heb 6:13-20.
[269] 2 Sam 7:14 (parallel 1 Chron 17:13).
[270] See Col 1:15

significant and that will be a necessary component of his ultimate qualifications and mission. This detail is in v. 20:

> I have found David My servant; with My holy oil I have anointed him.

The "*holy* oil" mentioned here must refer to the "holy oil" described in Exod 30:22-33 that consisted of a special blend of oil and spices, and was used—by the command of God—to anoint, and thus consecrate, the priests and temple furnishings. God commanded that it not be used for any other purpose, on pain of being "cut off" from the nation (v. 33). Yet here, according to Spirit-inspired Ethan, the holy oil is used to anoint David. When David was anointed king by Samuel, the record does not say that the oil used by the prophet was "holy," although it probably was since Samuel was a Levite who operated in a quasi-priestly capacity.[271] Ethan's description of this oil as "holy" quite likely anticipates the Messiah's priestly function: The priests were anointed with this oil for their priestly service, and so it will be with the Messiah. That the Messiah is a priest in addition to a king is declared plainly in Ps 110—a highly messianic psalm that we will consider in the next section.[272]

But first, we must consider the last main part (vv. 38-45) of Ps 89 that depicts the suffering of the Messiah (this suffering, as we will eventually see, will be the highest priestly duty of the Messiah). Thus far in Ps 89, we have been shown that, first, God is good, and second, that God made solemn promises to David and his "seed," i.e., the Messiah. Now in the last major section, we have what might prompt one to doubt the validity of God's promises to David of the second part: Ethan goes into distressing detail about how the Messiah has suffered and died, which then appears to be the end of the dynasty that God had said would last forever. Just before the "suffering" section begins, vv. 30-37 repeat approximately what Nathan's prophecy had said about David; but in addition there is a warning that David's sons will be punished by the "rod" and with "stripes" if *they* forsake the Law of God. Nevertheless God promises to never take his lovingkindness away from—one would expect "them," but the MT has "him." Now in this final Ps 89 "suffering" section, Ethan will describe various sufferings that are inflicted upon a single person, the Messiah (called by Ethan in v. 38 God's "anointed").

---

[271] Samuel, a Levite—and originally consecrated to God's service at the Tabernacle in Shiloh—probably remained in contact with the priests and was able to obtain the holy oil.

[272] The "holy oil" was perhaps used to anoint Solomon also, for when he was anointed king by Zadok, at the Gihon spring, the oil was obtained, according to 1 Kings 1:39, "from the tent," that is, most likely from the tent that David had erected for the Ark of the Covenant (2 Sam 6:17).

Each of the sufferings is inflicted by God, based upon the great "wrath" that God has towards his "anointed" (v. 38). The wrath must be based upon some grievous sin found in the Messiah, although Ethan does not say what it is—a feature which goes against the grain of the Tanakh's normal practice of describing sins committed that incur the judgment of God. Here, the wrath of God comes down harshly upon the Messiah: he is plundered by enemies, his strongholds are ruined, his splendor disappears, he suffers great shame and premature termination of life, and his throne and crown are cast to the ground. After this comes the final great dishonor: God "spurns" the covenant that he had made with David (v. 39).

In all this, Ethan describes these blows coming down upon an individual whom he calls God's "anointed" and "servant." Who is he? David was already gone by this time, and in any case neither he nor Solomon (who sinned greatly) suffered loss to this extent.[273] Rehoboam, Solomon's son, as already mentioned, fits the picture painted here pretty well: he "did evil in the sight of the LORD," lost the northern ten tribes to the rebel Jeroboam, was conquered by the Egyptians—suffering great loss in the process—and did not live to old age.[274] Similar suffering could be attributed to several wicked kings of Judah, like, for example, King Zedekiah who ruled when Judah was conquered by the Babylonians.[275] But there is something here in Ethan's psalm that makes these candidates unlikely. Ethan, in vv. 38-39, speaks to God, saying:

> But You have cast off and rejected, You have been full of wrath against Your anointed. You have spurned the covenant of Your servant; You have profaned his crown in the dust.

Of importance here is that the covenant made with David has been "spurned" by God. The JPS '85 says that God has "repudiated" the covenant, and the Judaica Tanakh makes the break final: God "abrogated" the covenant with his servant. Even if God could do this, we have to ask if he did do this at any time during the united and divided monarchies. From what the Tanakh records, the answer is no: Even though Judah and the Davidic kings had seasons of apostasy which were part of a general decline until the Babylonian exile, the Scripture testifies that God's relationship with Judah and her kings was always based on the reality and the continued viability of the Davidic covenant. And this viability continued on through the exile into the time of the rebuilding of the temple (under the Davidic governor Zerubbabel, and the High Priest Joshua) and the rebuilding of the city and its walls (under the guidance of Nehemiah).

---

[273] Much as Solomon sinned, he was not subject to much of what is described here.
[274] 1 Kings 12-14; 2 Chron 10-12
[275] 2 Kings 24-25; 2 Chron 36

For example, when Jehoram succeeded the good King Jehoshaphat (ca. 850 BC), he did "evil in the sight of the LORD." His "evil" began right away: When Jehoram ascended the throne, he killed all of his brothers. The Chronicler then says,

> Yet the Lord was not willing to destroy the house of David because of the covenant which He had made with David, and since He had promised to give a lamp to him and his sons forever.[276]

So Jehoram lived for a few years longer, and his son Ahaziah succeeded him, and the "house" of David lived on. About a century and a half later, King Hezekiah (who ruled when the Assyrians threatened the existence of Judah) was told by God (through Isaiah) that he was going to die.[277] The king grieved bitterly over the news, and pleaded with God not to take his life. God listened and had Isaiah return and tell the king this:

> I have heard your prayer, I have seen your tears; behold, I will heal you. On the third day you shall go up to the house of the LORD. I will add fifteen years to your life, and I will deliver you and this city from the hand of the king of Assyria; and I will defend this city for My own sake and for My servant David's sake.[278]

God would preserve the city, i.e., preserve the king and what was left of his kingdom, for his own sake and for David's sake—for YHWH had made a covenant with David that could not be broken. One more example should be mentioned, one that is especially apropos regarding the point being made here. Even as the history recorded in the Tanakh closes just after the time of the return from exile, the viability of the Davidic covenant and the Davidic line is still evident in regard to events that were prophesied by Zechariah to still be far out into the future. At a far-future date when Jerusalem is defended by God against the nations' attack, the LORD says:

> I will pour out on the house of David and on the inhabitants of Jerusalem, the Spirit of grace and of supplication, so that they will look on Me whom they have pierced; and they will mourn for Him, as one mourns for an only son, and they will weep bitterly over Him like the bitter weeping over a firstborn.[279]

It is assumed here that the "house of David" is still legitimate. And from what God says just before this, the house of David is powerful:

---

[276] 2 Chron 21:7
[277] 2 Kings 20
[278] 2 Kings 20:5-6
[279] Zech 12:10

> In that day the LORD will defend the inhabitants of Jerusalem, and the one who is feeble among them in that day will be like David, and the house of David will be like God, like the angel of the LORD before them.[280]

Yet Ethan, in our psalm, says that at some point the covenant will be (as the Judaica Tanakh puts it) "abrogated." If this did not occur during the history that the Tanakh records, and if the Davidic covenant is still in effect in eschatological times, then when is it abrogated? When the angel Gabriel spoke to Daniel near the time when the Babylonian exile was at an end (ca. 535 BC), it is probably the case that he referred to this Davidic covenant abrogation when he told Daniel that the Messiah would be "cut off and have nothing" some five centuries later.[281] Be that as it may, we will discover further along in this book that the prophets in the Tanakh have much more to say about the suffering of the Messiah, even suffering unto death. We have learned so far that he suffers; the prophets will tell us how and why he suffers, and Daniel will tell us, as just mentioned, when he suffers.

Ethan appears to end his psalm in despondency when he questions the LORD, saying (v. 49), "Where are Your former lovingkindnesses, O Lord, which You swore to David in Your faithfulness?" But it's really a rhetorical question that, in the context of the psalm and in view of who God is, expects an answer that confirms that God is still God: He is love, he is faithful, he is righteous, and so his "lovingkindnesses" will be revealed again and his Messiah will one day flourish and fulfill all that was promised by oath to David.

PSALM 110—THE MESSIAH IS AN ETERNAL PRIEST

We come here to another psalm of David, one that is highly messianic, and the one other psalm in the Psalter that has the ethereal and eschatological tone of Ps 2. This psalm will add a surprising and vitally important component to our "forensic picture," and will also imply something about the essence of the Messiah that the prophets will later make explicit. King David obviously wrote this psalm, for the superscription at the beginning says so: "A Psalm of David." About half the psalms in the Tanakh contain this superscription, and they should be taken as indicating authorship. Yet some today take the Ps 110 superscription to mean that the psalm is about David, not by him—an opinion

---

[280] Zech 12:8
[281] Dan 9:26. I assume here, like many others, that the "sevens" denominated by Gabriel are sevens *of years*. For a fuller discussion of Daniel's prophecy, see chapter 2's, "the Messiah is the 'Son of Man.'"

that runs against this Scripture's plain meaning and one that is driven by the assumption that God's Messiah can in no way be divine.[282]

Like Ps 2, Ps 110 is short and to the point. The two psalms share the same basic outline: First, the Messiah is presented in the midst of opposition; second, YHWH decrees remarkable things about the Messiah; and last, the Messiah is described as conquering all enemies from many nations.

In view of what we know about the Messiah so far, messianic features of this psalm can be quickly discerned. The king who is the subject matter of the psalm is presented as being very close to God and as having dominion over all the earth. Right at the start, the Messiah, whom David calls "Lord," sits at the right hand of YHWH. Of course, this could hyperbolically refer, for example, to Solomon's rule—on "the throne of the LORD"[283]—at his palace not far from YHWH's "throne" in the Temple. But the tone of the psalm is so otherworldly that this interpretation does not seem appropriate at all. Literally, the Messiah is said to be at YHWH's "right hand"—a fact that should prompt one to recall what YHWH had said (as recorded in 1 Chron 17) about David's son after that son built a "house" for YHWH: "I will install him in my house." In other words, for one thing, Ps 110 is messianic because the Messiah is presented as being spatially and relationally extremely close to God—right at God's right hand. And from this position of favor and high authority, the Messiah doesn't alone put all enemies under his feet and extend his ruler's staff over the world, but YHWH does both for him (vv. 1-2). Their relationship makes them as one in authority and action, and this results in the Messiah gaining the victory over kings and peoples of the *goyim* (v. 6). Just as Gen 49:10 said that the "obedience of the peoples" would be his, so the Messiah here conquers the nations and forces them to bow the knee before him.[284]

Now let's add some amazing new details to the messianic portrait that we have been slowly developing. First, what David says in v. 1 should be seriously considered. It involves something remarkable that is easily overlooked when the verse is first read. David says:

---

[282] If an unknown Ps 110 Hebrew author is speaking of David, then it is appropriate for the writer to call King David his "Lord" (v. 1). In this case, the subject of the psalm is David as simply himself or as the archetype of the Messiah. If the author is David, and the subject of the psalm is the son of David, who is the Messiah, then it is inappropriate for David to call him "Lord"—unless there is something extraordinary about him. In any case, it seems to be the case that Jesus and Peter in their separate appeals to Ps 110 assumed that their Jewish auditors understood that David wrote the psalm (see Luke 20:41-44; Acts 2:34).

[283] 1 Chron 29:23

[284] In Ps 2 the *goyim* rage against, and then are defeated by, YHWH and his Messiah. YHWH says this in Isa 45:22-23: "Turn to Me and be saved, all the ends of the earth; for I am God, and there is no other. I have sworn by Myself, The word has gone forth from My mouth in righteousness and will not turn back, that to Me every knee will bow, every tongue will swear allegiance."

> The LORD [YHWH] says to my Lord [*adoni*]: "Sit at My right
> hand until I make Your enemies a footstool for Your feet."

David here records the words of YHWH, who commands his Messiah: "Sit at my right hand ...." We know from earlier Scripture that the Messiah—who will rule all nations—is the son of David, that is, one of his descendants.[285] Yet King David (who is the one speaking in v. 1 from the start) calls the Messiah—who is his own son—"Lord." A son may call his father "Lord," but a father will never call his son by that title. Yet David here calls his son "Lord," which indicates that—familial protocol notwithstanding—he recognized something in this king at God's right hand that was extraordinary and something that transcended time: David called him "Lord" even though David would be dead and gone by the time this son would arise. Nothing in Solomon or Rehoboam or any of the other kings of Judah would have warranted David calling them "Lord" (if he could have somehow foreknown their characters and works). If David wrote this psalm after he had secured the kingdom and gained independence from all competing forces, foreign and domestic, he was at that point under no obligation to call anyone "Lord"—except, of course, *the* LORD (YHWH). So what we have here is an *indication* that David perceived in the Messiah something more than mere humanity. He perceived, through the Spirit, something extraordinary in one of his future offspring that prompted him to indicate his submission to this person—even before this person was born.

There is something else to learn from Ps 110 that is especially wonderful, although already hinted at in Ps 89:20 ("with My holy oil I have anointed him"). David says (and then quotes YHWH) in v. 4:

> The LORD has sworn and will not change His mind, "You are a priest
> forever According to the order of Melchizedek."

First note that YHWH decrees this with an oath: "The LORD has sworn ...." With or without an oath, God will perfectly fulfill his promises; but with an oath, he gives assurance to us weak human beings who are prone to doubt his word. God, here, wants us to especially be confident that he will make the Messiah a priest who can intercede between God and man. This priestly function of the Messiah is decreed to last "forever," and this forever will really be forever because YHWH will never "change his mind" about it. Jewish and Christian versions are agreed up to this point; but there is much disagreement regarding the "Melchizedek" clause—disagreement that we should briefly consider, for much rides upon the translation and interpretation. The MT of this clause as well as several English translations are shown just below:

---

[285] 1 Chron 17:11

אַתָּה־כֹהֵן לְעוֹלָם עַל־דִּבְרָתִי מַלְכִּי־צֶדֶק

NASB: "You are a priest forever according to the order of Melchizedek."
KJV: "Thou art a priest for ever after the order of Melchizedek."
JPS '85: "You are a priest forever, a rightful king by My decree."
Judaica: "[Y]ou are a priest forever because of the speech of Malchizedek."
Artscroll: "You shall be a priest forever, because you are a king of righteousness."

The Christian translations connect the Messiah's priesthood to that of the ancient king of Salem, Melchizedek (Gen 14:18-20). On the other hand, the Judaica Tanakh makes it look like the Messiah is a priest because of something Melchizedek said (thus not specifying what order of priest the Messiah is), and the JPS '85 and Artscroll versions avoid any relationship with the historical Melchizedek altogether by simply applying the literal Hebrew meaning of מַלְכִּי־צֶדֶק, *melchi-zedek*, to the Messiah as a personal characteristic: The Messiah is (as the Artscroll has it) a "king of righteousness." For some reason these Jewish versions labor hard to keep from drawing any connection between the Messiah and the historical Melchizedek.

A couple of common sense things need to be mentioned before going into some detail about the MT language. First, *melchi-zedek*, other than here, is only found in Gen 14, where Abraham's encounter with Melchizedek, the priest of "God Most High" in Salem, is recorded. The occasion for the encounter was the following: King Chedorlaomer of Elam, with three other kings from nations surrounding the Promised Land, came against the king of Sodom, while Abraham's nephew Lot lived there, and defeated the king of Sodom and those kings allied with him. Lot was carried away captive by Chedorlaomer and his allied kings. When Abraham was notified of this, he and the fighting men with him, along with the fighting men of Amorite friends of his, went after Chedorlaomer, and overcame him and those kings with him sufficient to retrieve Lot as well as many other Sodomite prisoners, and the booty that Chedorlaomer had taken from Sodom as well. Upon his return, Abraham (who was then called "Abram") was visited by the king of Salem (Jerusalem), as Gen 14:18-20 records:

> And Melchizedek king of Salem brought out bread and wine; now he was a priest of God Most High. He blessed him and said, "Blessed be Abram of God Most High, possessor of heaven and earth; and blessed be God Most High, Who has delivered your enemies into your hand." He gave him a tenth of all.

The king of Sodom also came to meet Abraham, but Abraham did not honor him in any way. But to Melchizedek, Abraham gave ten percent of all that he had acquired in the rescue expedition, and unlike his refusal to accept anything from the king of Sodom, Abraham accepted from Melchizedek the bread and wine that he offered, and accepted Melchizedek's blessing as well. Thus, Melchizedek comes briefly upon the biblical historical stage, and then disappears—until he is mentioned in the Tanakh one more time, in Ps 110. Who was this king of Salem, i.e., king of "peace," who had the distinction of being both a king and a priest to his people? There is something "otherworldly" about him too. Other than what is said here, the Tanakh tells us nothing, so there is not much we can say: nothing is recorded about his genealogy or his posterity.[286] All we know is that he was a priest and king, and Abraham submitted to him as a legitimate priestly representative of the One true God, who he called "God Most High," i.e., YHWH.

That Ps 110 makes a connection between this priest-king and the Messiah is patently obvious, translational differences of the versions notwithstanding. One reason for this simply comes down to common sense. It might be recalled that Ps 2's main subject matter was the Messiah, mainly through what God said about him. In that psalm, YHWH calls the Messiah his "son." So when the Aramaic word for "son" showed up at the end ("kiss the son"), I argued that this word (*bar*) certainly means "son," for the Son of YHWH has been the subject of the psalm all along. The logic that connects the Messiah in Ps 110:4 to Melchizedek is similar: In the first clause, there is the clearly presented fact—a fact decreed by YHWH with an oath—that the Messiah is not only a king, but a priest as well . . . and not just temporarily, but forever. With this solemnly declared, any biblically knowledgeable reader would immediately think of Melchizedek in Gen 14—the priest-king who met Abraham with the bread and wine. And when this reader read *melchi-zedek* at the end of the verse, he or she would naturally understand that God (through David) is making a connection between the priest-king Messiah and the priest-king Melchizedek. What are the chances that this text would have as its subject a priest-king Messiah, and then mention the name of the only other priest-king in the Tanakh, *melchi-zedek*, but not intend for the king of Salem to be thought of at all? It is extremely unlikely. I might add that because the Tanakh is so concerned about priestly *order* (usually having to do with the Aaronic order), it would seem a reasonable first understanding of this text that God is saying that the Messiah is of the priestly order *of Melchizedek*, which is unique in that it is a *royal* priesthood.

---

[286] The author of the book of Hebrews in the NT tells us a little more about Melchizedek and verifies that the Messiah is of the priestly order of that king of Salam. See Heb 5-7.

So there should be no doubt that v. 4 presents some kind of connection between the Messiah and Melchizedek. But what is the nature of this connection? The answer must be found in the meaning of the Hebrew compound word עַל־דִּבְרָתִי, *al-dibrahthe*. The first part is easy enough: the preposition *al* being ubiquitous in the Tanakh, meaning basically "on" or "upon." The second part is an inflected form of the rare feminine noun *dibrah* (דִּבְרָה)—the final *hey* changing into *tav* in the construct form (in other languages, usually called the genitive/possessive: "the order *of* Melchizedek"), and the *hiriq-yod* at the end being, according to some lexicographers, a poetic device to smooth transition from one word to another.[287] The feminine noun *dibrah* is obviously based on the often-used masculine noun for "word," *dabar*, and so their meanings are probably not that far apart. But as a stand-alone word, *dibrah* is only used once in the Tanakh, in Job 5:8, and as a compound word with *al*, only employed here and a few times in Ecclesiastes, the most germane being Eccl 3:18. So to get an idea of what the meaning is in Ps 110:4, let's consider for a moment the meaning of *dibrah* and *al-dibrah* in these other texts.

> Job 5:8 (*dibrah*):
> NASB: I would place my *cause* before God.
> JPS: I would lay my *case* before God.
> Judaica: to God would I commit my *cause*.

The context of Job 5:8 makes translation of the stand-alone *dibrah* fairly straightforward: It denotes Job's "case" or "cause"—one might say "situation" or "reality"—that he wants God to know about. Now with *al*, as a compound word, its meaning in Eccl 3:18 is a little different:

> Eccl 3:18 (*al-dibrah*):
> NASB: I said to myself *concerning* the sons of men.
> JPS: So I decided, as *regards* men.
> Judaica: I said to myself, [that this is] *because of* the children of men.

The compound *al-dibrah* is used here to point the reader to the situation of somebody or something that the writer is concerned about. Eliphaz (Job's friend), to take a fictional case, may want to address Job's "case," *dibrah*, but as he broaches the subject with his hearers, he might say, "now, *on the case* (*al dibrah*) of Job, we should take into account God's providence." The better way to say this, of course, would be "now, *regarding* Job, we should ...." Admittedly, all this is approximate because there is so little data to go on. But when we consider the most basic meanings of *dabar* (which has plentiful data) and then what little we can glean from the few uses of *dibarah* and *al-dibarah*, it's pretty

---

[287] BDB, דִּבְרָה, citing Gesenius.

clear that these latter two words simply provide a generic marker to represent in one word the general situation of a person or thing.

If that is generally so, we might not be that far away from the mark if we woodenly translate Ps 110:4b, "You are a priest forever *upon the reality* of Melchizedek." This is very close to the JPS 1917 version, which translates using better (old) English: "Thou art a priest for ever *after the manner* of Melchizedek." Most English versions assume that priestly *order* (as in, for example, the Aaronic *order*, but here, the Melchizedekian order) is what is meant here. The NASB, for example, has "You are a priest forever *according to the order* of Melchizedek." Given the context, this is probably an accurate translation, for the "reality" of Melchizedek that YHWH is obviously concerned about (in his declaration that the Messiah is a "priest") is Melchizedek's vocation/calling of *king-priest*. As Melchizedek is that, so, says YHWH, is the king who sits at his (YHWH's) right hand.

The JPS '85 and Artscroll Tanakh versions don't even refer to the historical Melchizedek here; but for the reasons already stated, this simply cannot be right. The Judaica Tanakh understands this as referring to Melchizedek: "[Y]ou are a priest forever because of the speech of Melchizedek." Perhaps "because of the speech" is an acceptable translation of *al-dibrah*, but the problem with this is that it does not correlate to anything biblical: The Tanakh records nothing about Melchizedek saying anything about passing on his priesthood to the Messiah or anyone else. Plus, in Ps 110:4, it is YHWH who makes the designation with an oath, a decision on his part that is unchangeable. Melchizedek has nothing to do with making the Messiah a priest, but God has everything to do with making the Messiah a priest-king like Melchizedek.

The Holman Christian Standard Bible perhaps captures the meaning of the passage best with its simple translation: "Forever, You are a priest like Melchizedek." Perhaps the Messiah is "like" Melchizedek in more ways than the king-priest commonality: Perhaps he too is a "king of peace" and a priest who intercedes for his people and brings them "bread and wine" in their famished state. Be that as it may, it is surely the case that Ps 110 gives us a new and amazing addition to our "forensic picture": The Messiah is a king who functions in his royalty as an intermediary between God and the people within his domain—which eventually will be worldwide. As a priest, he is intimately bound up with the processes by which men and women are reconciled to God and thereby overcome the post-fall decree of death. He is "anointed" with the "holy oil" so that he can offer whatever sacrifice might be required to realize the reconciliation between man and his Maker.[288]

Finally, Ps 110 offers one more new bit of information that should greatly encourage us. In v. 3 the Messiah is told this:

> Your people will volunteer freely in the day of Your power; in holy array, from the womb of the dawn, Your youth are to You as the dew.

Here we see that the "people" of the Messiah serve him—probably as fellow warriors—on the day that he battles his enemies. Vv. 5-6 and Ps 2:8-9 depict the Messiah roundly defeating his enemies; here, it shows that he is not alone. The second part of the verse is highly esoteric, adding to the "otherworldly" tone of the psalm. If the "holy array" of the second clause refers to the clothing of the Messiah's people, then some kind of priestly identity might be indicated in them: For the same apparel description—probably some kind of linen garment that resembled the priests' ephod—is used in regards to the Levitical singers who went before Jehoshaphat and his army as the LORD fought the Ammonites, Moabites, and Edomites on their behalf.[289] If this is so, it should not come completely as a surprise, because God called his people at Sinai "a kingdom of priests and a holy nation."[290] With this thought in mind, it might be best to conclude this section with a quote from Daniel that pertains to the final judgment brought by the "Ancient of Days" and the "Son of Man" (to whom is "given dominion, glory and a kingdom, that all the peoples, nations and men of every language might serve Him" [Dan 7:14]):

> Then the sovereignty, the dominion and the greatness of all the kingdoms under the whole heaven will be given to the people of the saints of the Highest One; His kingdom will be an everlasting kingdom, and all the dominions will serve and obey Him.[291]

---

[288] About five centuries after David wrote Ps 110, the prophet Zechariah said (symbolically) that the two offices of king and priest would be combined in the Messiah (there, called "the Branch"). See Zech 6:9-14.

[289] "[T]he Levite singers went forth before the army in 'holy attire' in 2 Chron. 20:21; here, however, the people without distinction wear holy festive garments. Thus they surround the divine king as dew that is born out of the womb of the morning-red. It is a priestly people which he leads forth to holy battle, just as in Apoc. 19:14 ...." (Carl Friedrich Keil and Franz Delitzsch, *Commentary on the Old Testament* [Peabody: Hendrickson, 1996], Ps 110:3-4.) For "holy attire," Ps 110 and 2 Chron 20:21 both have *hdr-qodesh*.

[290] Exod 19:6

[291] Dan 7:27. See also Ps 149:5-9; Rev 19:14.

CONCLUSION TO CHAPTER ONE

Before we enter into the time when the prophets of the failing kingdoms of Israel and Judah prophesied of these nations' destruction, and of their last-days resurrection with YHWH and the Messiah at the helm, allow me to first briefly sketch what prophetic information has been brought to light about the Messiah so far.

The Messiah is called "the Anointed One,"[292] the Hebrew being *mashiach,* which is, of course, where we get our word "Messiah." He is anointed by the "holy oil" and the Holy Spirit into his worldwide kingly ministry.[293] The Messiah is sometimes called "David,"[294] sometimes the "seed" of David,[295] and in a number of instances said to be the "servant" of God.[296] YHWH calls him "my firstborn" who, although "the highest of the kings of earth,"[297] is violently opposed by nations and their kings.[298] Yet the Messiah is righteous, compassionate, just,[299] and does not just benevolently rule his people, but is a priest who intercedes on their behalf.[300] In this capacity he has all the authority and power of YHWH,[301] yet is intimately concerned about the death of each of his people—people not only of Israel, but the gentile nations as well.[302] God's desire is to have a "house" in which he and his people can live together: The Messiah will build this house, and he will live in this house as well.[303]

Even though the Messiah is righteous and eminently just, he is for yet some unknown reason subject to God's wrath.[304] In the process of being judged and punished by God, the Messiah loses his kingdom and his life is cut short.[305] Thus the covenant that God made with David concerning his "throne" and his "seed" is "abrogated."[306] Yet in the long run God does honor the covenant, for God's love is never taken away from the Messiah.[307] Somehow through all this, the Messiah "redeems" his people.[308]

---

[292] 1 Sam 2:10; Ps 2:2; Ps 89:20, 38, 51; Ps 132:10, 17
[293] Ps 89:20
[294] Ps 89:3, 20, 35, 49; Ps 132:10, 17
[295] 2 Sam 7:12; 1 Chron 17:11; Ps 89:29, 36-37
[296] 2 Sam 7:5, 8; 1 Chron 17:4, 7; Ps 89:3, 20, 39; Ps 132:10
[297] Ps 89:27
[298] Gen 3:15; Ps 2:1-3; Ps 89:50-51; Ps 110:1-2, 5-6
[299] Ps 72:1-2, 4, 12-14
[300] Ps 89:20; Ps 110:4; Ps 72:12-14
[301] Ps 2:6; Ps 89:21, 24; Ps 110:2
[302] Ps 72:8, 14, 17
[303] 2 Sam 7:13; 1 Chron 17:12; Ps 132:1-8
[304] Ps 89:38, 46
[305] Ps 89:39-45
[306] Ps 89:39
[307] 2 Sam 7:13-16; 1 Chron 17:11-14; Ps 89:3-4, 24, 28, 33-37, 49; Ps 132:10-12
[308] Ps 72:14

At some point in the distant future the Messiah will sit at the right hand of YHWH.[309] From there he will, through the power of God, go to war against all enemy nations.[310] In this war, the Messiah's "people" will fight alongside him.[311] The enemy nations will be subject to his wrath, utterly defeated, and brought into submission to him.[312] The Messiah's exaltation and essence will be so glorified that even King David, moved by the Spirit, calls him "Lord."[313] Zion will be the home and throne of the Messiah.[314] From there he will judge the nations.[315] If any king of any nation does not honor ("kiss") the Son, he will be subject to God's wrath and destruction.[316] The nations will be righteously ruled by the Messiah, and everlasting peace and prosperity will finally be established.[317] The Messiah's throne and kingdom will last forever.[318] In the course of all this, the Evil One, who is the devil, will at some point be overcome and mortally wounded.[319]

This distillation of what can be learned from the messianic passages considered from the time of Adam and Eve to King Solomon tells us much about the "seed" of Eve who will one day "bruise" the head of the devil. It should be said here that there are many symbolic elements of the Torah—like the items in the Tabernacle and the sacrifices offered under the Mosaic Law— that are messianic in various ways; the Psalms also contain many more messianic features than we have already discussed. Before ending chapter 1, let me mention a few interesting things from the latter that could be kept in mind as we proceed on into chapter 2. These have to do with interesting similarities between YHWH and the Messiah.

Among other things, the messianic psalms discussed above showed that the coming Messiah is to be a great king, that he is to rule from Mount Zion, and that he will have dominion over the whole earth. Not a few other psalms show that YHWH will be/do the same. For example, David asks in Ps 24:10, "Who is this King of glory?" He then answers, "The LORD of hosts, he is the King of glory." "The LORD," says David in Ps 29:10, "sits as King forever." And in Ps 93:2, David says that YHWH's "throne is established from old" and that the Almighty is "from everlasting." Not only do the Messiah and YHWH both possess the office of King, they also have the similarity of abiding in and

---

[309] Ps 110:1
[310] Ps 2:9; Ps 89:23; Ps 110:2, 5-6
[311] Ps 110:3
[312] Ps 2:4-6, 8-12; Ps 72:8-11; Ps 89:23, 25, 27; Ps 110:1-3, 5-6
[313] Ps 110:1
[314] Ps 2:6
[315] Ps 110:6
[316] Ps 2:12
[317] Gen 12:3; 22:18; 49:10; Ps 72:2-3, 6, 7, 16-17
[318] 2 Sam 7:13, 16; 1 Chron 17:12, 14
[319] Gen 3:15; Ps 72:4; Ps 132:17-18

ruling from the same royal location, which is, *Zion*. YHWH in Ps 2:6 announced the installment of the Messiah as king upon Zion, God's "holy mountain." While YHWH's throne is certainly in the heavens,[320] he has, according to several psalms, also chosen Zion for his eternal dwelling place. God has established forever the "city of the LORD of hosts," "Mount Zion in the far north," "the city of our God," "the joy of the whole earth," "the city of the great King"—who is YHWH.[321] Ps 132:13 declares that "the LORD has chosen Zion," and then quotes YHWH saying (v. 14): "This is My resting place forever; here I will dwell, for I have desired it."[322] The spheres of earthly dominion of the Messiah and YHWH appear to completely overlap: The Messiah's rule, as we have seen, will be successfully wielded over the whole world; likewise, as the Psalms show, the rule of YHWH is universal. He is the judge and king of "all the earth."[323] He "sits on his holy throne" and "rules over the nations."[324] "His sovereignty," as David says, "rules over all."[325] YHWH has the authority to give the nations, as we have seen in Ps 2, to his Messiah. And we should remember that it is not the Messiah alone that extends his scepter from Zion and makes all enemies a "footstool" for his feet, but YHWH does these for him (Ps 110:1). So YHWH and the Messiah have much in common. This commonality perhaps becomes *identity* in Ps 45, which is a love psalm to the Davidic king by the "sons of Korah." After offering praise to this king, they say to him (vv. 6-7):

> Your throne, O God, is forever and ever; a scepter of uprightness is the scepter of Your kingdom. You have loved righteousness and hated wickedness; therefore God, Your God, has anointed You With the oil of joy above Your fellows.

Here they speak to the Messiah as God, and at the same time they speak of him as one separate from God.

---

[320] Ps 11:4: "The LORD is in His holy temple; the LORD's throne is in heaven." Ps 103:19: "The LORD has established His throne in the heavens, and His sovereignty rules over all." Ps 113:5-6: "Who is like the LORD our God, who is enthroned on high, who humbles Himself to behold the things that are in heaven and in the earth?" Ps 123:1: "To You I lift up my eyes, O You who are enthroned in the heavens!"

[321] Ps 48:1-2, 8

[322] The Psalms do not say literally that God's "throne" is at Zion. But YHWH dwelt above the Mercy Seat and between the Cherubim of the Ark of the Covenant (Exod 25:22; 1 Sam 4:4; Ps 80:1; Ps 99:1; Isa 37:16). So when the Ark was in Jerusalem—beginning with David until it disappeared no later than the Babylonian destruction of the temple and city—God was necessarily "enthroned" (Pss 80:1; 90:1) at Zion. Isaiah's vision of YHWH in chapter six might also be considered: "In the year of King Uzziah's death," Isaiah "saw the Lord sitting on a throne, lofty and exalted, with the train of His robe filling the temple." Also consider Ezek 43:7.

[323] Ps 47:7

[324] Ps 47:8

[325] Ps 103:19

And finally, perhaps as a sign of the future Messiah's identity with YHWH, the Tanakh records this upon the ascension (to the throne) of King Solomon (1 Chron 29:23):

> Then Solomon sat on the throne of the LORD as king in place of David his father. And he prospered, and all Israel obeyed him.

Chapter Two

THE MESSIAH CONCEPT FROM SOLOMON TO THE RETURN FROM EXILE

INTRODUCTION

When the queen of Sheba visited King Solomon, he and his kingdom were at the apex of glory and power and God's blessing. She had heard in her own land of his wisdom and prosperity, but it turned out that she didn't know the half of it until she came to Jerusalem; then she was stunned at what she heard and saw.[1] She probably didn't know much, if anything, about the promises that God had made to the Hebrew patriarchs regarding wonderful future blessings. But many of Solomon's subjects surely must have wondered if Solomon was *the* Messiah who would preside over the promised kingdom of unending peace, prosperity, and worldwide influence. The greatest promises of God now appeared fulfilled: Israel and her king now occupied a nation that extended (approximately), as promised, "from the river of Egypt as far as the great river, the river Euphrates";[2] the people were as numerous as the stars of the heavens; they now had a glorious anointed king, brimming with majesty and wisdom; the kingdom burst with bountiful material blessings; and Israel was ever more bringing blessings to the nations that she touched. Not long before the queen of Sheba's visit, the people must have stood in amazement at the Temple dedication when they saw the glory of what Solomon had built, and they heard the profound prayer that he, kneeling on his platform with arms stretched out toward heaven, offered up to YHWH—a prayer that Solomon ended with an acknowledgment that he was the LORD's "Anointed."[3] And at the end of the prayer, when the fire of Heaven came down and consumed what was on the brazen altar,[4] and then when they saw the smoke of God's presence

---

[1] 1 Kings 10:1-13
[2] Gen 15:18
[3] 2 Chron 6:42 (NKJV)
[4] 2 Chron 7:1-3

enter the Temple, some must have felt like the unending glorious messianic age had arrived—and a few might have even wondered if this glorious king and his kingdom would endure forever. But there may have been a few among these— although highly impressed with the spectacle, and hopeful for the glorious messianic age—who thought in their hearts, *Is this all there is?* It was all so wonderful; and yet, it was all so earthbound and temporal.

Solomon and his kingdom could not have been the messianic apex that God had already spoken about—albeit somewhat enigmatically—by that time. What the people beheld in Solomon and his palace and temple, and wealth and wisdom beyond measure, was obviously the fulfillment of some things that the holy writings had said about the Messiah; yet nothing in it appeared to give men and women any explicit information about how to be forgiven for *all* their sins and thereby achieve blessed life with God after earthly death. A few, maybe more, surely wondered about this, for the Scripture that they had by that time began with Adam and Eve's fall from eternal life, and there were hints in a few places of the possibility of restoration to eternal life: the devil, the great deceiver, would one day be silenced;[5] Moses mentioned God's "book" that probably contained the names of those slated for blessed eternal life;[6] Job declared the reality of a resurrection of the righteous;[7] and a few of David's songs appeared to teach that, for the righteous man, the "valley of the shadow of death" and "Sheol" were no threat to the soul.[8] Yet, regarding this matter, these were very small flashes of light on an otherwise dark scriptural horizon: The whole of the Torah, the record of the time of the judges and the first two kings of Israel, and the Psalms, were nearly completely silent on the subject.[9] There was, however, enough there to prompt awareness of eternal concerns, and thus to question why something so important to Scripture as the Messiah phenomenon would not have any ultimate human concerns associated with it, and with that, to be prompted to wonder why the Scripture up to that point was so focused on temporal life, and not eternal life.

Why the Earthly, Temporal Focus?

At this point let me ponder for a few moments the question about why God in his Holy Word, up to the time of Solomon, hardly spoke about life after death, and kept all concerns of the Israelites focused on matters concerning their

---

[5] Gen 3:15

[6] Exod 32:32

[7] Job 19:25-27

[8] Pss 16, 21, 23

[9] Silent, but it could be argued even a bit negative, if some words of David and Solomon are considered that speak about the inactivity that obtains in the grave. See Pss 6:5; 30:9; Eccl 9:2-6.

earthly existence. They were taught to believe in YHWH and to follow his Law, but all the blessings and curses delineated only had to do with earthly life and death. And what was known (as we have seen in chapter 1) about the Messiah appeared to be mainly about his person and his reign in this temporal life: he would rule and bless all nations, bring worldwide peace, and be the son of David. Yes, he would be the Son of God also, and as such establish a throne and a kingdom that would last forever;[10] but when David's son came to the throne, and fulfilled Nathan's prophecy (at least the short-term, literal prophecy) by building YHWH a glorious "house," Solomon and the Temple and what he said at the Temple's dedication—and all that the history describes about Solomon and his kingdom after that—all had to do with worshipping God and obtaining his favor *in the here and now.* There was never any mention (as far as what is recorded) about the reality of a blessed afterlife and what one must do to obtain it.[11]

So why did God subject Israel, from its beginning on through the time of Solomon and beyond, to his heavy hand, yet keep the people's focus on earthly blessings and curses, and not on the grand concern of man regarding life after death? As far as I know, the Tanakh does not give us the answer. But let me speculate a bit as to why this was. We know that before God began to work with Abraham, few men honored God: most men were idol worshippers and unrighteous.[12] It seems that God's plan was to take one man, Abraham, and slowly build up "seed" after him that would also be his "seed" in the sense that they shared his faith in God.[13] But while the Israelites waited in Egypt until "the iniquity of the Amorite" reached its full measure,[14] whatever knowledge of YHWH they had inherited from the patriarchs was largely forgotten, and they took to the belief in, and fear of, the gods that abounded there.[15] Plus, during their four centuries in Egypt, they had come to enjoy and expect daily "the cucumbers and the melons and the leeks and the onions and the garlic" that the fertile banks and delta of the Nile provided without fail.[16] They relied on the Egyptian river and the Egyptian gods. So in order to continue to grow up his adolescent "son,"[17] YHWH reintroduced himself to Israel (and introduced

---

[10] 2 Sam 7:13-14; 1 Chron 17:11-14; Ps 2:7; Ps 89:27-29. Compare with Isa 9:6-7.

[11] Throughout the Tanakh it could be the case that some or all mentions of temporal/material blessings, based upon the people's willingness to trust God and obey, were intended by the Holy Spirit to represent eternal/spiritual blessings. The Tanakh, however, does not say if this is so or not.

[12] Gen 10:5; Josh 24:2

[13] During the divided monarchy, God called Israel "not my people," even though they were descended from Abraham, because they had rejected YHWH as their God (Hos 1:8).

[14] Gen 15:16

[15] Ezek 20:7-8; Amos 5:25-26; Deut 32:15-18

[16] Num 11:5. Also, Exod 16:3.

[17] Exod 4:22-23

himself to Egypt) by supernaturally empowering Moses, bringing plagues upon Egypt, dividing the Red Sea, and by wondrously appearing to Israel at Sinai— an appearance that was so stupendous that it left the people and Moses quaking with fear.[18] So frightened were the people that they begged Moses to intercede for them so that YHWH would stay at a distance.[19] YHWH and Moses acceded to their plea, apparently understanding that some kind of half-way relationship between God and his people was—considering the circumstances—the best plan for the time being.[20]

It was enough through the Exodus on through the conquest of the Promised Land for Israel to learn the following: first, that God is, and that his name is YHWH; second, to know that he is a righteous God who has many laws by which God's people must live (the laws Israel was to live by were given mainly at Mt. Sinai); third, to learn that they were without exception enslaved to sin, for they would soon find out that no one could fully keep all of God's laws; and finally, to learn that—as far as earthly blessings and curses were concerned—they could stay in God's good graces by keeping a reverent relationship with him and, at the same time, by offering appropriate substitutionary sacrifices which God would accept as atonement for some of their sins. All this seemed to be sufficient for God's purposes, knowing what he knew about the heart of Israel at the time, and knowing what they would think and do in the future.[21] God permitted their knowledge about ultimate questions to be in proportion to their nearness to him: As long as they kept God at a distance, then his illumination of them regarding ultimate questions would be correspondingly distant. Given their "stiff-necked" and "rebellious" character, they would have in one way or another abused YHWH if he had come to them—like he had come then to Moses—so close as to be "face to face": They might have worshipped him as just another Egyptian god and immediately made idols in his image, or they might have become overly familiar with him as apparently the sons of Aaron did,[22] or they might have even tried to kill him.[23] In other words, they would have acted not only wickedly, but immaturely.

So the reason why God kept his distance—dwelling in the Tabernacle Holy of Holies where only the High Priest was allowed to enter once a year in order to atone for Israel's sins—is perhaps because this is what was then best for

---

[18] Exod 19-20; Deut 9:19

[19] Exod 20:18-19

[20] Deut 5:22-28

[21] Deut 4:25-31; 9:4-6

[22] Lev 10:1-3

[23] The people came close to stoning YHWH's representatives during the Exodus (Exod 17:4; Num 14:10). During the divided monarchy, God's representatives, the prophets, were often treated badly, and sometimes killed (see, e.g., 1 Kings 18:4; 2 Chron 24:21; 25:16; Neh 9:26; Jer 26:23). See also Heb 11:32-38.

the people, and for the development of Jewish people far down the line who would one day have the spiritual maturity and knowledge sufficient to respond appropriately to a closer relationship with God. The process of coming to fear the one true God, of coming to be fully aware of one's own sinfulness,[24] and as a result coming to cry out to God for deliverance from death and the possibility of post-death unending life separated from God (damnation), is the process that God, it seems, intended for his people Israel. But this process would take a long time, and at the time of Solomon it wasn't very far along.

So with Solomon, we have Scripture substantially fulfilled, and most who were there at the Temple dedication were content to leave it at that: God had a permanent place in the Temple, and his Messiah was now presiding over a peaceful and prosperous kingdom. And yet in the eyes of probably not a few, this must have fallen short of what they understood about God and his ultimate will for mankind. Samuel's words echoed in their minds: "[Y]our wickedness is great which you have done in the sight of the LORD by asking for yourselves a king."[25] And, they remembered God's words to Samuel: "[T]hey have not rejected you, but they have rejected Me from being king over them."[26] Solomon, in all his glory, was still human—especially as later events would bear out—and as such was something of a usurper, for God should have always been Israel's king.[27] And there was the lack of awareness about the blessed afterlife and how to achieve it. Solomon ruled over an earthly kingdom, and the relationship with YHWH was such that earthly blessings could be achieved if the people and their leaders prayed to YHWH and brought sacrifices to the priests at the Temple so as to make atonement for at least some of their sins. But YHWH was not king, and the Law never said that their sacrifices would earn them eternal life and reconciliation with God. Thus, a few discerning men must have perceived that Solomon's glorious kingdom could not endure, for it was far short of what God really wanted.

---

[24] Israel's experience under the Old Covenant showed them that, left to their own devices, perfection before God could not be achieved (Lev 18:5; 1 Kings 8:46; Ezek 20:13). But thanks to God's lovingkindness, it would be achieved under God's New Covenant (Jer 31:31-34) by a supernatural, Spirit caused, change of heart. Man is to blame for his sin and resultant condemnation by God. On the other hand, only God can receive the credit for man being righteous and justified before God, for it is God's Spirit alone that enables a man to think and act righteously and thereby be justified in God's sight (John 6:44; 15:5; Phil 2:13).

[25] 1 Sam 12:17

[26] 1 Sam 8:7

[27] A usurpation that God permitted. This thought would apply to Saul, David, Solomon, and all the kings of Judah.

God Pulls the Rug out from under Israel

At the end of Solomon's forty-year reign, God began to pull the rug out from under the nation of Israel. Now, of course, he did not do this to a righteous people, but to a nation that quickly became unrighteous. The LORD, during this time between Solomon and the exile, taught his people new things, and forced them to mature—all according to God's perfect sovereign plan known to him since "ancient days"—yet in earthly time and space he worked out his perfect plan within the context of the human experience. To put this in philosophical terms, God and his foreknown and fore-ordained purpose for mankind was the "final" cause of Israel's post-Solomonic fall; the "efficient" cause, however, was the wickedness of Israel from Solomon's time down to the time of the Babylonian exile and beyond. Or, to put this succinctly, God worked for good what the people intended for evil.[28] God used the occasion of Solomon's apostasy later in life to begin a process whereby Israel would again be taken through the "wilderness" in order to make the nation better and stronger. In the first wilderness wanderings, God forced the people to believe in and obey YHWH alone, so that life "under the sun" would go well; in the second "wilderness" experience, God continues the lessons of the first, but goes further: Israel must come closer to God, and accept him—and him alone—as their king, and do this, and obey him, sufficient to warrant a pardon at the final judgment.[29] So God "pulled the rug" out from under Israel a second time in order to raise two great concerns in the minds of the people: *Who, ultimately, is my king?* And, *What must I do to be saved?*

Solomon and Israel were fabulously wealthy when the process began that led to this second wilderness experience. David sought God with all his heart, and Solomon did too at first, so God greatly blessed them. David provided for the Temple construction that his son Solomon would undertake with the stupendous amounts, as recorded in 1 Chron 22:14, of "100,000 talents of gold and 1,000,000 talents of silver, and bronze and iron beyond weight."[30] Yet another indicator of the abundance in Israel at that time was the number of animals sacrificed when the ark was brought to the Temple: Solomon and the people sacrificed "so many sheep and oxen that they could not be counted or numbered."[31] As we will soon see, the gold and silver and animals (available for sacrifice) in Israel diminished greatly after the kingdom split and began the slow death march leading to exile. But this precipitous fall after such blessings was

---

[28] Judg 14:4; 2 Kings 12:15, 24; 2 Chron 25:20; Jer 29:11
[29] Zech 14:16-17; Isa 25:6-9
[30] This amount of gold and silver would be worth roughly 250 billion dollars today.
[31] 2 Chron 5:6

no surprise to God, for he had long before predicted it and warned the people about it in these words:

> Beware that you do not forget the LORD your God by not keeping His commandments and His ordinances and His statutes which I am commanding you today; otherwise, when you have eaten and are satisfied, and have built good houses and lived in them, and when your herds and your flocks multiply, and your silver and gold multiply, and all that you have multiplies, then your heart will become proud and you will forget the LORD your God who brought you out from the land of Egypt, out of the house of slavery. He led you through the great and terrible wilderness, with its fiery serpents and scorpions and thirsty ground where there was no water; He brought water for you out of the rock of flint. In the wilderness He fed you manna which your fathers did not know, that He might humble you and that He might test you, to do good for you in the end. Otherwise, you may say in your heart, "My power and the strength of my hand made me this wealth." But you shall remember the LORD your God, for it is He who is giving you power to make wealth, that He may confirm His covenant which He swore to your fathers, as it is this day. It shall come about if you ever forget the LORD your God and go after other gods and serve them and worship them, I testify against you today that you will surely perish. Like the nations that the LORD makes to perish before you, so you shall perish; because you would not listen to the voice of the LORD your God.[32]

And at the zenith of Israel's glory, God warned Solomon of what would be the result if he turned his back on God:

> [I]f you or your sons indeed turn away from following Me, and do not keep My commandments and My statutes which I have set before you, and go and serve other gods and worship them, then I will cut off Israel from the land which I have given them, and the house which I have consecrated for My name, I will cast out of My sight. So Israel will become a proverb and a byword among all peoples. And this house will become a heap of ruins; everyone who passes by will be astonished and hiss and say, "Why has the LORD done thus to this land and to this house?" And they will say, "Because they forsook the LORD their God, who brought their fathers out of the land of Egypt, and adopted other gods and worshiped them and

---

[32] Deut 8:11-20

served them, therefore the LORD has brought all this adversity on them."[33]

Thus, when Solomon and his subjects began to grow spiritually lazy because of their prosperity, God set in motion events that would eventually lead to the loss of everything.

Included in this total loss were three very important things that God at several points had unconditionally promised to Israel. He promised that a king would always sit on David's throne (2 Sam 7:13, 16; 1 Chron 17:12, 14), that the land would be theirs forever (Gen 15:18; Deut 1:8), and that there would be a permanent "house" in which God and the Messiah would dwell forever (1 Chron 17:14). These things that were promised unconditionally were the main things that were lost—which makes one wonder if these things that were lost were really what God promised unconditionally to start with.

The miserable "death march" began with the defection of Solomon. He started well, and with the best intentions. But, as 1 Kings 11:2 and 4 say regarding his many foreign wives, "he held fast to these in love," and so they "turned his heart away after other gods." Solomon eventually had 700 wives and 300 concubines.[34] Many of these were foreign women who worshipped foreign gods. Solomon, to keep them happy, built houses for the worship of their gods, and in time ended up worshipping those gods himself.[35] So the LORD brought troubles upon him, including enemies that rose up from both inside and outside of his empire.[36] As mentioned earlier, upon Solomon's death, his son Rehoboam increased the various burdens (taxes, labor and army conscription, etc.) on the already-overburdened people. So the northern ten tribes revolted against Judah (and Simeon which was located within Judah), and took as their leader an Ephraimite named Jeroboam who had previously served in Solomon's administration.[37] It seems a curious thing that God promised Jeroboam an unending dynasty that had the potential of flourishing as fully as the Davidic dynasty.[38] But the Jeroboamic covenant was, from the beginning, *conditional*: God would bless him and his sons *if* they worshipped and honored YHWH. But any chance of achieving what God said was possible was wrecked right from the start by Jeroboam's establishment of an alternate— i.e., radically non-Mosaic—YHWH cult built around the worship of golden calves at Bethel and also at Dan in the far north. Levites wanted no part of this, so Jeroboam established a priesthood for the cult consisting of anyone who was

---

[33] 1 Kings 9:6-9
[34] 1 Kings 11:3
[35] 1 Kings 11:1-13
[36] 1 Kings 11:14-40
[37] 1 Kings 12:1-24
[38] 1 Kings 11:38

willing and able-bodied.[39] Being worried about his ability to rule over the northern tribes successfully, Jeroboam established this cult in order to keep the people under his domain from going down to worship in Jerusalem, where they might have been tempted to re-submit to the Davidic monarchy.[40] Needless to say, God was not happy with this. So he sent a prophet to Bethel, while Jeroboam was there offering a sacrifice, who foretold of the cult's eventual destruction—even naming the Judean king (Josiah) who would destroy the cult and its priesthood three centuries later.[41]

The two-or-so centuries history (ca. 930-710 BC) of the northern kingdom, Israel, is one of idolatry, intermittent usurpations of the throne, and general decline. During this time, there were nineteen kings, eight of whom were killed by non-family usurpers.[42] The usurpation began right away: Because of Jeroboam's sin of leading Israel into the calves worship, the lasting dynasty that he was promised, contingent upon his and his sons' good behavior, lasted only one generation. When Jeroboam died after a 27-year reign, his son Nadab was murdered by the usurper Baasha within two years. During Baasha's 24-year reign, there was continual warfare between him and King Asa of Judah. The latter sent a substantial gift to the king of Aram and asked him to break his treaty with Israel. The king of Aram complied and attacked Israel and took for himself most of the northern half, including Dan and the region around the Sea of Galilee.[43]

Apostasy, violence, and loss of territory characterized the history of Israel. The kings, according to the Tanakh, were all evil, and the people by and large accepted the heretical YHWH-golden-calves cult in flagrant disregard of all that the Scripture said about idols and about the procedure and place of proper worship. The blatant worship of foreign gods, however, was somewhat subdued in Israel because the idolatrous impulse of the people could to some degree be satisfied by the worship of the golden calves.[44] Still, this syncretism between Mosaic YHWH worship and idolatry was an abomination in God's sight, and it seems that all the kings of Israel participated in this "sin of Jeroboam." But some went further: King Ahab (ruled 874-853 BC), the seventh king of Israel (i.e., the northern kingdom), at the prompting of his Sidonian Baal-loving wife Jezebel, brought Baal worship into Israel in a big way. He built a temple for Baal in Samaria and sanctioned a large Baal priesthood. At the same time Jezebel

---

[39] 1 Kings 12:31
[40] 1 Kings 12:25-33
[41] 1 Kings 13:1-10
[42] Nadab, Elah, Zimri (died by suicide when besieged by Omri), Jehoram, Zachariah, Shallum, Pekahiah, and Pekah.
[43] 1 Kings 15:16-16:12; 2 Chron 16:1-6
[44] A thought offered by Keil and Delitzsch, First Kings, introduction to chapter 12.

labored to exterminate the prophets of YHWH.[45] As a result, God destroyed the house of Ahab within a generation. Jehu, an army commander, was commissioned by God to kill all the sons of Ahab. Jehu also killed all of the priests and worshippers of Baal when he lured them all into Baal's temple (probably the one Ahab had built in Samaria) under the pretense of holding a great festival to Baal. When all were inside and it was verified that no YHWH devotees were with them, Jehu's lieutenants killed them all. The temple was then razed and turned into a latrine. This was according to God's will, but Israel carried on with the golden-calves worship. Because Jehu in general carried out God's order to destroy the house of Ahab and take its place, God told him that his dynasty would last another four generations. Yet because his zeal in exterminating Ahab and Jezebel's offspring was apparently to some extent motivated by selfish ambition, and because "he did not depart from the sins of Jeroboam, which ... made Israel sin," the LORD enabled the king of Aram to defeat Jehu on many occasions, and the LORD saw to it that Jehu's dynasty did not endure beyond the allotted generations.[46]

There was, however, a resurgence of the nation during the 41-year reign of Jehu's great-grandson, Jeroboam II (reigned 793-752)—not because of any goodness in him, but because of the LORD's compassion. He took back from Aram and other surrounding nations most or all of the land lost. But this renaissance was not to last long.[47] Not long after, the giant and ruthless power of Assyria began to affect, first, Israel, and then Judah. Pul,[48] king of Assyria, advanced against Israel, and in order to satisfy him, Menahem, king of Israel, paid the Assyrian king a thousand talents of silver—a very modest amount compared to the abundance during Solomon's days when silver was "as common as stones in Jerusalem."[49] About forty years later the last king of Israel, Hosea, quit paying tribute to the king of Assyria. So Shalmaneser V besieged the royal capitol of Israel, Samaria, and three years later finally broke through the walls and committed the people either to death or to exile.[50] King Hosea was taken prisoner to Assyria and was never heard from again. At that point "Israel" (the northern kingdom consisting at that time of the twelve tribes

---

[45] 1 Kings 16:29-33; 18:4, 13; 19:10, 14

[46] 2 Kings 9-10; Hos 1:4. See Keil and Delitzsch on Hos 1:4.

[47] 2 Kings 14:23-28

[48] Generally regarded as Tiglath-Pileser III. Paul R. House, *1, 2 Kings*, vol. 8 of *The New American Commentary* (Nashville: Broadman & Holman, 1995), 2 Kings 15:19-22.

[49] 2 Kings 15:13-22; 1 Kings 10:27

[50] "The city fell in 722 BC at about the time of Shalmaneser V's death. In Assyrian sources Sargon II, his brother and successor, claims credit for the city's capture." (John J. Bimson, "1 and 2 Kings," in *New Bible Commentary: 21ˢᵗ Century Edition*, ed. D. A. Carson *et al* [Downers Grove: Inter-Varsity Press, 1994], 2 Kings 17:1-6. For the annals of Sargon II, see Daniel D. Luckenbill, *Ancient Records of Assyria and Babylonia*, vol. 2 [Chicago: Univ. of Chicago Press, 1926], accessible at www.archive.org.

minus Judah, Simeon, and Levi) ceased to exist.[51] A few poor people survived the disaster, but brambles and weeds took over all the arable land, and the wild animals roamed at will. Why did the nation fail? The historian of 2 Kings gives us the answer:

> The sons of Israel did things secretly which were not right against the LORD their God. Moreover, they built for themselves high places in all their towns, from watchtower to fortified city. They set for themselves sacred pillars and Asherim on every high hill and under every green tree, and there they burned incense on all the high places as the nations did which the LORD had carried away to exile before them; and they did evil things provoking the LORD. They served idols, concerning which the LORD had said to them, "You shall not do this thing."[52]

And so,

> The LORD rejected all the descendants of Israel and afflicted them and gave them into the hand of plunderers, until He had cast them out of His sight. The sons of Israel walked in all the sins of Jeroboam which he did; they did not depart from them until the LORD removed Israel from His sight, as He spoke through all His servants the prophets. So Israel was carried away into exile from their own land to Assyria until this day.[53]

The history of the southern kingdom, Judah, is also one of general decline, but the road is bumpier, with higher highs and lower lows.[54] The dying process took about a century and a half longer than her northern sister (931-586 BC). Nineteen kings—all from the Davidic dynasty—ruled during that time, and one (evil) usurping queen, Atheliah, who was the daughter of Ahab and Jezebel of Israel. Of these nineteen kings, eight were judged to have done "right in the sight of the LORD" (Asa, Jehoshaphat, Joash, Amaziah, Uzziah, Jotham, Hezekiah, and Josiah), although all of them stumbled at one point or another, either in minor or major ways. The rest were judged as evil. Whereas the heretical YHWH worship of the golden calves prevailed in the northern kingdom, and was not pleasing to God, nor good for man, the orthodox worship of YHWH taught in the books of Moses prevailed in Judah throughout its history—although it became dormant from time to time when evil kings

---

[51] 2 Kings 17:1-6
[52] 2 Kings 17:9-12
[53] 2 Kings 17:20, 22-23
[54] The LORD informed Ezekiel that in the final analysis Jerusalem's behavior was worse than Samaria's (Ezek 16:51).

ruled. But Judah had Jerusalem and the Temple, and the Levites and priests congregated there after Solomon's kingdom split and Jeroboam foisted the golden calves and non-Levitical priesthood on his subjects.[55] So when good Judean kings ruled, YHWH worship, based on the Mosaic code, could (but didn't always) flourish. But there was always a sizable portion of the people whose hearts craved idolatry, and who felt the need to bow down to something tangible. So when wicked kings ruled who also had idolatrous hearts, shrines of false foreign gods popped up everywhere—even in Jerusalem, and on a few occasions, even at the Temple—and the people and their wicked kings served these gods and forgot the LORD.

Four of the writing prophets who made significant contributions to the Messiah concept (who we will soon consider in detail)—Isaiah, Jeremiah, Ezekiel, and Daniel—lived during or right at the end of the divided monarchy, and all were from Judah: Isaiah served at about the two-thirds point in Judah's history, and Jeremiah, Ezekiel, and Daniel prophesied at the end and for some time after—the latter two having their ministries in exile.[56] In order to set the context of the social and political conditions in which they lived and ministered, it might be beneficial to briefly mention several of the more interesting kings of Judah who either facilitated the degradation of the nation, or who helped reverse for a time the downward trend. Keep in mind God's goal of "pulling the rug out" from under the nation: Viz., to get the people, and future generations, to see that human kings inevitably fail, and that as they fail, their kingdoms fail; but with this knowledge, men and women will begin to live more for the heavenly eternal kingdom instead of the earthly temporal kingdom. The history of the Davidic dynasty in Judah is in general an object lesson of the foolishness of relying on human kings and their kingdoms for all one's security, pleasure, and lifelong contentment.

The disillusionment, of course, began later in Solomon's reign, and his son Rehoboam (began to reign, 931 BC) continued the process. Because of his heavy-handed policy from the start, his kingdom immediately shrank to only about a quarter of its original size. Jeroboam took the northern three quarters of the land and people, retaining the name "Israel," and Rehoboam was left in his native Judah, with Simeon within it. Rehoboam, as already mentioned, also retained the loyalty of most of the Levites and priests. Five years after the split, the LORD sent Pharaoh Shishak against Judah because Rehoboam and the people had begun to apostatize. Pharaoh soon overcame all Judean defenses and ravished the land and, as the Chronicler records, "took the treasures of the house of the LORD and the treasures of the king's palace. He took everything; he

---

[55] 2 Chron 11:13-17

[56] The closing part of Jeremiah's prophetic ministry occurred in Egypt.

even took the golden shields which Solomon had made."[57] Rehoboam's grandson, Asa (r. 911-870), reversed the trend by serving YHWH with enthusiasm. He commanded his people to do the same, and, unlike most of even the good kings, he removed the "high places" that served as local YHWH worship sites. But late in life when attacked by Baasha, the king of Israel, "Asa took all the silver and the gold which were left in the treasuries of the house of the LORD and the treasuries of the king's house," and sent them to Ben-hadad, king of Aram, in order to buy an ally against Baasha. So the kingdom became poorer. The prophet Hanani rebuked Asa for his failure to trust God, and informed him that from then on he would be embroiled in constant wars. For this word, Asa had the prophet locked up in prison.[58]

Rehoboam, Abijah, and Asa were often at war with Israel. But with Asa's son, Jehoshaphat (r. 873-848),[59] came a man thoroughly devoted to serving the LORD; but also came the beginning of troubles, because he established peace with Israel—cemented by King Ahab's daughter's (Atheliah) marriage to his son Jehoram—and with that set the stage for later disasters. Jehoshaphat promoted orthodox YHWH worship in many ways, and even commissioned a travelling seminary to teach the people God's ways and the Law of Moses. But he got mixed up with an ill-fated military expedition led by Ahab (in which Ahab was killed by the Arameans), and later a ship-building program that Ahab's son, Ahaziah, initiated (which the LORD foiled). He was rebuked with these words: "Should you help the wicked and love those who hate the LORD and so bring wrath on yourself from the LORD?"[60] Jehoshaphat's son Jehoram (r. 854-842),[61] after his father's death, killed all of his brothers and then brought into Judah the Baal religion of his wife Athaliah and mother-in-law Jezebel (wife of Ahab). So wicked was his reign that God prompted Elijah—normally the prophet serving the kings of Israel—to rebuke him (via letter) for his folly and to inform him that he would die a horrible death of an acutely prolapsed bowel. Just before this mortal disease came upon him, Philistines and Arabs overran the land and emptied the king's house of anything valuable, then took his wives and killed his sons, except Ahaziah, the youngest.[62] Ahaziah (r. 842-841), when he came to the throne of Judah a little later, didn't last long, for he was swept up in Jehu's slaughter of the house of Ahab, and was killed.[63] His mother, Atheliah (r. 841-846), was a scheming, ambitious soul—like Jezebel, her mother—who killed all of her son's (Ahaziah's) sons—save one—and then

---

[57] 2 Chron 12:9
[58] 1 Kings 15:8-24; 2 Chron 14-16
[59] According to Thiele, Asa and Jehoshaphat co-reigned for three years.
[60] 2 Chron 19:2
[61] According to Thiele, Jehoshaphat and Jehoram co-reigned for six years.
[62] 2 Chron 21; 22:1
[63] 2 Kings 8:24-29; 9:16-28; 2 Chron 22:1-9

seized the Judean throne. The grandson who escaped the grandmotherly purge was the youngest, Joash (r. 836-796), who was for the next several years raised in secret by the priest Jehoiada. This priest raised Joash in the fear of the LORD and with the knowledge of God's word. When Joash was only eight years old and his grandmother still reigned with an iron hand, the priests made all possible sympathetic arrangements, and presented the boy to the public and declared him king. Fortunately, the people and many of the ruling class were glad to see that the Davidic line was still alive, so they immediately gave their support to him. Jehoiada then had the usurping queen put to death.[64] As Joash matured he continued to follow the LORD as long as Jehoida instructed him. But when the aged priest finally died, Joash's heart drifted away from God: He turned to idol worship and became despotic.

When Zechariah, the son of Jehoida, rebuked Joash at the Temple for his apostasy, Joash had him killed. And so, God again brought problems on Judah: Hazael, king of Aram, "set his face" to go against Judah, so Joash took all the "sacred things" that he and his fathers had dedicated to YHWH, as well as all the gold in the king's house and in YHWH's house, and sent them to Hazael.[65] The story with the next king, Amaziah (r. 796-768), was similar. He began well, and the LORD blessed him. But after he defeated the Edomites, he began worshipping the Edomite gods. A prophet of God rebuked him, and Amaziah came close to killing him. Like several of the Judean kings, he began well, but his heart became proud later on. So with an idolatrous and arrogant heart, Amaziah made war against the king of Israel (Joash [not King Joash of Judah]), but was defeated. Joash then went on to tear down a long section of Jerusalem's wall as well as to make off with what gold, silver, and cultic utensils remained in the Temple.[66] Whatever peace that existed between Israel and Judah that began with Ahab and Jehoshaphat was now finished.

During Amaziah's reign, Judah came to almost nothing; but God was intent on preserving the "Holy Seed." With Amaziah's son, Uzziah (r. 791-740),[67] God gave Judah a lengthy reprieve, based substantially upon Uzziah's obedience to the LORD. And at the same time, God brought Israel into a period of renewed life and expansion, despite the fact that her long-reigning king, Jeroboam II, had only done evil in God's eyes. But their glory, as independent kingdoms, would not last much longer: Israel and Judah would finally fall prey to, respectively, the titanic powers of Assyria and Babylon. But

---

[64] 2 Kings 11; 2 Chron 22:10-23:21
[65] 2 Kings 12; 2 Chron 24
[66] 2 Kings 14:1-20; 2 Chron 25
[67] According to Thiele, Uzziah (some Bibles: "Azariah") co-reigned with his father Amaziah from 791 till 768. From then till 751 Uzziah alone ruled. From 751 till 740 Uzziah co-reigned with his son Jotham.

during his long reign, Judah's King Uzziah would fortify the nation militarily and spiritually, until, as was so typical of Judah's kings, his heart became proud: He burned "strange fire," that is, incense, before the LORD at the temple—a rite, according to the Law, that was solely a prerogative of the priesthood. When he resisted the rebuke of the priests, leprosy broke out on his forehead. From then until his death a few years later, he lived in isolation and his righteous son, Jotham, carried out the royal duties on his behalf.[68]

"In the year that King Uzziah died" (Isa 6:1), the year ca. 740 BC, YHWH commissioned Isaiah to speak his Word to Jerusalem and beyond, but especially to the kings of Judah. Isaiah had the pleasure of ministering to Uzziah's good son Jotham for a brief time, but then he had to deal with the next in line, King Ahaz, who proved himself wickeder that all who had gone before. Second Chron 28:2-3 records:

> [Ahaz] walked in the ways of the kings of Israel; he also made molten images for the Baals. Moreover, he burned incense in the valley of Ben-hinnom and burned his sons in fire, according to the abominations of the nations whom the LORD had driven out before the sons of Israel.

And so, God sent the kings of Aram and Israel, Rezin and Pekah, against him, and the Judean army was crushed. Ahaz lost 120,000 men in the fighting, and nearly twice that number of men and women were marched off as slaves.[69] When Rezin and Pekah threatened Jerusalem, Isaiah told King Ahaz (as a part of a tremendously important prophecy that we will soon consider) that the threat from the two northern marauders would soon melt away.[70] Ahaz didn't listen, but instead took from the gold and silver in God's house, as well as from his own house, and paid the Assyrian king, Tiglath-Pileser, to come to his rescue—thus committing Judah to be a vassal state of Assyria. As the Chronicler records: The king of Assyria only "afflicted him instead of strengthening him."[71] In time, "in deference to the king of Assyria,"[72] Ahaz recast the Jerusalem Temple worship in the image of the worship of the gods of Damascus, and at length finally closed down the Temple altogether.[73]

Isaiah breathed a twenty-nine-year sigh of relief during the reign of Ahaz's son, Hezekiah (r. 716-687), for "he did right in the sight of the LORD, according to all that his father David had done."[74] Hezekiah immediately

[68] 2 Kings 15:1-7; 2 Chron 26
[69] 2 Chron 28
[70] Isa 7-8
[71] 2 Chron 28:20
[72] 2 Kings 16:18 (NIV)
[73] 2 Kings 16; 2 Chron 28
[74] 2 Kings 18:3; 2 Chron 29:2

commissioned the Levites and priests to cleanse and consecrate the Temple so it could again be opened; and, as soon as possible, the Passover, after a long hiatus, was celebrated. Even the destitute survivors of the Assyrian destruction of Samaria and Israel were invited, and some actually attended. When Solomon dedicated the Temple 250 years before, he sacrificed 22,000 bulls and 120,000 sheep as his own offering. As a sign of the relative poverty of Judah during Hezekiah's time, he and the "princes of the city" offered only "seven bulls, seven rams, seven lambs and seven male goats" at the Temple's rededication. The number of animals sacrificed by the rest of the congregation was a paltry 70 bulls, 100 rams, and 200 lambs.[75] Hezekiah, it appears to be the case, continued to pay the tribute to Assyria that his father had initiated. But about a decade into his reign, he felt confident enough about Judah's recovery to withhold payment to the Assyrians. We do not know what he paid in regular tribute, but when King Sennacherib of Assyria invaded Judah in retaliation, Hezekiah confessed to the angry king that he had done wrong, and stripped the Temple of all remaining silver and some of the remaining gold—a hundred talents of silver and thirty talents of gold—and immediately sent it to Sennacherib, who demanded of him just that much. If the Assyrian king had seriously threatened Judah at the time David made provisions for the temple of 1,000,000 talents of silver and 100,000 talents of gold, he would have asked for much, much more. But Sennacherib's demand of Hezekiah shows that he knew that Judah had much less than before. At all events, Sennacherib despised the payment and sent his army to besiege Jerusalem. After listening to the taunts of the Assyrian commander, and his mockery of YHWH, Hezekiah and the people fasted and prayed, and Isaiah then prophesied that the city would be spared. That night, the Angel of YHWH killed the entire Assyrian army around Jerusalem, 185,000 men.[76] Other than the Angel of YHWH's two visits to Elijah,[77] this was his only recorded appearance since he killed 70,000 Israelites as a consequence of David's census.[78] Not too long after, Isaiah informed Hezekiah that the good king would soon die, and so he should set his house in order. Hezekiah was crushed, and begged the LORD to let him live on. When the LORD saw his sorrow and tears, he acquiesced. But it's probably the case that he should have exited as originally scheduled, for in the time of his life extension, Hezekiah foolishly showed off Jerusalem's remaining treasures to envoys from Babylon, and he fathered Manasseh (r. 697-642) who, after his father's death, became

---

[75] 2 Kings 18:1-6; 2 Chron 29-31

[76] 2 Kings 18-19; 2 Chron 32:1-23; Isa 36-37

[77] 1 Kings 19:7; 2 Kings 1:3, 15. The Angel of YHWH appears again in Zech 3, but in a prophetic dream/vision of the prophet.

[78] 2 Sam 24:15

king,[79] and who, for most of his fifty-five-year reign, brought idolatry, oppression, and misery to his people.[80] Isaiah most likely died under his murderous administration, perhaps violently.[81]

The idolatry and associated abominations that Manasseh forced on Jerusalem and Judah were so bad that they eclipsed those of the Amorites and other peoples who lived in the land before the conquest.[82] He even set up altars to the celestial bodies next to the Temple, set an Asherah carved image *in* the Temple, and sacrificed his son "in the fire" of the Ammonite abomination Molech. "Moreover, Manasseh shed very much innocent blood until he had filled Jerusalem from one end to another." There is no telling how many prophets of the LORD that he persecuted and killed.[83] The Chronicler records that Manasseh repented (probably late in his reign) after the Assyrians "captured [him] with hooks, bound him with bronze chains and took him to Babylon."[84] The LORD enabled him to return to his throne and have a short time to undo some of the evil that he had brought upon his country; but permanent damage had been done, and, in any case, the LORD had decided, based on Manasseh's and the people's wickedness, to abandon them to their enemies.[85] Amon (r. 642-640), Manasseh's son, following the wicked example of his father, lasted only two years before being assassinated.[86] His son Josiah (r. 640-609), at eight years old, then sat on Judah's throne, and a few years later began to seek the LORD and not long after that to serve the LORD and work to rid the nation of the evil that his father and grandfather had promoted. He refurbished the Temple, reinitiated orthodox YHWH worship there, and travelled north to Bethel in order to destroy the YHWH golden calves cult altar that Jeroboam

---

[79] According to Thiele, Manasseh co-reigned with his father, Hezekieh, for ten years.

[80] 2 Kings 20; 2 Chron 32:24-33; Isa 38-39

[81] Justin Martyr of the 2nd-century church (*Dialogue with Trypho*, 120) and the *Babylonian Talmud* (Yevamot 49b) profess that Isaiah was murdered—the latter says by the hand of King Manasseh. The tradition may find its source in the *Ascension of Isaiah*, one of early Christian-era books considered to be pseudepigrapha (books with false attribution of authorship), where Isaiah's death at the hands of Manasseh is described. In the NT, Heb 11:37 has a possible allusion to this.

[82] 2 Kings 21:11. King Manasseh showed himself to be *more* wicked than the Amorites, whereas King Ahab of Israel—as bad as he was—was only *as* wicked as the Amorites (1 Kings 21:26).

[83] 2 Kings 21:1-18

[84] 2 Chron 33:11. Manasseh was probably under the thumb of the Assyrians during his entire reign, except for a brief rebellion that resulted in his exile to Babylon and change of heart. Paul House says that he is mentioned by the Assyrian kings Esarhaddon and Ashurbanipal regarding, respectively, building materials owed and Judah's military contribution to Assyria's war against Egypt. (Paul R. House, *The New American Commentary*, 2 Kings 21:1-6.) See Luckenbill, *Ancient Records of Assyria and Babylonia*, vol. 2.

[85] 2 Kings 21:1-18; 2 Chron 33:1-20

[86] 2 Kings 21:19-26; 2 Chron 33:21-25

had built long before—thus fulfilling prophecy.[87] Because of Josiah's righteousness and wholeheartedness in serving YHWH, the LORD did not bring Judah to an end in his days, but promised to bring it to an end shortly thereafter.[88] The prophet Jeremiah, who told of the disaster and restoration to come (and the "new covenant" that would ground that restoration), received his prophetical call while still a youth living under Josiah's administration.[89] He would go on to prophesy to Jerusalem and her four evil kings—Jehoahaz, Jehoiakim, Jehoiachin, and Zedekiah—during the last twenty-two years of Judah's existence.

These last four kings of Judah ruled at a time when the power of Babylon was on the rise. By the time of Josiah, Assyria was seriously in decline. About 610 BC the Babylonians, who had not long before successfully throne off the Assyrian yoke, conquered the Assyrian capitol of Nineveh, with the help of the Medes and others, and destroyed "that great city" utterly. Remains of the Assyrian army retreated to Carchemish (on the Euphrates, northeast of Damascus) and tried to make a stand against the pursuing Babylonians there. Pharaoh Necho took his army up to Carchemish in order to assist the Assyrians; but on the way he was opposed by King Josiah, even though Pharaoh had told him that he was on a mission from God and that Judah should not stand in the way. Josiah nevertheless attacked the Egyptians and was killed and his Judean army defeated.[90] Josiah's son Jehoahaz was then placed on the throne, but three months later was deposed by Pharaoh Necho and replaced with his brother Jehoiakim. At that time, Pharaoh imposed tribute on Judah to the tune of one talent of gold and one hundred talents of silver—an amount that shows the relative poverty of the nation. Just after this (606 BC) the Egyptian and remnant Assyrian armies were decisively defeated by the Babylonians—led by prince Nebuchadnezzar—at Carchemish. Egypt quickly faded from the scene at that point, and Judah came increasingly under the power of Babylon. After Pharaoh Necho took Josiah's son, Jehoahaz, as a prisoner to Egypt, his brother Jehoiakim sat on Judah's throne for the next eleven years, and "did evil in the sight of the LORD." A low point for him came when he burned the God-given words of the prophet Jeremiah which had been carefully written down on a scroll.[91] Nebuchadnezzar, soon after his victory at Carchemish, came up to Jerusalem (606 BC) and forced Jehoiakim to submit. At that time, gifted young men of the royal family and other prominent families were taken to Babylon in

---

[87] 1 Kings 13:2; 2 Kings 23:15-16
[88] 2 Kings 22:1-23:30; 2 Chron 34-35
[89] Jer 1:1-3
[90] 2 Kings 23:29-30; 2 Chron 35:20-24
[91] Jer 36. For this distain for God's word, God told Jehoiakim (through Jeremiah) that his body would not be properly honored after his death, and that no descendant of his would ever sit on the throne of David (36:29-30).

order to serve the king there. Among them was the prophet Daniel who was about fifteen years old at the time.[92] Three years later, Jehoiakim rebelled, so Nebuchadnezzar came to Jerusalem a second time (599 BC). Shortly before, or perhaps during, the siege, Jehoiakim died, and his son Jehoiachin took his place—but for only three months, for he gave himself and the city up to the Babylonians, and was immediately deposed and taken away to Babylon. Many others were also marched away to exile including Ezekiel. This priest and prophet was finally settled with a community of Jews on the Chebar River (which was near what would today be the border of Iraq and Armenia), and prophesied there concerning the soon-to-come destruction of Jerusalem and her future restoration.[93]

Nebuchadnezzar, king of Babylon, put Jehoiachin's uncle, Zedekiah,[94] on the throne and made him swear allegiance by God. But despite the many pleas by the prophet Jeremiah to stay submitted to the Babylonians (pleas that brought on him severe persecution), Zedekiah yielded to the pressure of powerful men around him, and rebelled, believing that Egypt would come to his aid. Pharaoh turned out to be a "splintered reed," so in Zedekiah's eighth year, Nebuchadnezzar returned to Jerusalem and besieged it. Again and again Zedekiah refused to submit to God's word, given through Jeremiah, to give up the fight and surrender to the Babylonians.[95] A year and a half into the siege (when the situation in the city had become so desperate that some had turned to cannibalism), the Babylonians broke through the walls and entered the city. Much of the city was given to the sword, many were exiled, and a little while later the city—including the Temple—was burned and its walls razed.[96] Nebuchadnezzar was aware of Jeremiah's long-term attempt to get the kings to submit to Babylon, thus he was spared and set free. But Zedekiah (who had tried to flee the city) and his sons were caught and taken before Nebuchadnezzar at Riblah where the sons were executed and Zedekiah's eyes put out.[97] The blind king was then led in chains to Babylon, and there he died. Judah and the Davidic kingdom had seemingly come to a permanent end.[98]

Why did the unthinkable come, which seemed to be at total variance with the great promise that God had made to Israel and its Davidic "Holy Seed"?

---

[92] Dan 1:1-7

[93] Ezek 1:1-3; 2 Kings 23:31-24:16; 2 Chron 36:1-10

[94] Jehoahaz, Jehoiakim, and Zedekiah were sons of Josiah.

[95] See Jer 21; 27; 32; 34; 36-38.

[96] Jeremiah says in Lamentations 1:1, 3 that those exiled and those remaining in Jerusalem were enslaved as "forced laborers" under "harsh servitude." He also says, in 5:8, that "Slaves rule over us." See also Isa 47:6.

[97] Nebuchadnezzar had accompanied his army when the Jerusalem siege was begun (2 Kings 25:1), but apparently had returned to his campaign headquarters at Riblah (near Damascus) before the end of the siege (2 Kings 25:6).

[98] 2 Kings 24:17-25:21; 2 Chron 36:10-21; Jer 37-40

The answer is stated here in a word of YHWH which came to Jeremiah after the fall of Jerusalem and after he was forced to go to Egypt with a remnant of Jews:

> Thus says the LORD of hosts, the God of Israel, "You yourselves have seen all the calamity that I have brought on Jerusalem and all the cities of Judah; and behold, this day they are in ruins and no one lives in them, because of their wickedness which they committed so as to provoke Me to anger by continuing to burn sacrifices and to serve other gods whom they had not known, neither they, you, nor your fathers. Yet I sent you all My servants the prophets, again and again, saying, 'Oh, do not do this abominable thing which I hate.' But they did not listen or incline their ears to turn from their wickedness, so as not to burn sacrifices to other gods. Therefore My wrath and My anger were poured out and burned in the cities of Judah and in the streets of Jerusalem, so they have become a ruin and a desolation as it is this day."

But the "unthinkable," thankfully, was really not the end of the story. God is love and he is the faithful God who keeps his promises. In a very dark world at that point, two glimmers of light pierced through: First, the Jews could hold on to the prophecy of Jeremiah that said that the captivity would last only seventy years;[99] and second, Jehoiachin, after thirty-six years of imprisonment in Babylon, was freed by King Evil-Marodoch, and the fallen monarch of Judah thereafter regularly dined at the king of Babylon's royal table.[100]

The Prophets Point towards a Much Greater "Israel"

So God pulled the rug out from under Israel, but it was all done for a great and noble purpose: to get God's people closer to him, and get them closer for eternity. At the time of the great King Solomon, times were good, and YHWH had to a large measure achieved the goal of raising up a people who knew and worshipped him as the one true God, and who to a great degree (at that time) rejected the legitimacy of the gods of the nations that they removed from the Promised Land. But at that time, there were still two great shortcomings: YHWH was not their king, and they did not live for eternity, but for the earthly blessings that they were promised through their relationship with YHWH. So in order to resolve these shortcomings, God took them through another great "wilderness" experience. During this experience (the

---

[99] Jer 25:11; 29:10
[100] 2 Kings 25:27-30

"rug" being pulled out experience), they learned that their kings were far from perfect, and they witnessed the collapse of the Davidic kingdom altogether, leaving them without a king to fight their battles for them. During this process of the slow erosion of the divided kingdoms, they slowly lost their beloved Promised Land too. And as a part of that, Solomon's great Temple—the physical dwelling place of God—became dilapidated, increasingly unused, increasingly irrelevant regarding the spiritual needs of the people, and at long last, completely destroyed by the enraged Babylonians. The most horrible component of this wilderness experience—from a *salvation* standpoint—was the fact that both Israel and Judah broke their covenant with God (the Mosaic covenant), and so God gave Israel a "writ of divorce" and wiped "Jerusalem as one wipes a dish, wiping it and turning it upside down."[101]

These were the second "wilderness" events that happened, and the prophets of this period at various times and in many ways warned of these events before they happened. But they also prophesied that, although God would sternly punish his people, yet would he by and by feel great compassion for them and restore them as his beloved, but under conditions that would be far more wonderful and lasting—the restoration of a much greater "Israel" in which God would be much closer to his people than before. God would restore his people to their *land*, but a land in which they could be with God—the land being, in a sense, simply the means to that end, with little prophetical importance given to the physical land as such. God would, in the restoration, again inhabit his temple; yet the prophets (other than Ezekiel and Haggai) say relatively little about the new temple, but much about the fact that YHWH will be with his people: The physical place of God's throne fades into the background as the prophetic fact of God's spiritual presence with his people—through the indwelling of his Spirit—comes to the fore. "Land" and "temple" with the divided monarchy and exilic prophets become nearly synonymous with "God with us." And this all takes place within a "new covenant" that God establishes with his people as a merciful improvement upon the original Mosaic covenant which Israel and Judah broke. This covenant proves to be the means by which the people come to the land and the temple and choose to worship God and do so forever. For God promises in the new covenant to indwell his people with his own Spirit such that they will no longer even think of rejecting God again, let alone do so. So men will come into God's presence, in a sense, physically, in that they will approach his throne in the Promised Land at "Mount Zion." At the same time, regardless of place, God will "pour out [His] spirit upon all flesh,"[102] and "they will all know [Him], from the least of them

---

[101] Jer 3:8; 2 Kings 21:13
[102] Joel 2:28 (KJV)

to the greatest of them."[103] Within this context will come the Messiah, who, as the prophets show, will minister in both the domains of the physical and the divine-spiritual. Before turning to what the prophets had to say about the Messiah, let me say a few words more about how the eschatological "land" and "temple" and "covenant" have less to do with those literal things themselves, and more about simply being with God.

The prophet Jeremiah told of a new covenant to come by which God would change men's hearts and cause them, through the transforming work of his Spirit, to know and worship him.[104] At Jeremiah's time, it was painfully clear that the covenant that the people had hitherto lived under had by and large failed to reconcile men to God—not because there was any deficiency on God's part, but because Israel and Judah had "broken God's covenant."[105] Now this Old Covenant in general assumed the ongoing validity of the promises, or separate covenants, that God had made to the patriarchs. It is interesting how this collective Old Covenant contained so many earthly details. Abraham was promised the land of Canaan, and this was confirmed with Moses at Mt. Sinai and afterward: God would give to Israel the defined piece of land between "the river of Egypt as far as the great river, the river Euphrates," and from the "Great Sea" to the Jordan, and perhaps even some land on the east bank of the Jordan.[106] As Israel entered the Promised Land, each tribe was assigned its place. The history from there to the exile is intimately bound up with this land. The Law given at Sinai contained 600+ statutes regarding many subjects, including sexual morality, liability issues, inheritance rights, and, of course, many statutes regarding the proper worship of YHWH. Regarding this latter subject, Israel was to have a "holy place" in which YHWH would dwell, and there was to be a priesthood—from the tribe of Levi, and from a certain Levite, Aaron—to mediate between YHWH and Israel. The priests' most vital function was to offer up animal sacrifices so that atonement might be provided for the sins of the people. When Israel conquered the land of Canaan, many continued to go to the Tabernacle at Shiloh, and then later to the Temple in Jerusalem after Solomon had built that. And during the divided monarchy, the Temple continued, off and on, to be a focal center for YHWH worship, but was finally destroyed by the Babylonians about four centuries after it was built.

It is true that the prophets during the divided monarchy, the exile, and at the time of the return from exile, never said that the Old Covenant (which, as just mentioned, assumed the validity of the patriarchal promises) was to be abolished. In the prophecies of the final restoration to come, its validity seems

---

[103] Jer 31:34
[104] Jer 31:31-34
[105] 2 Kings 17:15; Jer 11:10; Jer 31:32
[106] Gen 15:18; Exod 23:31; Num 32, 34; Deut 1:7; Josh 1:4; Ezek 47:13-20

to be assumed, and the final prophet finding expression in the Tanakh, Malachi, admonished Israel to never forget the Law of Moses.[107] But that being said, one cannot help but notice the stark differences between what the prophets said about the New Covenant and what was the reality living under the Old Covenant. Let us briefly consider some of what the prophets foretold about the New Covenant to come.

The New Covenant, sometimes called the "everlasting covenant," is intimately bound up with the fact that, upon its activation, the Spirit of God will be poured out upon men and women such that their hearts will be turned to God, and they will worship God without ever looking back.[108] When the prophets in several places mention this covenant, there is little mention of any particular laws that they must obey, but only the fact that God will unilaterally change men's hearts. As a result, YHWH declares this: "They shall be My people, and I will be their God."[109] Now regarding the conditions that will obtain during the time of this covenant, if we set aside the Ezekiel 47 prophecy of the end-time's Temple for the moment, there is not a lot said by the prophets about the land or the Temple. Most of what is said about the New Covenant conditions has to do with the fact that God is present and that the situation is idyllic. Regarding the physical location of God's dwelling place—which is the place where God's people from all nations will go to worship him—the prophets speak of God's "Holy Mountain" and "Mount Zion," which will then be the highest mountain on earth—an earth that has already, along with the heavens, been remade.[110] Zion will be the "throne of the LORD."[111] His glory there will shine so brightly that there will be no need for a sun or moon to provide light; in fact, they will not exist.[112] God's glory, in the form of smoke and fire, will exist as a permanent canopy over Zion, and everything there will be "holy to the LORD."[113] Isaiah says to Zion: "Nations will come to your light, and kings to the brightness of your rising." God's house there "will be called a house of prayer for all the peoples."[114] All seems restored to Eden-like conditions:[115] the wolf lies down with the lamb, and children lead lions by the

---

[107] Mal 4:4: "Remember the law of Moses My servant, even the statutes and ordinances which I commanded him in Horeb for all Israel."

[108] Isa 32:15; 44:3; 55:3; 59:21; 61:8; Jer 24:7; 31:31; 32:40; 50:5; Ezek 11:19; 16:60; 36:25-27; 37:26; 39:29; Hos 2:18-19; Joel 2:28; Zech 12:10

[109] Jer 32:38; Ezek 37:27

[110] Isa 2:2; Mic 4:1-7. See also Isa 24:23; 27:13; Ezek 20:40; 40:2; Zech 8:3; 14:10. Regarding a remade earth and heavens, see Isa 65:17; 66:22.

[111] Jer 3:17. Also see Ezek 43:7.

[112] Isa 60:19-20

[113] Isa 4:5; Zech 14:20

[114] Isa 60:3, 14; 56:7

[115] Ezek 36:35

mane.[116] Isaiah says that people will live a long time,[117] yet he also says that in that day, "the LORD of hosts will reign on Mount Zion and in Jerusalem," and he will,

> ...prepare a lavish banquet for all peoples on this mountain; a banquet of aged wine, choice pieces with marrow, and refined, aged wine. And on this mountain He will swallow up the covering which is over all peoples, even the veil which is stretched over all nations. He will swallow up death for all time, and the Lord God will wipe tears away from all faces, and He will remove the reproach of His people from all the earth; for the LORD has spoken.[118]

So in this New Covenant we have conditions that were lacking under the Old Covenant, even at the time of David and Solomon. God is reconciled to his people, both physically and spiritually: The entire world comes to Zion to be with him and to learn from him; yet at the same time, God is with them all, no matter where they are, because his Spirit has been poured into them. And, in that day, God's people will fully know about eternal life and actually have it. Under the Old Covenant, people were obligated to follow hundreds of rules, regarding nearly every facet of life, so that they could obtain God's favor and thereby prosper during their lives "under the sun" in the Promised Land that God had given them. Under the New Covenant, God's Spirit—which "circumcises" the hearts of all—will propel men and women to be with God and to serve God perfectly. They will all be "oaks of righteousness" and "priests of the LORD" because each one will be allowed unfettered fellowship with God—first, through his or her possession of the Spirit of God, and, second, because each person will have access to God at Zion.[119] This will be for the Jew first, but also for the Egyptian and the Assyrian, and even for the unclean (by the Mosaic Law's standard) eunuchs of the world.[120]

The one prophecy that appears to run against what I just said—that appears to be more in keeping with the Old Covenant instead of the New—is Ezekiel's long description of the New-Covenant-era temple and land in chapters 40-48. There are many details about the Temple and its rites, and, at the end, there is a detailed description of the eschatological division of the Promised Land among the thirteen tribes of Israel.[121] Most Christian commentators over the eons have one way or another interpreted Ezekiel's

---

[116] Isa 11:6-9; 65:25
[117] Isa 65:20
[118] Isa 25:6-8; 24:23
[119] Isa 2:3; 31:34; Hos 2:14-20
[120] Isa 19:25; 56:3-8
[121] Levi is included in the land allotment, unlike when the land was allotted under Joshua.

depiction of temple and land to be a highly symbolic representation of the Church. In the last century and a half or so, other Christians, who take the Old Testament prophecies more literally, agree with many Jews that there will indeed be an end-times temple built (according to the plans shown to Ezekiel) and that the Promised Land will again be occupied and the land divided among the tribes like Ezekiel 48 describes. I find myself somewhere between these views, knowing that the New Testament by and large bestows the blessings promised to Israel (taken figuratively for salvation) upon the Church (consisting of both Jews and gentiles) because of her acceptance of, and service to, Christ. At the same time, I find it highly unlikely that so many detail-laden OT prophecies regarding the final permanent restoration would be intended by God to *only* be taken figuratively. It is my view that God will indeed bring about a final gathering of Israelites in the Promised Land, and that "David" will be their king at Zion; but this cannot be all there is, because it ostensibly leaves Israel yet without YHWH as her *only* king, and the question about life after death is still, in the main, left hanging.

Regarding Ezekiel's temple prophecy, the plethora of descriptions of its furnishings and rites makes it hard to understand this as applying to anything other than a physical future temple. That being said, it seems fair to say that even here, there is a noticeable feeling of etherealness that goes along with all the nuts and bolts description. This is made evident by several features.

The first one I'll mention is a minor point although worthy of note. In his first mystical transport to the pre-destruction Temple, it is said that he was transported "in visions of God to Jerusalem";[122] but when he was transported "in visions of God" to the restored Temple, its location is described only as being "on a very high mountain" that had on its southern slope "a structure like a city."[123] The "city" is never referred to as "Jerusalem," but only as the "city," and that sixteen times. Neither is the mountain or the city called "Zion" or "Moriah" or any other name, except the name that God gives it in the last verse of Ezekiel's prophecy: יהוה שָׁמָּה, *YHWH-shamah*, "The LORD is there."[124] As in other prophesies of the end-time restoration, geographical location fades in importance compared to the truth that God is there.

Second, God never told Ezekiel to tell his comrades back on the Chebar river to "build" or "make" the temple of the vision, but only that they should "observe its whole design and all its statutes and do them." By doing this, they would be induced to "be ashamed of their iniquities."[125] God showed Moses

---

[122] Ezek 8:3
[123] Ezek 40:2; 43:12. "Jerusalem" is mentioned in Ezekiel some 26 times, but never in the eschatological Temple/Land-allotment vision in the last eight chapters.
[124] Ezek 48:35
[125] Ezek 43:10-11

the "pattern" of the Tabernacle while Moses spoke with God "face to face" on Mount Sinai; God showed Ezekiel the pattern of the eschatological Temple while he spoke with God, perhaps face to face, on "the very high mountain." Maybe in both cases, the "pattern" is that of the higher heavenly reality. When pondering this question, God's words to Isaiah might be kept in mind:

> Heaven is My throne and the earth is My footstool. Where then is a house you could build for Me? And where is a place that I may rest? For My hand made all these things, thus all these things came into being.[126]

Thirdly, there is no mention by Ezekiel's bronze-colored guide, or by YHWH after his Spirit reenters the Temple, of the Ark of the Covenant—which under the old Covenant was the dwelling place of God and a necessary instrument in the process of providing forgiveness of Israel's sins on the Day of Atonement. Going back for a moment to actual history, the Ark had disappeared when the Temple was destroyed (or perhaps before) in 586 BC, and Jeremiah, not long before Ezekiel's temple vision, had prophesied that the day would come when the Ark would no longer be remembered, and, in any case, never again be remade.[127] Now if there is no Ark, there is no "throne" for God within the Holy of Holies; also, the necessary instrument for the mass forgiveness of sins, according to the Law, is unavailable.[128] So if God is not there, and the means of forgiveness is not there, then it seems that the Temple, according to requirements of the Mosaic Law, would serve no ultimate purpose. If so, then the mediating Aaronic priesthood has no function: They cannot approach God because, first, God is not there, and even if he were, they could not approach God because there is no Mercy Seat upon which they can sprinkle the bull's blood for their own sins—which, on the Day of Atonement, had to be accomplish first before they could sprinkle the goat's blood before the Mercy Seat for the sins of the people.[129] The Ark of the Covenant was at the very heart of the Mosaic Law, because any satisfaction of God regarding the corporate sins of Israel vitally involved that small wooden chest. If God was not satisfied by the proper offerings on the Day of Atonement, then try as the priests and the Levites and people might, all their good deeds would be as "filthy rags" and thus no merit would attach to them—and they would live and die in their sins. The temple that Ezekiel described may be a temple that will be built in the future,

---

[126] Isa 66:1-2a

[127] Jer 3:16

[128] The writer of the NT book of Hebrews (9:7) indicates that only unintentional sins were covered on the Day of Atonement: "but into the [Most Holy Place], only the high priest enters once a year, not without taking blood, which he offers for himself and for the sins of the people committed in ignorance."

[129] Lev 16

but, if so, it is not a temple that can operate according to the most critical dictates of the Mosaic Law.[130]

One other reason puts the literalness of this temple in question. In chapter 47, there is a small spring that emanates from under the Temple, which thence flows east, growing in size as it goes, that finally falls into the Dead Sea far below where the trickle has become a torrent that is so mighty that it turns nearly all of the Dead Sea into fresh water. The spring-turned-massive river that the bronze guide showed to Ezekiel certainly must represent something more than just fresh H$_2$O that reduces the salinity level of the Salt Sea. Given the context of Scripture, it surely must be a metaphor for the Spirit of God who emanates from his dwelling place and goes into the dead world, bringing physical and spiritual healing such that the death curse is overcome. God is, after all, "the spring of living waters" (Jer 2:13).[131] The river in Ezekiel's account is lined with fruit trees that bring "healing"—a scene that brings to mind the Tree of Life in the center of the Garden of Eden. In fact, as the Ezekiel text says, "everything will live wherever the river goes."[132] If this "spiritual" interpretation is at least partially right, then maybe the Temple, whence the water flows, should likewise be understood in some sense figuratively. Be that as it may, it remains the case that, while the Old Covenant was focused on the many rites and laws that would allow Israel to enjoy earthly blessings, the New Covenant era, as described by the prophets, is focused much more on the fact that God will permanently be with his people.

And, finally, the era that begins with the final return from exile after "the Day of the LORD" has passed will be the era when the Messiah will "sit upon his glorious throne" on Mount Zion in order to judge the nations. As the prophetic words concerning the eschatological "covenant" and "land" and "temple" find their highest reality in man's presence with God (and the unending life that is a product of that presence), so the prophetical words that

---

[130] It might be noted also that not only is the "Holy of Holies" in the Temple "most holy" (41:4), but the entire Temple complex atop the mountain is designated as "most holy" as well (43:12). In other words, the entire complex is one giant "Holy of Holies." If we interpret Ezek 40-47 literally, interesting questions arise. For example, if the Old Covenant (the Mosaic Law) is still in effect at the time of the operation of this temple, how can people bring their sacrifices and/or worship there? According to the Law, only the High Priest was allowed into the Holy of Holies, and that, only after extensive consecration and various rituals and the bringing of blood. Assuming that the New Covenant is in effect at this time, but with the Old not superseded, it could be that people are allowed to come there because they have been changed by God's Spirit and have become "oaks of righteousness." That is, they are sinless, and can therefore enter the Temple grounds at the top of the mountain and not defile it and not die. If this is so, then there is no need at all for expiatory sacrifices, no need for Aaronic priests to function as intermediaries, and no critical purpose of the Temple (in my *Kindness Towards Israel*, I discuss at some length the function of the Ezek 40-47 Temple).

[131] In Isa 44:3-4, water is symbolic of God's Spirit. Also see John 4 in the NT.

[132] Ezek 47:9

speak of the coming Davidic king provide strong indications that the reality of the Messiah is best understood as ultimately the reality of "God with us." What the prophets of the divided monarchy and exilic/post-exilic periods said about the Messiah—that he is human, but so much more—is the subject to which we now turn.

THE MESSIAH IS IMMANUEL (GOD WITH US)

"In the year of King Uzziah's death" (740 BC) the prophet Isaiah, who served Judean kings for over fifty years, in an awesome vision (Isa 6) saw God "sitting on a throne, lofty and exalted, with the train of His robe filling the temple." Surrounding him were heavenly angelic creatures called "Seraphim" whose duty it was to always be expressing the absolute holiness of YHWH: "Holy, Holy, Holy is the LORD of hosts," they continually cried out to one another. Isaiah, like others before him who saw God, immediately felt that he was "ruined," for he had "seen the King, the LORD of hosts." The prophet was then commissioned to speak God's words to his fellow Judeans—a people who, because of hardness of heart, would not listen. And so God told the prophet that harsh judgment would fall upon them such that their cities would soon be "devastated and without inhabitant," and their land become "utterly desolate." At the end of the vision, however, God assured Isaiah that a godly remnant—a "holy seed"—would survive, and be a "stump" out of which something new and greater would arise.

After recording this event, the book of Isaiah goes immediately (in chapter 7) into the account of Isaiah's prophecy given to the panicked grandson of Uzziah, Ahaz by name, who (along with his people) was terrified by the prospect of Jerusalem being conquered by the armies of Aram and Israel. This was about two decades after Uzziah's death, and now the life of the Holy Seed was in danger—because of Ahaz's and the people's wickedness (Ahaz went as far as to sacrifice his sons to false gods)—and the very center of the Holy Seed, the royal Davidic line, was in mortal danger as well. Things did not look good at all for the faithless Ahaz: Aram had already defeated him once and carried away many slaves to Damascus; King Pekah of Israel had also met him in battle and slain 120,000 Judeans; and the Philistines and Edomites had attacked and the former had taken a number of cities away from Judah.[133] But now that Pekah and King Rezin of Aram were besieging Jerusalem with the intent of deposing or killing Ahaz, the King of Judah was bent on employing desperate measures. So God sent Isaiah to not just anyone, and not just anyone of the house of David, but to King Ahaz, because the LORD was intensely concerned

---

[133] 2 Chron 28

about him and the fate of the Davidic line. Isaiah, as we'll see in a moment, told Ahaz that Aram and Israel were really no threat at all, for they would soon evaporate from the world stage. And he told Ahaz to trust God, and by that implied that Ahaz should not put his faith in man, that is, put his faith in the Assyrians. But Ahaz would not listen. Instead, he took gold and silver from the Temple and his own treasury, sent it all to King Tiglath-Pileser of Assyria as a gift, and convinced that king to attack Rezin and Pekah.[134] He obliged and soon thereafter defeated Aram and killed Rezin, and then conquered the northern half of Israel, killing or exiling massive numbers of Israelites in the process.[135] Tiglath-Pileser's son Shalmanesar was faithful to finish the job: He conquered the rest of Israel, including the capitol Samaria, about fifty years later, and killed or deported most of its inhabitants. With that the northern kingdom of Israel ceased to exist.[136] So Ahaz, because of his evil, facilitated the destruction of the northern kingdom, employing the brutal Assyrians whose regular siege tactics (as amply depicted in the annals and reliefs found at Nineveh) included flaying prisoners alive and/or impaling them on poles around besieged cities. Assyria finished off Israel, and a portion of the Assyrian empire that soon thereafter gained independence, Babylon, in time would finish off Judah (and Assyria too). If Ahaz had just listened to Isaiah, and trusted in God, the outcome might have been different.

Now let us look closely at what Isaiah said to King Ahaz as recorded in Isa 7. As the combined Rezin and Pekah siege was near or even underway, God told Isaiah to meet Ahaz at one of the main aqueducts of the holy city. There, Isaiah told Ahaz not to worry, for the siege would come to nothing. But Ahaz was in a panic, so God graciously offered to give him a spectacular sign to demonstrate to him that what Isaiah said was reliable and true. It is critical at this point to be reminded of God's concern for the Israelite holy seed, but specifically the part of that seed that was the Davidic line that would one day lead to the Messiah. As Isaiah here honored Ahaz with the offering of a sign and the giving of a great prophecy, he looked beyond Ahaz, for when the vital prophecy is introduced, Isaiah doesn't just speak to Ahaz, but to the whole "house of David."[137] And when he gives the prophecy, he gives it not just to Ahaz, but to "you-all," that is, to the House of David.[138]

The LORD offered Ahaz (through the mouth of the prophet) to choose his own "sign" that would confirm what Isaiah had already said about the deliverance from Rezin and Pekah. "Make it," the LORD said, "as deep as Sheol

---

[134] 2 Kings 16:5-9; 2 Chron 28:16-21
[135] 2 Kings 16:7-9; 2 Kings 15:29; 1 Chron 5:26
[136] 2 Kings 17:1-6
[137] Isa 7:13
[138] Isa 7:14

or high as heaven."[139] Now this was truly a rare and amazing offer: Ahaz had the chance to be provided a sign that would be of biblical proportions, the likes of which few had ever been given.[140] Ahaz here could have asked for God to open the earth in order to make "Sheol" visible, or he might have requested that the heavens be "rolled up as a scroll," or he could have demanded that people be resurrected from nearby graves. The point to grasp here is this: God really wanted to give a special sign in order to show that the promise (regarding the preservation of Ahaz and the House of David) was true, and he felt that the promise was so important that he was willing to provide a sign of utterly stupendous proportions. So God offered the sign, but Ahaz was too foolish and selfish to take him up on the exceedingly precious offer. He said (v. 12), "I will not ask, nor will I test the LORD." Ahaz here tries to sound pious, but he doesn't understand that as long as the LORD offered to give a sign, it would not at all be a "test" of the LORD to accept it (it would have been a test if Ahaz had unilaterally demanded it).[141] In any case, Ahaz had probably already made up his mind to seek aid from the Assyrians and did not want any sign from God to in any way dissuade him from that path (by the sign demonstrating that what Isaiah said was true, and thus, that there was no real Aram/Israel threat and no reason to seek external help).

At this point is when God essentially says, "You, O most pathetic Ahaz, may not want a sign, but I will give one anyway—not for your benefit, but for the benefit and encouragement for the whole House of David!" So Isaiah goes ahead and declares what the sign will be:

שִׁמְעוּ-נָא בֵּית דָּוִד .... יִתֵּן אֲדֹנָי הוּא
לָכֶם אוֹת הִנֵּה הָעַלְמָה הָרָה וְיֹלֶדֶת בֵּן
וְקָרָאת שְׁמוֹ עִמָּנוּ אֵל

Listen now, O house of David! .... The LORD Himself will give you a sign: Behold, a virgin will be with child and bear a son, and she will call His name Immanuel.

---

[139] Isa 7:11

[140] Hezekiah was given a cosmos-altering sign in Isa 38:7-8. Joshua asked for and experienced a cosmos-altering event in Josh 10:12-13. Regarding the latter, it is interesting to note that the halting of the sun *and* the moon conforms nicely with Copernican cosmology, not the reigning cosmology of ancient times. If Earth's rotation is stopped, both sun and moon will appear to become stationary.

[141] As a biblical concept, testing God occurs in just about any situation in which a person doubts the goodness of God. If Ahaz had demanded a sign, he would have essentially been saying (as corrupt as he was): "if you don't give me a sign, I'll know that you are not a good God." Thus, he would have "put God to the test."

We must keep firmly in mind that this sign, whether Ahaz wanted it or not, was meant to confirm the continuance of the Davidic royal line, and was meant to be utterly stupendous and unforgettable. The sign necessarily has everything to do with the preservation of the House of David within the nation of Israel; and Isaiah's prophecy in chapter 9 of a special "child" being born, who is of the line of David, will confirm this as we will soon see. So is this sign "stupendous and unforgettable" or not? I and, of course, most Christians think that it is. Much depends upon the translation of the Hebrew word *almah*. Most Christian versions translate it (as here in the NASB) as "virgin"; Jewish versions translate it as "young woman" or the like. The Jewish versions are technically correct, for *almah* in general in several places in the Tanakh denotes a young unmarried woman. The Christian translation, on the other hand, is based upon a couple of weighty considerations. First, in those days (very much unlike our own), the concept of a "young unmarried woman" was near synonymous with the concept of virginity. In Israel, virginity was highly valued, and under the Mosaic Law the voluntary loss of virginity before marriage was punishable by death.[142] Here, as in most other places in the Tanakh where *almah* is used, it's pretty well certain that a virgin is being referred to.[143] This line of thinking is then reinforced by another consideration weighed by Christian translators: It is clear that God intensely wanted to give a sign that no one would ever forget and that would be, one way or another, for the benefit of the House of David and all who look to that House for their hope and encouragement. But if the sign is only that a generic woman—married or not—will bear a son *naturally*, and give him a nice, yet somewhat pretentious, name like "Immanuel," then it is no "sign" at all. On the other hand, if the sign consists of a virgin having a son, then the sign is "stupendous and unforgettable," and the name of the child then becomes intensely interesting. Does this name tell us something about this amazing miracle child? We will soon see.

The rest of the Isa 7 prophecy does not give us any clear information regarding who the woman is, and there is nothing more said about the child other than the fact that by the time he grows up, Aram and Israel will be no more (vv. 15-16), and that the king of Assyria will continue south and turn even Judah into a wasteland of "briars and thorns" (v. 24). Perhaps there is some literal/short-term fulfillment of the prophecy/sign in the child mentioned at the beginning of chapter 8 that is fathered by Isaiah after he goes into "the prophetess"; but there appears to be nothing remarkable about this, and the name given to the child is not "Immanuel," but "Maher-shalal-hash-baz"—translated by the NASB, "swift is the booty, speedy is the prey," a name that

---

[142] Deut 22:13-30
[143] This is especially so in Gen 24:43 where it is obvious that Eleazer waited upon God's provision of a virgin for Isaac.

seems to foreshadow Assyria's future victories over Aram and Israel, but is otherwise enigmatic. At all events, the prophet shows in chapter 8 that the Assyrians will rampage through Judah, reaching up "even to the neck," and as time goes on, conditions in Judah will become so bad that the people will see, as Isaiah says in 8:22, only "distress and darkness, the gloom of anguish; and they will be driven away into darkness." Yet through all this Isaiah twice says that "God is with us," thus invoking the name of the sign-child (vv. 8, 10). That the highest fulfillment of the prophecy (and the advent of the sign) of "Immanuel" refers to the distant future, is indicated by the fact that Isaiah decides to "bind up the testimony" and to "seal the law" among his disciples, and decides as well to "wait for the LORD who is hiding His face from the house of Jacob."[144]

The connection of Immanuel with anyone at the time of Isaiah—perhaps one of Isaiah's children—is tenuous at best, so we must look for further prophetical clues. Fortunately, we don't have to look far. YHWH and Isaiah in chapter 7 were obviously deeply concerned about the preservation of the House of David, and, thus, the prophecy about Immanuel all but necessarily must have to do with that concern. In chapter 8, Isaiah's children are mentioned, but they have nothing to do with the Davidic bloodline. But in chapter 9, Isaiah prophesies the advent of an amazing child who will be a "great light" (v. 2)— first appearing in the Galilee region—for all Israel as well as for all nations. This child will sit upon "the throne of David," bringing an ever-increasing influence of his government and peace such that justice and righteousness obtain as everlasting conditions.[145] V. 6 tells us his name:

$$\text{וַיִּקְרָא שְׁמוֹ פֶּלֶא יוֹעֵץ אֵל גִּבּוֹר אֲבִי עַד שַׂר־שָׁלוֹם}$$

And His name will be called Wonderful Counselor, Mighty God, Eternal Father, Prince of Peace. (NASB)

[T]he wondrous adviser, the mighty God, the everlasting Father, called his name, "the prince of peace." (Judaica)

He has been named "The Mighty God is planning grace; The eternal Father, a peaceable ruler." (JPS '85)

---

[144] Isa 8:16-17
[145] Isa 9:7

Before discussing the validity of each of these translations, let us first briefly observe the relationship between the child of chapter 7 and the child of chapter 9.

In each case, the child comes during a time of darkness brought about by marauding enemies. The child in chapter 7 enters the world while Judah is being ravaged by Aram and Israel. Yet the coming of the child is part of a prophetical message of some hopeful glimmer of light: Before the child attains maturity, says Isaiah, the threat from Aram and Israel will evaporate; but the specter of Assyria arises, and Isaiah tells us that this great and heartless power will lay waste the people and land of Israel. In the darkness and gloom that is a result of this, we are told in chapter 9 that a "great light" appears in the person of a child who is "born to us," a son who is "given to us." This child, we are told, will be of the House of David and will bring unending government and peace. The first child is called "God with us" and the second child, among other components of his name, is called "Mighty God." The first child is a sign that represents a temporary salvation (from Aram and Israel); the second child *gives* final salvation (from Assyria specifically, but, as Isa 9:1-7 shows, from all threats generally). In both of these prophecies, the house of David is shown to survive; but with the chapter 9 prophecy, we learn that it survives and endures without end in the single person of the child who is born. The virgin with child of Isa 7 is the sign, the child of Isa 9 is he to whom the sign points.[146] The point is that the Davidic line will be preserved and find its highest fulfillment in a child who will be a "great light" (9:2) to the world. Now let's evaluate each of the translations of Isa 9:6b shown just above, in light of the immediate context and then in light of what we have already learned in chapter 1 of this book.

The three translations represent the three main ways that the "name" has been interpreted through the ages. In the Judaica Press translation, a large portion of the name (that has to do with divinity) is actually understood to be the subject of the clause, i.e., the one doing the naming; in the JPS '85 version, the entire name is the name of the child, but, like many other Hebrew names it does not say anything about the person named, but only something about God (e.g., Isaiah, "Salvation of YH"); finally, there is the typical Christian translation, represented here by the NASB, that understands that the "name" consists of four or five sub-names that tell us much about the child. Let us now take a closer look at each of these options. Maybe there are some good reasons to prefer one over the others.

---

[146] Christians believe that the sign of Isa 7:14 appeared in the world at the moment that Mary miraculously conceived. The miraculous conception, in conjunction with the son's name, was a sign that signaled the deity of the child in Mary's womb. So the sign and to whom the sign pointed came at the same time.

In the Judaica Press translation, most of the name—up to the "prince of peace"—is understood to be the one doing the naming, i.e., God. Because the subject of the verb is otherwise not specified, perhaps "the wondrous adviser, the mighty God, the everlasting Father" could indeed be the subject of the verb who is doing the naming, and if so, the name of the child ends up being reduced to "prince of peace." But does this option fit the laws of biblical Hebrew syntax? It would if "the wondrous adviser, the mighty God, the everlasting Father," which is the subject of the clause, came right after the verb (or before), which is the usual order. But in this case, it comes after the quasi-object of the verb, "his-name." In some 300+ cases of "call" plus "name" sentences/clauses in the Tanakh, I could not find one that puts the subject of the verb after "name," but, if made explicit, places it—if not before the verb—right after the verb and before the object of the verb.[147] Most of these "call" plus "name" sentences/clauses do not expressly state who is doing the calling, although it is usually understood by the context. A good example is Isa 7:14:

$$\text{וְקָרָאת שְׁמוֹ עִמָּנוּ אֵל}$$

and she calls his name "God-With-Us"

Occasionally the verb's subject is expressed. If it isn't found somewhere before the verb, it is only to be found immediately after it, as we see here in Gen 22:14:

$$\text{וַיִּקְרָא אַבְרָהָם שֵׁם־הַמָּקוֹם הַהוּא יהוה יִרְאֶה}$$

and Abraham called the name of that place "YHWH-Provides"

Notice here that the name of the person doing the calling, Abraham, is shown right after the verb and right before "the name of that place." If the subject of the verb in Isa 9:6b is, as the Judaica Press has it, "the wondrous adviser, the mighty God, the everlasting Father," then we have a case of significant syntactical deviation because the subject of the verb occurs after the object of the verb. And regarding the 300+ "call" plus "name" sentences/clauses in the Tanakh, it would be (as far as I can tell) the only one of its kind. So it is far better *not* to view any part of the "name" as being the subject of the clause—that is, being the one who does the naming—but to understand that the words that come after "his name" are components of the child's name.[148]

---

[147] Based on Logos Bible Software search results.

[148] According to Edward Young, the order of the words here provides a "fatal objection" to the (typically Jewish) view that some of what comes after "his name" applies not to the Messiah, but to the one doing the naming, that is, to God. (Edward Young, *The Book of Isaiah*, vol 1 [Grand Rapids: Wm. B. Eerdmans, 1992], 332.)

The JPS '85 translation reflects Jewish translations over the eons which present the name such that it is clear that the qualities contained within the name are not qualities of the person named, but of God. This is in keeping with many Hebrew names that tell us something about God, but usually nothing about the people who bear the names. For example, "Zedekiah" means "YH is righteous"; but, of course, the man Zedekiah, final king of Judah, was neither "YH" or "righteous." Obviously, names like this as well as, for example, names like Elijah ("my God is YH"), Elisha ("my God Saves") and Daniel ("my Judge is God"), don't *necessarily* tell us anything about those men of the Bible who bore those names. On the other hand, there are Hebrew names here and there that do obviously say something about the name bearer: Abraham was the "Father of a Multitude"; Isaac's birth provoked "laughter"; Jacob was a "supplanter" who was later called Israel, the one who "contends with God." So the long name in Isa 9:6 may or may not say something about the child named. If it does not, and, as the JPS has it, only says something about God—"The Mighty God is planning grace; The eternal Father, a peaceable ruler"—then we have a strange case here of much being said about God (through this name that one only with difficulty can verbalize in one breath) in a Bible passage that is laser-focused on the hope of the House of David and the nation of Israel. In other words, given the context, it would only be natural here to reveal critical information about the child. But the JPS would have us believe that here is a suitable place to give us a number of attributes about God through the presenting of the name. But what would be the point of this at this point in the narrative? Regarding God, there is nothing here that cannot be gleaned from what has preceded in the Tanakh. And even if there were something new here to be learned about God, why present it here where the total focus is upon the wonder-child who will be the eschatological Davidic Messiah?

The NASB, and most other Christian translations, interpret this with far less contextual and grammatical awkwardness by understanding that the whole "name" is not really intended to be a firm personal name for the Messiah (which, by the way, would be the longest personal name in the Bible by far),[149] but four pairs of identifications or characteristics attributable to the Messiah— each of these four pairs being a name that the Messiah would be called: "Wonderful counselor," "Mighty God," "Everlasting Father," "Prince of Peace." Breaking down the big "name" to these smaller name-units at least makes things more like most Hebrew names. That is, with this division we have names that consist of two basic units of thought, something that is the usual

---

[149] Mahershalalhashbaz (Isa 8:1, 3), Cushanrishathaim (Judg 3:8-10), and Zaphenathpaneah (Gen 41:45) are three of the longest names in the Bible. If Isa 9:60b in its entirety is to be taken as a personal name, it, at thirteen syllables, would be more than twice the length of these, and be written something like this: Peleyohaizelgiborahveeathsarshalom.

practice with Hebrew names in general: e.g., Jeremiah ("YH Loosens"), Ezekiel ("God Strengthens"), Jehoshaphat ("YH Judges"), and Joshua ("YH Saves"). It is only with incredulity that one wonders if the Messiah's name in the eschaton is "The Mighty God is planning grace, the eternal Father, a peaceable ruler," for elsewhere the names for the Messiah are mercifully short—e.g., "David," "Branch," "Joshua."

So of the translations that we are considering, the one that sees the "name" as substantially the subject of the verb should be rejected due to its grammatical un-tenability: the verb's subject is simply not going to appear after the verb's object. With this option off the table, the "name" can only be the name or a description of the child, with the verb being translated as passive (he is called) or active (he calls)—in either case the subject of the clause being unstated.[150] The question now is whether the name only says something about God or says something about the person named, that is, the child. I have stated just above a couple of reasons why the latter possibility should be preferred; but it's tough to make a firm decision from the immediate context of the prophecy. On the other hand, if we briefly recall several of the attributes and manifestations of the Messiah that we have seen in this study so far, it may be somewhat easier to perceive that the names within this child's "name" can apply to the Messiah in some mysterious ways.

First, is there anything that has gone before that might help us see that "wonderful counselor" is something that can be said about the Messiah? For starters, I think that there would be little disagreement, in view of all he is and what he does, that he would be a counselor par-excellence. If Solomon, the wisest man who ever lived, is a type of the Messiah, then the antitype will greatly excel him. If we factor in what we know about the Angel of the LORD, we might recall that God told Moses and the Israelites to "obey his voice."[151] He is not someone who is going to steer people wrong. Now as far as him being called "wonderful"—or in many instances, "wonder" (= "miracle")—we can think of all that the Messiah is prophesied to do and agree that his conquering of Satan and the evil nations, and his worldwide rule of the nations in perfect justice and righteousness, is a "wonderful" thing. But especially wonderful, and mysteriously miraculous, is the fact that he will be "David" and the son of David and the Son of God. Finally, let us also take note of the fact that only one other individual in the Tanakh was called "wonderful," and that was the Angel of the

---

[150] The vowels of וַיִּקְרָא (originally added—along with all other vowel and accent marks in the Tanakh—several centuries into the Christian era by Jewish scholars called "Masorites") indicate an active verb. The consonantal text, however, could be active ("and he calls") or passive ("and he is called").

[151] Exod 23:21

LORD who described his name as such when questioned by Manoah.[152] So, yes, the Messiah is "wonderful," and a superlative "counselor," or one might say, a "wonderful counselor."

That the Messiah is "Mighty God" is, of course, what this book is trying to humbly demonstrate. Before I mention a few things about the Messiah's possible divinity from what has gone before, I feel compelled to say once again what a strange thing it would be, literarily speaking, for the name in Isa 9:6 to be only a name that says something about God and not the child-Messiah. Given the immediate context—that is, the context that shows that the child will bring final peace to the world and rule on the throne of David forever—it should not be completely surprising that he is called, among other things, "Mighty God." Now one could say that he is called "God" here something like Ps 82 calls the elders of Israel "gods." It is true that men are called "gods" in a few places in the Tanakh,[153] but in these rare cases, *Elohim* is the Hebrew word used. In Isa 9:6, however, *El*, the singular of *Elohim*, is used (a far rarer word than *Elohim*). *El* is not a word used to identify man, but "God" or "a god."[154] That Isaiah here really means "Mighty God" is confirmed by his use of the same Hebrew words in Isa 10:21, where it is prophesied that a remnant of Jacob will one day return to the "Mighty God." In any case, the wider scriptural context gives us reasons to not completely recoil when we consider that God perhaps intended that the identification of "Mighty God" be something that could be said about his Messiah.

It might be recalled that the Messiah has the power to kill the devil, to conquer and rule all nations, and at last to bless all nations in that he brings them unending peace and a government of perfect justice and righteousness. He is at least super-human. What's more, he is more than once identified as God's Son—a son who will not only build God's "house," but live in that house as well. Knowing this through the Spirit, David in the 110th Psalm calls his own son, who sits at the right hand of YHWH, "my Lord"—an exaltation that would certainly be inappropriate unless there was something truly extraordinary about his son. If we could preview for a moment what is yet to come in our study, we might notice that he, according to Isaiah 11, is full of the seven-fold Spirit of YHWH, and also notice that Daniel (Chap. 7) saw him, in a heavenly vision, being presented before the "Ancient of Days" and coming "with the clouds of heaven" in order to judge the earth. In the Tanakh, clouds are more often than not mentioned in connection with some kind of manifestation of

---

[152] Judg 13:18
[153] E.g., Exod 21:6; 22:8-9; Ps 82:1, 6
[154] BDB lists a few possible applications of *El* to men, but says these are "uncertain." Young observes that: "In Isaiah [*El*] is found as a designation of God and only of Him." (Young, *The Book of Isaiah*, vol. 1, 336.)

God. The presence of God comes with—or in the form of—clouds at Sinai, in the desert with the new Israelite nation, and at the Temple. YHWH is said to ride upon the clouds and that a cloud is his "chariot."[155] Daniel shows that God has a kingdom and dominion that will endure forever, and that the "Son of Man," who comes upon the clouds of heaven, will have a kingdom and dominion that last forever.[156] Are there two kings ruling the world, or one? God says, through Ezekiel, that he will be Israel's shepherd in the days when Israel is restored, but then says that David, God's "servant," will be their shepherd, and that they will have "one shepherd."[157] These messianic prophetical passages will be discussed in more detail a little later. For now, let's move on to the next name within the "name" of Isa 9:6b.

To believe that the Messiah is "Everlasting Father" is surely a tough pill to swallow for many monotheists. The burden of proof is on the Christian to show that this has sufficient biblical support to overcome worries about the seeming impossibility of the Son of God being identified as God the Father. I confess that there is no way for the Christian to argue for this rationally, and most Christians would not be anxious to do so anyhow because Christian orthodoxy believes in the separate personhood of the Father and of the Son, notwithstanding the fact that Jesus said some things that seemed to blur the line,[158] and also notwithstanding the present text which most Christians believe applies to the Messiah. So if Christians think that "Everlasting Father" applies in some mysterious way to the Messiah, we are backed substantially into a corner, because we know that as much as God expects us to "work out [our] salvation with fear and trembling" based upon what he has revealed in Scripture, we also know that God does not want us to throw rationality out of the window in the process.[159] We choose the Bible, after all, over other religious writings because it is more reasonable: It addresses the ultimate questions of mankind with superior logical and historical precision. Of course, whether faith or reason comes first has been the subject of endless debate through the ages. At all events, whether we are led to truth by God's Word or we are led to it by reason, our basic understanding of God as truth and as good prompts us to

---

[155] Isa 19:1; Ps 104:3. See also Deut 33:26; Nah 1:2-3.
[156] Dan 4:34; 6:26; 7:14, 27. King Darius says (Dan 6:26) regarding "the God of Daniel": "His kingdom is one which will not be destroyed, and His dominion will be forever." Daniel says (Dan 7:14) regarding his vision of the Son of Man coming "with the clouds of heaven": "His dominion is an everlasting dominion which will not pass away; and His kingdom is one which will not be destroyed."
[157] Ezek 34. See especially v. 23.
[158] John 10:30; 14:7-11. But see John 14:28 and Jesus' prayer in John 17.
[159] Phil 2:12

know that he will not require us to accept obvious contradictions.[160] But he will lead us to accept mysteries that are far beyond our ability to fully comprehend.

Being faced with "mysteries" should be no surprise, for the Tanakh teaches that we, compared to God, are but a "breath" that ends "with a moan": the years "quickly pass and we fly away."[161] Yes, we are made in the image of God, but the LORD declares:

> My thoughts are not your thoughts, nor are your ways My ways. For as the heavens are higher than the earth, so are My ways higher than your ways and My thoughts than your thoughts.[162]

With this, God shows that he has infinite wisdom and knowledge, and we possess next to nothing in comparison. We know something about human fatherhood and sonship, but in view of God's knowledge compared to our own, how much can we honestly say that we know about that, let alone about divine fatherhood and sonship?

In his Holy Word, God right from the start indicates some kind of plurality within himself when he says, "Let Us make man in Our image, according to Our likeness," and then says after the fall, "Behold, the man has become like one of Us, knowing good and evil."[163] And God said to Isaiah when Isaiah saw God: "Who will go for Us?"[164] "Us," in these cases, cannot mean God *and* the angels, for angels did not create man, man is not made in the "image and likeness" of angels, man did not become like the angels when he first sinned, and, regarding Isaiah's vision, man does not "go" on behalf of angels, but on behalf of God alone. I could also mention that the usual Hebrew word for God is not the singular *El*, but the plural *Elohim*. If all this does in fact indicate some diversity within the unity of God, who are we to know—being the extremely limited creatures that we are—how that really goes?

The mixing of the human and divine is not unknown in the Tanakh, as a few examples here illustrate. When God's Spirit fell upon Saul, Israel's first king, he immediately began prophesying, something that he had never done before. It was Saul prophesying, yet it was God speaking through him at the same time—yes, using Saul's brain and nerves and vocal cords, yet God was the cause of it.[165] The same could be said of David and the prophets who uttered

---

[160] Seeming contradictions that relate to Jesus' person and/or his deeds and/or his demands are, for example, divinity and humanity; omniscient knowledge and limited knowledge; faith and works; predestination and freewill; Mosaic Law preservation and the Law's irrelevance; promises made to Israel and promises made to Christians; love and damnation.

[161] Ps 39:11; 90:9-10 (NIV)

[162] Isa 55:9

[163] Gen 1:26; 3:22

[164] Isa 6:8

[165] 1 Sam 10, 19

words based upon the Spirit's prompting.[166] In all these, it was they who spoke, and yet it was God who spoke. The Messiah is born into the world as a child and is a distinct person. He is filled, according to Isaiah, with the seven-fold Spirit of YHWH.[167] God's Spirit is upon him to such an extent that he has the power to declare, as he does in Isa 61:1-3, the release of the human race from its bondage—something that only God can do. Does the Messiah-Son do this or does God the Father do this? And, finally, the personality of the Angel of YHWH who visited Balaam and Gideon is blended with YHWH when that Angel speaks in several instances as the Angel and in other instances as YHWH.[168] Who visited them—the Angel or YHWH or both in the same "man"?[169] When the same Angel visited Manoah and his wife, Manoah believed that they would die because they had seen God, and there is nothing in the text to indicate that he misidentified the Angel.[170]

That YHWH is the "Father" of his people is a biblical fact (Deut 32:6; Isa 63:16), and it is a fact, as we have already seen, that YHWH is a Father to his Son who will sit on David's throne forever and one day bring all the nations of the earth into submission to him.[171] If YHWH is the Father of his Son, the Messiah, and his Son has the fullness of YHWH's Spirit dwelling within him—and he does as God does: he comes on the clouds of heaven, he redeems mankind, and he rules the world forever—is it beyond the pale to perceive some *commonality* between them?[172] Maybe not because he *is* in an absolute sense the Father, but because he is so infused by the Father's Spirit and so obedient to his Father that all he says and does is *only* what the Father would say and do. In any case, as I admitted at the start, calling the Son the Father seems preposterous; but maybe there's more going on here than meets the eye. The NT sheds some light on this, but it still remains a mystery *how* it could be. Now let's look at the last part of the "name" of Isa 9:6.

Few, whether Jewish or Christian, would disagree that "Prince of Peace" is a suitable epithet for the Messiah. But first YHWH must put all of his enemies under his feet, which includes the enemy nations and the arch-enemy, Satan. As a part of the Day of the LORD, the Messiah will "shatter [the nations] like earthenware," "heaping up the dead."[173] But once the "obedience of the

---

[166] "[N]o prophecy was ever made by an act of human will, but men moved by the Holy Spirit spoke from God" (2 Pet 1:21). David said of himself in his last recorded words (2 Sam 23:2): "The Spirit of the LORD spoke by me, and His word was on my tongue."

[167] Isa 11:2

[168] Num 22; Judg 6

[169] Judg 13:6

[170] Judg 13:22-23

[171] 2 Sam 7:14; 1 Chron 17:13; Pss 2:7; 89:26

[172] Regarding the Messiah redeeming mankind, we will learn more about this in "The Messiah is God's 'Servant'" section below.

[173] Pss 2:9; 110:6 (BSB)

peoples" is his, he will be "Shiloh"—or, if you will, a new Solomon—who will settle Israel at last in a permanent peaceful place, and through his righteous and compassionate government, bring ever expanding peace to the earth.[174] The time of his administration is described in Isa 11:6, 9 as one in which "the wolf will dwell with the lamb" and no one will,

> ...hurt or destroy in all [God's] holy mountain, for the earth will be
> full of the knowledge of the LORD as the waters cover the sea. Then
> in that day, the nations will resort to the root of Jesse, who will stand
> as a signal for the peoples; and His resting place will be glorious.

In conclusion, we should recall that the Isa 7-9 prophecy was all about encouraging men—like King Ahaz—with the news that the nation and its Davidic bloodline would not come to an end, but would be preserved despite the onslaught of even the world's most powerful and merciless nations. When Israel and the House of David would finally emerge from the darkness and gloom into the "great light," a Davidic ruler would come who would establish a government and peace that would be ever expanding. Because of the power and glory and goodness of this ruler, it is probable that the names given to him at birth—"God with us," "Wonderful counselor," "Mighty God," "Everlasting Father," "Prince of Peace"—are names that to some degree indeed tell us something about this very special child. What the prophets say next about the "Branch of David" and the "Root of Jesse" will serve to bolster this view.

THE MESSIAH IS THE "BRANCH"

The Messiah as "Branch" or "Sprout" or "Root" is mentioned in Isa 4 and 11, Jer 23 and 33, as well as Zech 3 and 6. The Zechariah mentions are unique in that they involve an actual person—the High Priest Joshua—who is figurative of the Messiah to come. We'll look at Zechariah's "Branch" at the end of this chapter, but for now concentrate on what is said about him in Isaiah and Jeremiah.

The presentments of the messianic "Branch" in Isaiah and Jeremiah all consist of the same basic package: both of these prophets first bring a stark contrast to the degraded state of Israel with the good news of the Messiah. In each case the advent of the messianic age is introduced with the solemn formula, "In that day," or something similar. Then the Branch, or similar designation, is mentioned followed by a short or longer description of his wonderful characteristics. Many wonderful blessings that come upon Israel at the time of

---

[174] Gen 49:10; Pss 2:8; 72:7; Isa 9:7; 11:1-10; 66:12. Regarding the Messiah being a new Solomon, see, in the New Testament, Luke 11:31.

the Branch's advent are then spoken of, and so, each "package" is completed. We'll begin with what Isaiah had to say about the Branch; but first, a little historical background is in order.

"In the year of King Uzziah's death," that is, about 740 BC, Isaiah was commissioned (Chap. 6) directly by God to go to his people in order to warn them about the judgment to come and to give them the encouraging news that, even though the nation would perish, a remnant would survive that would re-inhabit the Promised Land under the righteous leadership of the Messiah. Isaiah's harsh depictions of the sinfulness of Judah and the consequent judgment to follow, as well as his first mention of the Branch who would come in the restoration that followed the judgment, were given just after his commissioning. One would think that given the relatively good times that obtained under Uzziah and his son Jotham (both were recorded as having done "good in the sight of the LORD"), Isaiah would have had better things to say about the people and their leaders in his descriptions of them in Chapters 1-3. Even though Jotham was a good king, whom the LORD made "mighty" and under whom Isaiah gave his first prophecies, nevertheless, as is recorded in 2 Chron 27:2, "the people continued acting corruptly." Other than the "sneak preview" of the messianic times presented at the beginning of chapter 2 (also recorded nearly verbatim in Micah 4) and of the Branch in chapter 4, the entirety of the first five chapters is about the wickedness of the people of Judah. Their character could be boiled down to what Isaiah says right at the start:

> Listen, O heavens, and hear, O earth; for the LORD speaks, "Sons I have reared and brought up, but they have revolted against Me. An ox knows its owner, and a donkey its master's manger, but Israel does not know, My people do not understand." Alas, sinful nation, people weighed down with iniquity, offspring of evildoers, sons who act corruptly! They have abandoned the LORD, they have despised the Holy One of Israel, they have turned away from Him. [175]

Isaiah then goes on to tell them that their tithes and offerings are of no value, for their hands are "covered in blood." They who were once righteous are now "murderers," and their leaders "rebels" and "thieves." God would in time judge them harshly for this, but the day would come when he would demonstrate his great compassion and restore them to a permanent state of prosperity and tranquility in their land. [176] "In that day" will come the glorious Messiah (4:2):

---

[175] Isa 1:2-4
[176] Isa 1:26-27; 2:2-4; 4:2-6

In that day the Branch of the LORD will be beautiful and glorious, and the fruit of the earth will be the pride and the adornment of the survivors of Israel. (NASB)

On that day, the sprout of the Lord shall be for beauty and for honor, and the fruit of the land for greatness and for glory for the survivors of Israel. (Judaica)

In that day shall the growth of the LORD be beautiful and glorious, And the fruit of the land excellent and comely for them that are escaped of Israel. (JPS '17)

Here, the "Branch" is introduced: He is "beautiful and glorious" and, according to the next couple verses, will exist at a time when all sin has been purged from the land, everyone is holy, and God's glory (in the form of a cloud by day and fire by night) will hover as a protective cover over Zion. Two things here tremendously bless the "survivors" of Israel, that is, the righteous remnant remaining after God's judgment is over: the Branch of YHWH and the tremendous "fruit" of the earth, i.e., the great food abundance that God will cause to spring forth from the earth at that time.

Some Tanakh versions—the JPS '17 is an example—interpret the first part of the verse as a parallel to the second part: If the second part is about the great food crops that abound at that time, the first part must be about that too. So the JPS '17 version uses the phrase, "growth of the LORD," which seems to imply that the "fruit of the land" mentioned in the second part begins as an agricultural "growth of the LORD" of the first part—and thus has nothing to do with the Messiah. Further on in the obviously messianic texts of Isa 11 and Jer 23, 33, the JPS '17 uses the typical messianic words "shoot" and "twig," and could have done so here like the NASB and Judaica have done. It is unlikely that Isa 4:2 is *only* about grain, vegetables, and fruit production, for something greater than that must be in view here. A historical and prophetical hint that indeed something greater is presented here is found in the last words of David which were uttered about 250 years before:

[The God of Israel] has made an everlasting covenant with me, ordered in all things, and secured; for all my salvation and all my desire, will He not indeed make it grow?[177]

The root verb here for "make it grow" is צָמַח, *tsamach*, meaning "to sprout forth"—the noun version being צֶמַח, *tsemach*, "a sprout," which is the same word used by Isaiah in 4:2a.[178] David testified here that he knew beyond a doubt

[177] 2 Sam 23:5
[178] BDB, Gesenius

that the LORD would in time bring to pass what he had promised—what David calls the "everlasting covenant" (2 Sam 7; 1 Chron 17): viz., that God would establish his dynasty forever by raising up (causing to "sprout") the son of David who would rule on David's throne forever. And this fulfillment of the covenant would have everything to do with David's personal "salvation" and "desire"—a foretaste of the redeeming work that the Messiah would one day accomplish. Given the facts that Isaiah was the prophet of four kings of the Davidic dynasty (Isa 1:1) and that he was intensely interested in the dynasty's preservation, it has to be the case that Isaiah was acutely aware of David's last recorded words, and thus was more than apt to say of the Messiah when he came upon the scene that he had at last "sprouted," and could thus be called a "sprout" (or something similar). We could also look a little forward in time when Isaiah (11:1) plainly used "sprout" (or something similar, depending on the versions) as a technical term for the Messiah (as did Jeremiah in Chapters 23 and 33).

So in view of David's last words and also in view of how this term would be employed later in prophecies that are plainly about the Messiah, it must be the case in Isa 4:2 that the "sprout" that would one day emerge from the House of David is here in view.[179] One more observation could be made regarding Isa 4:2—albeit frankly speculative, but worth considering in view of all that we have learned about the Messiah. In what Isaiah says here, both clauses of the verse may refer to the Messiah, the second clause being more figurative. Borrowing for a moment from Isa 9:6, the prophet said that the "wonderful" Messiah-child would not only be a son who would be "born to us," but also a son who would be "given" to us. Isa 4:2 perhaps parallels this in the following way: The "fruit of the earth" refers to the emergence of the Messiah from the "dust of the ground," that is, from the seed of the human Davidic line. At the same time, he is a son that is "given" in that God is his Father and is the source of his divinity. He is not only the "Branch of David," as he will be called later,[180] but also the "Branch of YHWH." He is the fruit of the ground, and the fruit of heaven.[181] Isaiah's formal presentation of the Branch in chapter 11 (that we turn to now) will serve to give credence to the idea that he is just as much a product of heaven as he is of the earth.

After God has sternly chastised Israel, such that there is a "complete devastation," God will in turn bring his judging hand upon the excessive cruelty

[179] Compare Isa 4:2 with Isa 28:5 (compare Isa 28:5 with Ps 132:18).
[180] Jer 33:15
[181] "The use of this double epithet to denote 'the coming One' can only be accounted for, without anticipating the New Testament standpoint, from the desire to depict His double-sided origin. He would come, on the one hand, from *Jehovah*; but, on the other hand, from *the earth*, inasmuch as He would spring from Israel." (Keil and Delitzsch, *Commentary on the Old Testament*, Isa 4:2.)

of his "instrument," the Assyrians, and at long last bring a small remnant back into the Promised Land. "Now in that day," declares Isaiah in 10:20,

> ...the remnant of Israel, and those of the house of Jacob who have escaped, will never again rely on the one who struck them, but will truly rely on the LORD, the Holy One of Israel.

Israel (i.e., all of Israel, both northern and southern kingdoms) will no longer be inclined to trust in heathen kings—like Ahaz had done—but will trust in the King of kings, the "Holy One of Israel." Then after spending several lines assuring Israel that Assyria would soon be destroyed and the godly remnant preserved, Isaiah introduces the Branch and his most vital characteristic with these words:

> Then a shoot will spring from the stem of Jesse, and a branch from his roots will bear fruit. The Spirit of the LORD will rest on Him, the spirit of wisdom and understanding, the spirit of counsel and strength, the spirit of knowledge and the fear of the LORD.

The "shoot" which will "spring from the stem of Jesse," is David and his royal "seed" that eventually leads to the Messiah. Jesse was, of course, David's father.[182] Perhaps Isaiah sources the royal line in Jesse so as to fully include David within the "shoot," also called "branch," that extends from Jesse to the One upon whom the seven-fold Spirit of YHWH will one day rest. The Hebrew here employs words for "shoot," *choter*, and "branch," *netzer*, which are all but synonymous with 4:2's *zemach*. And echoing 4:2's "fruit of the earth," the Branch is described here as one who "will bear fruit."

The Branch, according to 11:4, is a righteous judge who judges the poor and the "afflicted of the earth." We have already learned in Ps 72 that the Messiah will do this: he is a champion and defender of the poor and oppressed. Now what empowers him to do this is shown in v. 2—indeed something new for our study, and something new that will somewhat explain how the Messiah can be not just a Branch of Jesse, but also a Branch of the LORD. The Spirit of YHWH is said to rest upon him in a fullness that is unique to him and said of no other. This Spirit consists of seven elements, beginning with "the Spirit of the LORD," which, it is said, can be represented by the central lamp of the lampstand (the Menorah) in the Temple.[183] The three oil lamps on one side of the lampstand, one might say, are wisdom, understanding, and counsel; and on the other side, strength, knowledge, and the fear of the LORD. A total of seven Spirits making up the one Spirit that is central to the others, the Spirit of

---

[182] 1 Sam 16
[183] This thought comes from Keil and Delitzsch, *Commentary on the Old Testament*, Isa 11:2.

YHWH. As is well known, the number seven in general represents perfection, whether that number of units is involved with, for example, the amount of time that it took to create the cosmos and rest from that creation or the number of times the goat's blood was sprinkled before the altar on the Day of Atonement. Seven represents not only perfection, but completion. In this case, the fact that the Messiah has the seven-fold Spirit of God means that the imbuing is so perfect that it can be said to be complete, and in a way far more perfect and complete than the filling that others experienced as recorded in the Tanakh. The Spirit of craftsmanship, for instance, came upon Bezalel so he could bring great artistic skill to the building of the desert Tabernacle; Moses, Joshua, and the seventy elders of Israel were given God's Spirit of leadership; Othniel, Gideon, and Samson were enabled by God, through his Spirit, to do great warrior exploits; and both Saul and David had their hearts and minds changed by God's Spirit.[184] But none of these (nor any others mentioned later in the Tanakh who received God's Spirit) were given the Spirit in the perfection and completeness that is the case when the Spirit rests upon the Branch of Jesse, who is also the Branch of YHWH. This is what makes him the perfect and righteous judge of the poor. It is also what gives him "faithfulness" (*emunah*) as a "belt about his waist" (11:5)—just like Ethan the Ezrahite had already said about God (Ps 89:8): "O LORD God of hosts, who is like You, O mighty LORD? Your faithfulness [*emunah*] also surrounds You."

Not only will the Branch rescue the poor and afflicted, "He will strike the earth with the rod of His mouth and with the breath of His lips He will slay the wicked" (11:4). It has already been said in several places that the Messiah will conquer all nations: He will sit at his Father's right hand until all of his enemies become a "footstool" for his feet; in the days of his wrath, he will smash the nations "like pottery," "heaping up the dead" in the process; and at long last, the "obedience of the nations shall be his."[185] We know that his Father enables him to do this, so much so that it is said that his Father "gives" the nations to him "as an inheritance," and that it is his Father, YHWH, who puts his "enemies under [his] feet."[186] So far, the weapons of his warfare have not been revealed. But here we get a glimpse of them: He attacks the earth with "the rod of His mouth" and kills all of his enemies "with the breath of His lips." In other words, he is not like earthly kings who must employ armies to subdue the earth, but he simply does as he did in the beginning: "God said … and it was so."[187] Yes, potentates, like Nebuchadnezzar, could say who lives and dies,

---

[184] Exod 31:2-5; Num 11:16-30; 27:18; Judg 3:10; 6:34; 14:6; 1 Sam 10:9-12; 16:13
[185] Ps 110:1; Ps 2:9 (NIV); Ps 110:6 (NIV); Gen 49:10 (NIV)
[186] Pss 2:8; 110:1-2
[187] Gen 1:9

and men would go out with swords to do their bidding; but it is only God and the Messiah, according to the Tanakh, who conquer *merely* by speaking.[188]

The presentations of the Branch in Isaiah and Jeremiah, as already mentioned, include information about the Branch and information about the conditions of the time in which he reigns. We've already learned that the Messiah, after all enemies are under his feet, will be a man of peace, and that peace and tranquility and prosperity will be manifest throughout his realm.[189] Here in Isa 11:6-9 the prophet gives us a beautiful picture of what that peace will look like: All the animals—the wolf, bear, lion, leopard, ox, cow, calf, goat, lamb, etc.—in that day will be herbivores, and they will coexist peacefully with each other and with man. Even reptiles will be rendered harmless. In fact, no creatures of any kind will "hurt or destroy in all [of God's] holy mountain, for the earth will be full of the knowledge of the LORD as the waters cover the sea."[190] God will cause all of his remnant people (as described in vv. 11-16) to come to this new paradise from all the nations in which they were scattered, and he will draw the gentiles too:

> Then in that day The nations [*goyim*] will resort to the root of Jesse, who will stand as a signal for the peoples [*amim*]; and His resting place will be glorious.

Again, it's not so much about the land, but about the God and his Messiah who will be there. The nations are primarily drawn to a *who*, not a *what*—that "who" being the "root of Jesse," i.e., the Messiah. In that day, he stands "as a signal for the peoples." One thing worthy of note here, before we end this section on Isa 11, is the fact that he is a "signal" for the "peoples" who are in all "nations." The Messiah is someone who attracts everyone, and someone before whom all peoples and nations will one day bow. The Messiah *stands* as a "signal," yet it is God who *lifts up* this signal as revealed in v. 12 as well as in Isa 49:22. In all these cases, the same Hebrew word is used: נֵס, *nes*, "standard, ensign, signal" (BDB). Let us now turn to the prophet Jeremiah to see what he had to say about the Branch.

Isaiah prophesied of the judgment that would come upon Israel after his lifetime; Jeremiah about a century later also prophesied of this judgment, but lived to see the prophecies of "lamentations, mourning and woe" fulfilled during the days that he served the last kings of the House of David.[191] Isaiah

---

[188] The Messiah is said to conquer by mouth here and in Isa 49:2, and God is said to do the same in Isa 30:27-28, 31, 33 and in Job 4:9. The NT also says this of Jesus: 2 Thess 2:8; Rev 1:6; 19:15, 21. Consider also John 18:6.

[189] Gen 49:10; Ps 72; Isa 9:6-7

[190] Isa 11:9

[191] Ezek 2:10

foresaw that the House of David at some future point would be reduced to only a "stump";[192] Jeremiah foresaw something similar: the nation and its Davidic leaders would be a beautiful olive tree burned down—and this he witnessed with his own eyes.[193] The LORD warned Judah through Jeremiah, "The wind will sweep away all your shepherds,"[194] and, indeed, all five that Jeremiah served under were swept away: King Josiah—the only good king among them, although the people continued in wickedness—was killed by Pharaoh Necho; Jeremiah said that Jehoahaz, Josiah's son, would be taken to Egypt and never return—and so it was; Jeremiah said that Jehoiakim, who burned Jeremiah's words and who was a murderer,[195] would die violently and be buried like a donkey—and so it was; Jeremiah foretold that Jehoiachin would be exiled to Babylon and never return—and so it was; and, finally, he showed King Zedekiah that his family and leading men would be killed and that the feckless king would be led away in chains to Babylon where he would die—and so it was.[196] The shepherds of Judah were all swept away—shepherds who, as God said through Jeremiah, "ruined My vineyard" and "trampled down My field" and "made My pleasant field a desolate wilderness."[197]

The problem was that everyone was evil, not just the kings.[198] Each man's heart was, as the prophet said, "more deceitful than all else" and "desperately sick."[199] Instead of Isaiah's idyllic scene of fearsome animals living at peace with people—which some then might have thought to be something soon realized— Jeremiah saw something different that was about to come upon his people:

> [A] lion from the forest will slay them, a wolf of the deserts will destroy them, a leopard is watching their cities. Everyone who goes out of them will be torn in pieces, because their transgressions are many, their apostasies are numerous.[200]

If only one good man could be found in Jerusalem, said Jeremiah, then God would pardon the city.[201] But one couldn't be found. They had even sunk to the depraved level of offering up their own children to the burning arms of

---

[192] Isa 6:13

[193] Jer 11:16

[194] Jer 22:22

[195] Jehoiakim killed the prophet Uriah (Jer 26:20-23).

[196] 2 Kings 22:16-17; 23:29; Jer 22:11-12, 18-19, 24-30. Regarding warnings to Zedekiah, see: Jer 21:3-7; 38:17-18.

[197] Jer 12:10

[198] See especially Jer 32:26-35.

[199] Jer 17:9

[200] Jer 5:6

[201] Jer 5:1

Molech.[202] The prophets and priests were rotten too: The former continually told lies and led the people astray, and the latter shed the innocent "blood of the righteous."[203] All had broken God's covenant and their hearts were rock hard: "The sin of Judah is written down with an iron stylus; with a diamond point it is engraved upon the tablet of their heart."[204] In general, the kings of Israel and Judah had fulfilled the warning given by Samuel long before: the king would be oppressive and the people would be his slaves (1 Sam 8). Samuel then said:

> [Y]ou will cry out in that day because of your king whom you have chosen for yourselves, but the LORD will not answer you in that day.[205]

By the time of Jeremiah, the experiment of attempting to create a utopia upon earth with a human Davidic king had failed—a fact that only served to highlight and uphold the truth expressed long before that the only king that mankind should ever serve is God.[206] Because the kings and those they ruled did wickedly, all of them, as Samuel foretold, were "swept away."[207] So bad was it in Jeremiah's time that as the end neared, God declared that he would no longer listen to his people, and he commanded Jeremiah to no longer pray for them.[208] Their "wound," as the prophet lamented,[209] was "incurable"—a fact that profoundly grieved his heart:

> Oh that my head were waters and my eyes a fountain of tears, that I might weep day and night for the slain of the daughter of my people! My eyes run down with streams of water because of the destruction of the daughter of my people. My eyes pour down unceasingly, without stopping.[210]

All seemed lost, and it appeared that God was completely through with Israel and the House of David.

In the historical narrative at that time, however, all was not completely black. The last king of Judah, Zedekiah, as evil as he was,[211] had a glimmer of

---

[202] Jer 32:35. Jeremiah also said that they would eat the flesh of their sons and daughters during the siege (Jer 19:9—a fulfillment of Deut 28:53-57).

[203] Jer 3:8; 6:13; 14:13-16; 23:9-40; 28; 29:8-9, 21-32; Lam 4:13

[204] Jer 17:1

[205] 1 Sam 8:18

[206] 1 Sam 8:7; 12:12-25

[207] 1 Sam 12:25

[208] Jer 11:11, 14; 14:11-12

[209] Jer 30:12

[210] Jer 9:1; Lam 3:48-49

[211] Zedekiah was declared to be evil (2 Kings 24:19) and was included by God in the basket of "very bad figs which could not be eaten due to rottenness" (Jer 24:8).

light in him: He still seemed to have some fear of God and thus gave some measure of protection to Jeremiah—enough that the prophet was spared from those in Zedekiah's court who sought his life. He had some regard for Jeremiah's words, although he by and large did not act in accordance with them.[212] And Jehoiachin, who was dethroned after only three months by Nebuchadnezzar and imprisoned in Babylon eleven years before Jerusalem's destruction, was, upon the death of the great Babylonian king, released. He remained in Babylon and ate regularly at the King's table.[213] The news of this, as reported in 2 Kings and Jeremiah, seemed to telegraph the possibility that, even though the Davidic kings were "swept away," there remained, in him, a discernable "sprout" emanating from the burned out stump.[214] Prophetically speaking, there was also the word given by Jeremiah that informed his fellow Jews that the exile would not be permanent: it would only last seventy years.[215]

With Jeremiah, as it was with Isaiah, there were more than just historical hints of something better to come; in fact they gave rich prophecies of the time that Israel would be restored *permanently*. In general, they prophesied one "Day of the LORD"[216] and one final return from exile, such that some perhaps believed that all had been fulfilled when the Jews came back to Jerusalem after the Babylonian exile. But later events made it abundantly clear that the permanent resettling of the Promised Land and the coming of the Messiah would come at a time far in the future—so far in fact that the timespan between when the prophecies concerning the messianic era were made and when they would be fulfilled would allow lesser exiles and return-from-exiles in between.[217]

God gave Jeremiah several extended prophecies concerning the messianic times that informed the people that YHWH would one day bring a remnant back to the Promised Land, and there bestow upon them unending prosperity

---

[212] Zedekiah was overcome by hardliners on his court who believed that the Babylonians could be successfully resisted and who would not give up even when all hope was lost (Jer 38:22). They wanted to kill Jeremiah, but the king interceded—probably at the risk of his own life—on more than one occasion (37:21; 38:10, 16). Jeremiah prophesied disaster for him, yet comforted him with the word that he would die in peace and that his death would be lamented by his countrymen (34:4-5). Jeremiah knew that the LORD was firmly committed to bringing about the demise of the nation (14:10-12). When the prophet pondered this and Zedekiah's unwillingness to heed God's warnings, he might have recalled words that he had previously spoken to God: "I know, O LORD, that a man's way is not in himself, nor is it in a man who walks to direct his steps" (10:23). If so, he probably had some feelings of pity—perhaps even compassion—for the scheming, yet hapless, king.

[213] 2 Kings 25:27-30; Jer 52:31-34

[214] Although the curse that YHWH pronounced on Jehoiachin in Jer 22:30 seems to preclude this.

[215] Jer 25:11; 29:10

[216] Isa 13:6-16; Jer 30:5-8; 46:10

[217] Palestine and Jerusalem have experienced numerous significant changes in Jewish population during the Roman, Byzantine, Muslim, Crusader, and Ottoman epochs.

and joy.[218] This state would be permanent because God's people would no longer sin and rebel. And this would be made possible, as Jeremiah explained, because God would provide a "New Covenant" by which he would change men's and women's hearts so that they would all know the LORD.[219] In the process of this, the LORD would redeem Israel and, by doing so, would forgive all their sins and remember them no more.[220] This covenant would not be like the Mosaic Covenant—the covenant that they broke—but would be entirely new and unbreakable.[221] And so, things of the Old Covenant would fade away and soon disappear: Men would no longer swear by the fact that YHWH brought Israel out of Egypt, and the furniture item that was at the very center of the Mosaic Law, the Ark of the Covenant, would disappear, no longer be remembered, and never again be remade.[222] Thus, the complete forgiveness of sins and the new hearts provided to the people by God would not be accomplished as a product of the Old Covenant, but as a product of the New Covenant—a covenant under which the "righteous Branch" would rule on the throne of David, all the people would call YHWH their "Father,"[223] and Jerusalem would be the "throne" of the "everlasting King."[224]

So now we come to our special text, Jer 23:5-6 (and its near-parallel, 33:15-16), in which the arrival of the "Branch" is foretold as a part of the ingathering of the Jewish remnant after the great judgment. Beginning with a solemn formula similar to Isaiah's "Branch" prophecies ("in that day"), Jeremiah says:

> "Behold, the days are coming," declares the LORD, "when I will raise up for David a righteous Branch; and He will reign as king and act wisely and do justice and righteousness in the land. In His days Judah will be saved, and Israel will dwell securely; and this is His name by which He will be called, 'The LORD our righteousness.'"

In Jer 33:15 he is called the "righteous Branch of David." No doubt the Branch referred to here is the same Branch of Isaiah 4:2—there, the *samach* of YHWH, and here the *samach* of David. And this *samach* is the same as the *nezar* that sprouts out of the root of Jesse (David's father) in Isa 11:1. Several things here repeat what we already know about the Messiah: He will be a wise king who will rule the nations and his people with perfect justice such that peace and righteousness pervade his whole domain. Through this, "Judah will be saved,"

---

[218] Jer 3:14-19; 16:14-16; 23:1-8; 30:9-10, 18-22; 31; 32:36-44; 33; 50:4-5, 19-20
[219] Jer 31:27-40; 32:37-44
[220] Jer 31:11, 34; 33:8
[221] Jer 11:1-10 (Old Covenant broken); 31:27-40 (New Covenant to be established).
[222] Jer 3:16; 16:14-15; 23:7-8
[223] Jer 3:19
[224] Jer 3:17; 10:10

that is, rescued from extinction, and "Israel will dwell securely" just like God had foretold to David through the prophet Nathan.[225] In consideration of the fact that YHWH will forgive all sins (33:8), it may be that salvation of Judah and the security obtained for Israel may be more than just the earthly preservation of those nations. If so, then it is only made possible by the new righteousness in the people, a righteousness that allows them to be reconciled to God, but a righteousness that has its source not in the souls of the people, but in God alone.

This is indicated by the remarkable name of the Messiah that God reveals through Jeremiah in 23:6:

וְזֶה־שְּׁמוֹ אֲשֶׁר־יִקְרְאוֹ יְהוָה ׀ צִדְקֵנוּ

And this is His name by which He will be called, "The LORD our righteousness." (NASB)[226]

And this is the name by which he shall be called: "The LORD is our Vindicator." (JPS '85)

[A]nd this is his name that he shall be called, The Lord is our righteousness. (Judaica)

This is the name people will call him: Hashem is our righteousness. (Artscroll)

Here and there, some have understood that YHWH in this sentence is not part of the Messiah's name, but the subject of the verb, that is, the one who is doing the naming, rendering something like: "and this is his name that YHWH calls him: 'our righteousness.'"[227] While the form of the verb can accommodate this, it does not accord with several other similar sentences in the Tanakh that reveal a name for a place that also includes the whole Tetragrammaton (YHWH):

וַיִּקְרָא אַבְרָהָם שֵׁם־הַמָּקוֹם הַהוּא יְהוָה ׀ יִרְאֶה
Gen 22:14

(And Abraham called the name of that place "YHWH will Provide")

---

[225] 2 Sam 7:10-11; 1 Chron 17:9-10

[226] Hebrew text from BHS.

[227] Hengstenberg (*Christology*, 2:416-17) says that relatively few Jewish commentators through the ages have gone this direction; but most, because of the accents involved, understand the name to be "YHWH our righteousness," or something similar.

וַיִּבֶן מֹשֶׁה מִזְבֵּחַ וַיִּקְרָא שְׁמוֹ יְהוָה | נִסִּי
Exod 17:15

(And Moses built an altar and he called its name "YHWH is my Banner")

וְשֵׁם־הָעִיר מִיּוֹם יְהוָה | שָׁמָּה
Ezek 48:35

(And the name of the city from that day: "YHWH is There")[228]

As it is with these, so it is most likely the case with Jer 23:6: The Messiah is called "YHWH our Righteousness."

We can ask (as we asked with Isa 9:6) if this name says something about YHWH or something about the person named, or both. That the name says something about the person named is strongly indicated by this remarkable fact: There are over a hundred names of persons in the Tanakh that include part (YH) of the Tetragrammaton (e.g., Isaiah, Jeremiah, Zedekiah), and there are a handful of place and inanimate object names (as can be seen in the example texts just above) that include the entire Tetragrammaton; but there is only one place in the Tanakh that reveals a *person's* name that includes the *entire* Tetragrammaton—and that is here in Jer 23:6, the name given to the Branch, who is the Messiah.[229] Especially in view of all that we have considered so far, this name certainly must say something about the man that it is given to. At the very least, it indicates the excellence of the man in that he is the only man in Scripture who is worthy enough to have God's whole name within his own name. Pondering this, we might recall what God said about the Angel that he sent before the Israelites in the desert: "My name is in him."[230] If the Messiah (the "Branch," the "Angel of the LORD") is divine, then the name given in Jer 23:6 applies to both YHWH and the Messiah—who are (in ways too "wonderful" to fully comprehend) *our righteousness.*

The prophet Isaiah and the LORD made it clear that men and woman find righteousness only in God:

> Isa 45:24: They will say of Me, "Only in the LORD are righteousness and strength." Men will come to Him, and all who were angry at Him will be put to shame.

---

[228] My translations. The Hebrew texts of these three verses are from BHS.
[229] Arnold G. Fruchtenbaum, *Ha-Mashiach* (San Antonio: Ariel Ministries, 2017), 60.
[230] Exod 23:21

Isa 54:17: "No weapon formed against you shall prosper, and every tongue which rises against you in judgment You shall condemn. This is the heritage of the servants of the LORD, and their righteousness is from Me," says the LORD.

Isa 61:10: I will rejoice greatly in the LORD, my soul will exult in my God; for He has clothed me with garments of salvation, He has wrapped me with a robe of righteousness, as a bridegroom decks himself with a garland, and as a bride adorns herself with her jewels.

Worthy of note here is that "salvation" and the obtaining of "righteousness" go hand in hand.[231] And as has been mentioned before, "salvation" and the final defeat of death go hand in hand.[232] In the New Covenant spoken of by Jeremiah, we learn the *means* by which men's hearts are changed for the better:

Jer 31:33: "But this is the covenant which I will make with the house of Israel after those days," declares the LORD, "I will put My law within them and on their heart I will write it; and I will be their God, and they shall be My people."

Jer 32:39-40: [A]nd I will give them one heart and one way, that they may fear Me always, for their own good and for the good of their children after them. I will make an everlasting covenant with them that I will not turn away from them, to do them good; and I will put the fear of Me in their hearts so that they will not turn away from Me.

Jer 31:34: "They will not teach again, each man his neighbor and each man his brother, saying, 'Know the LORD,' for they will all know Me, from the least of them to the greatest of them," declares the LORD, "for I will forgive their iniquity, and their sin I will remember no more."

For a man to become righteous in God's eyes, God must change his heart and put his law in his heart. This is the means by which men come to seek and know God, for to know God is really what God requires:

Thus says the LORD, "Let not a wise man boast of his wisdom, and let not the mighty man boast of his might, let not a rich man boast of his riches; but let him who boasts boast of this, that he understands and knows Me, that I am the LORD who exercises lovingkindness,

---

[231] See 1 Cor 1:30; 2 Cor 5:21.
[232] Isa 25:6-9

justice and righteousness on earth; for I delight in these things," declares the LORD.[233]

God changes men's hearts, and he forgives their iniquity and remembers their sins no more. But this is not the whole story, for justice must occur for the sins that have been committed; otherwise God would be unjust, and evil would permeate the universe forever.[234] Someone must pay for the crimes committed against the Almighty. If men and women are to be "saved," someone must "redeem" them by paying God the penalty due. The psalmist tells us that the One who pays the debt is God:

> O Israel, hope in the LORD; for with the LORD there is lovingkindness, and with Him is abundant redemption. And He will redeem Israel from all his iniquities.[235]

So God changes men's hearts. This is done by the miraculous work of God's Spirit that turns a heart of stone, as Ezekiel said, into a heart of flesh.[236] And God "redeems" men from the penalty due for their sins. This is done by the amazing sacrificial work of the One who we will now get to know as the "Servant" of God.

THE MESSIAH IS GOD'S "SERVANT"

For the Christian, the priestly, and at the same time, sacrificial, work done by God's "Servant" in Isa 52-53 is a key OT prophecy that fits perfectly with what Jesus of Nazareth ended up doing about seven centuries after the prophecy was made: Isaiah told of God's Servant who would suffer and die as a "guilt offering" for everyone; Jesus, following perfectly his Father's will, suffered and died for the sins of the world. Now the legitimate question arises: Do the Christians, for starters, get it right when they perceive the Servant in these chapters as an *individual* Jew? To answer this question, we should first perform a brief overflight of the "Servant" texts that are found here and there from Isa 41 to Isa 53. Before we begin, it might first be mentioned that the main flow of early Rabbinic interpretation of Isa 52-53 (the "suffering servant" passage) understood the Servant there to be the Messiah (or one of two Messiahs), whereas most modern Jewish interpreters understand the Servant to be the nation of Israel that has indeed suffered terribly over the eons.[237] This last

---

[233] Jer 9:23-24
[234] Exod 32:34; Deut 32:35; Prov 11:21; Ezek 18:20
[235] Ps 130:7-8
[236] Ezek 11:19; 36:26
[237] David Baron (*Rays of Messiah's Glory*, chapter 7) had this to say: "That until recent times this prophecy [Isa 53] has been almost universally received by the Jews as referring to Messiah

opinion frankly has a tough time, considering the exegetical evidence, as we will soon see.

Let us first observe that a number of individuals and groups are called God's "Servant(s)" in the Tanakh. Among the individuals, we could mention Abraham, Isaac, Jacob, Moses, David, and even the Babylonian King Nebuchadnezzar.[238] Among the groups are the Levitical singers, the prophets, and even the whole nation of Israel.[239] Only a few in Scripture earned the designation of the LORD's Servant—a designation reserved only for those who went above and beyond in loving the LORD and doing his will.[240] It may be the case that the concept of God's "Servant" in the Tanakh is most closely attached to the person of King David, for the Tanakh identifies David as the Servant of God on several occasions and in varying contexts, including prophetical contexts that have to do with the messianic future. For example, in Nathan's prophecy regarding the permanence of the Davidic House, and in David's prayer of thanksgiving immediately following, David is called, or calls himself, God's "Servant" twelve times.[241] So here right at the beginning, if we look through a prophetical lens, we can know that inasmuch as it is the case that David's "throne will be established forever," it can equally be said that the throne of God's Servant will last forever. In other words, the concept of *God's Servant* is definitely a messianic one.[242]

So here and there various persons and groups are said to be God's servant/servants. But when it comes to Isa 41-53, one gets the feeling that, as far as the Servant of God concept is concerned, one is at *ground zero*. Here we see that it is not simply the case that someone or some group is merely, like others, serving God, but that there is revealed someone or some group that is *the* Servant, i.e., the *preeminent* Servant of God, higher than all others. Again we ask, "Who is this Servant?" When the germane passages are read straightforwardly, it is pretty well clear that the Servant identity is applied to two groups and one individual. The first group is the whole nation of Israel, also called Jacob. While the rest of the world is off making and worshipping idols, the LORD, through Isaiah, says in chapter 41:

> But you, Israel, My servant, Jacob whom I have chosen, descendant of Abraham My friend, you whom I have taken from the ends of the

---

.... In fact, until Rashi, who applied it to the Jewish nation, the Messianic interpretation of this chapter was almost universally adopted by Jews ...." Baron cites many ancient Jewish texts that give evidence for this.

[238] Respectively, Gen 26:24; 24:14; Exod 32:13; Exod 14:31; 2 Sam 7:5; Jer 27:6.
[239] Respectively, Ps 113:1; Ezek 38:17; Ps 136:22.
[240] This might be too much to say regarding Nebuchadnezzar.
[241] 2 Sam 7; 1 Chron 17
[242] See also Ps 89 where the messianic David is called God's Servant three times.

earth, and called from its remotest parts and said to you, "You are My servant, I have chosen you and not rejected you. Do not fear, for I am with you; do not anxiously look about you, for I am your God. I will strengthen you, surely I will help you, surely I will uphold you with My righteous right hand."[243]

Reading further in the same chapter, God assures his people that he will protect them against their enemies, thus there is nothing to fear. In chapter 44 we learn that God's Servant Israel was formed by God "from the womb," that God's Spirit and blessings will be poured out one day to the "seed" of Israel, and that the day will come when all of their sins will be wiped away. This eradication of sins will come about through the work of God, for YHWH is their "redeemer," the One who, after the eradication of sins is complete, can say: "Return to Me, for I have redeemed you."[244] So Israel, God's Servant, is blessed, protected, and saved.

The second group, as recorded in Isa 42:18-22, is a subset of Israel—a very large subset—that is blind to God and his ways, and that does not follow God's Law. They are, as v. 22 says, "a people plundered and despoiled." Despite this Servant's rebellion, he is still counted (v. 19) as a "servant of the LORD." So all of Israel can be called God's Servant, and the wicked population within Israel can be called the same; but probably only because they are part of Israel, the beloved of the LORD.[245]

The designation can also apply to an individual person, as several Isaiah texts indicate.[246] A key passage is Isa 49:5-6: The Servant leads fallen and exiled (from God) Israel back to God. Here, both YHWH and the Servant testify to this fact. The Servant in this case cannot be the nation of Israel, for fallen and exiled Israel cannot lead fallen and exiled Israel back to God. Can the "sinful nation" that has "abandoned the LORD," and whose "whole head is sick," lead back to God the same?[247] Of course, there is no way. The "blind" cannot lead the blind. So this last category cannot be Israel as a whole or as a wicked subset of Israel, but must be some other group or individual. That it is an individual will become clearer as we now consider what Isaiah has to say about him.

The individual Servant is born of woman, a truth that the Servant tells in the first person: "The LORD called Me from the womb; from the body of My mother He named Me."[248] At the same time, one could say that he is born of

---

[243] Isa 41:8-10
[244] Isa 44:2, 3, 22, 24
[245] Deut 32:10; 33:12; Ps 60:5; Jer 11:15
[246] Isa 42:1-7; 49:1-6; 50:4-11; 52:13-15, and all of chapter 53.
[247] Isa 1:4-5
[248] Isa 49:1

God, in that God puts his Spirit upon him.[249] He hears what the Lord YHWH speaks to him and then he speaks with the authority of God because he has the "tongue of the learned" and because God has made his "mouth like a sharp sword."[250] In all that he does, the Servant completely trusts in God.[251] In his flesh, however, he is not a handsome man: "He has no stately form or majesty that we should look upon Him, nor appearance that we should be attracted to Him."[252] Worse than this deficiency is the fact that "He was despised and forsaken of men, a man of sorrows and acquainted with grief."[253] Yet he is gentle and compassionate and encouraging to those around him.[254] Somehow this man leads the remnant of Israel like a flock back to God, and as a good shepherd finds the lost sheep of the gentile nations and leads them to God. By doing this, he is therefore a great "light to the nations" so that God's "salvation may reach to the end of the earth."[255] He appears to be sinless, for Isaiah says that—even though terribly persecuted—"He had done no violence, nor was there deceit in his mouth."[256] Being "despised," he is treated contemptuously and violently and "numbered with the transgressors."[257] But he suffers the blows of men quietly "like a lamb that is led to slaughter."[258] In this process, the Servant's appearance is "marred more than any man" because he endures horrible "scourging" and is "pierced through" and "crushed."[259] Due to this, he is "cut off out of the land of the living," and pours "out Himself to death."[260] But this is not the end of the story. This suffering and dying has a purpose. For in priest-like fashion, the Servant "sprinkles many nations" with his own blood—said by Isaiah to be a "guilt offering"—which thereby provides atonement for the "transgressions" and the "iniquity" of all men.[261] And so, Israel is restored to God and God is glorified in the process, and the Servant becomes a "covenant of the people" by the means of his shed blood which pays for the penalty incurred by men and women on account of their sins.[262] And this is not the end of the story also in

---

[249] Isa 42:1
[250] Isa 50:4 (KJV); 49:2
[251] Isa 50:8
[252] Isa 53:2
[253] Isa 53:3
[254] Isa 42:3; 50:4; 53:4
[255] Isa 42:6; 49:5-6
[256] Isa 53:9
[257] Isa 50:6-7; 53:3, 7, 12
[258] Isa 53:7
[259] Isa 52:14; 53:5
[260] Isa 53:8, 12
[261] Isa 52:15; 53:5-6, 10-12
[262] Isa 49:3, 5-6, 8; 52:10. In relation to the Servant, "covenant" is mentioned in Isa 42:6 and 49:8. JPS '17 in both verses and the Artscroll version in 42:6 has the Servant himself being the covenant for the people (thereby agreeing with the typical Christian translation). The JPS '85, on the other hand, has "I [YHWH] … appoint you a covenant people" for both verses,

this way: though he dies, yet he lives on and is glorified by God.[263] In view of all this, the nations come to his light, and "the coastlands … wait expectantly for his law."[264] By and by, the Servant brings ever-expanding light and justice such that YHWH's "salvation" reaches "to the end of the earth."[265]

Early rabbinical commentary, as mentioned above, understood the suffering servant to be the Messiah; but most modern Jewish commentators believe that Isaiah referred here to the corporate nation of Israel that has suffered mightily over the ages. Here are some reasons why this "corporate" view is unlikely. First, while it is true that several texts in Isaiah show Israel to be God's servant, the portrayal of the Servant in Isa 52-53—that goes on uninterrupted for fifteen verses—so thoroughly describes the characteristics and deeds of a solitary man that it is difficult from a literary standpoint to see this as anything other than a prophecy concerning an individual. Second, there are several elements here that certainly cannot apply to Israel corporately. The Servant is said to be as innocent as a lamb, with no deceit in his mouth; yet how could this be said of Israel, who—although loved by God as a beloved "son"—is in general condemned by God as being thoroughly corrupt?

> Alas, sinful nation, people weighed down with iniquity, offspring of evildoers, sons who act corruptly! They have abandoned the LORD, they have despised the Holy One of Israel, they have turned away from Him.[266]

It should not be said that Israel had no "deceit in his mouth," for there were plenty of liars in Israel in Isaiah's day, and in Jeremiah's day too when all the people, including kings, priests, and prophets, were corrupt.[267] Certainly Israel has suffered much over the ages, but has she always suffered quietly, not opening her mouth, going to the slaughter, as Isaiah says, "like a lamb"? This could be said about the conduct of the Jews during the Holocaust, and no doubt now and again through the ages when the Jews were so heavily oppressed that

---

thereby equating the Servant with the people of Israel who are already God's "covenant" people (Artscroll essentially does the same with 49:8). With both verses, the Judaica version, similar to the JPS '85, does not associate "covenant" with the Servant, but with the people whom he serves. Christian versions indicate that the Servant is himself a covenant who is given on behalf of the people. Who is right? If the translation "appoint you a covenant people" (JPS '85) were correct, we would expect in the Hebrew to see "covenant"—which would function in this case as an adjective—after "people" (i.e., עַם בְּרִית). But the Hebrew word order is the opposite, and thus the preposition לְ ("as," "for," "to") is attached to "covenant." The most natural view is to understand that "covenant" is in the construct state with "people," and so, the most natural translation is "I [YHWH] appoint you as a covenant of the people."

[263] Isa 49:5; 52:13; 53:10-12
[264] Isa 42:4, 6
[265] Isa 42:3-4; 49:6
[266] Isa 1:4
[267] Jer 6:13; 8:10

they had no choice but to submit. But in general, Bible history, as well as later secular history, shows that the Israelites have tenaciously resisted their enemies, and complained and lamented mightily when their world was crumbling around them. And can it somehow be the case that the people of Israel suffer and are sacrificed as atonement for the sins of the whole world? If this is true, why isn't such a tremendously important doctrine (for the fate of mankind) taught plainly in Scripture? If Israel is the sacrificial "lamb," how could the sufferings and deaths of a relatively few people, who are, in general, unclean, pay for the sins of the billions of sinners who have ever lived? Even if the suffering men and women of Israel were clean, could they, by their suffering, atone for the sins of all mankind? Supposing they could, would this not completely violate the principle established by the psalmist that declares that the sins of a man cannot be atoned for by the life of another man?[268] And wouldn't this be a giant-scale case of human sacrifice, which is plainly condemned in Scripture?[269] Finally, it should be mentioned again that Israel cannot bring Israel back to God. For, as said before, how can the blind lead the blind? But the most important biblical truth to consider is this: The prophets said time and again that *God* brings Israel back to himself and back to the Promised Land. It is only a remnant of Israel that returns, but they certainly do not bring about this return on their own—it is completely a work of God's grace, a gift from God in order to fulfill his promises made to the patriarchs and to glorify his holy name in the eyes of the nations.[270] More reasons for seeing the Servant as an individual in these passages could be offered, but it seems best now to go on to the next important question: How do we know that this individual Servant is the Messiah?

The connection of the title "Servant" with the Davidic Messiah, as we have already seen, is plainly presented in Ps 89. It is recorded there that God anointed and made a covenant with David, whom God calls "My Servant"; but something goes awry and the covenant of the Servant is "spurned" and his crown "profaned ... in the dust."[271] Between the many times that David calls himself God's "Servant" in his prayer of thanksgiving in response to God's giving of the Davidic covenant (2 Sam 7; 1 Chron 17), and the connection between "Servant" and "Messiah" in Ps 89, it can be said with confidence that "Servant" is a technical term for the Messiah. But there's more: the connections multiply when it comes to the Servant passages of Isa 41-53.

For starters, it is interesting to note that the (individual) Servant, according to 53:2, grew up before God as a "tender shoot, and like a root out

---

[268] Ps 49:7-9
[269] Lev 18:21; Deut 12:30-31
[270] Deut 9:5; Ezek 36
[271] Ps 89:3, 20, 39

of parched ground." It must be more than a coincidence that the description of the Servant here is near-identical to that in Isa 11:1, where, as might be recalled, the prophet says: "a shoot will spring from the stem of Jesse, and a branch from his roots will bear fruit." That is, the "shoot" (= "Branch") there is the "shoot" (= "Branch") here. But in addition to this, there is this extremely vital commonality: both of these Branches are specially given the Spirit of God. Isaiah says regarding the Branch that will come from Jesse, "The Spirit of the LORD will rest on Him"; and regarding the Servant who will suffer and bring back the lost sheep of Israel, God says through Isaiah, "I have put My Spirit upon Him."[272] So, just like the Messiah, the Servant has the Spirit of God and is also identified as a "Branch."

It is presented clearly in Isaiah's "suffering servant" passage that the Servant *suffers*, and suffers terribly at the hands of those who hate him. He was "wounded" and "bruised" and covered with "stripes," no doubt from the scourge.[273] And finally, he "poured out his soul unto death" and thus "was cut off out of the land of the living."[274] From previous investigation, we know that the Messiah is greatly opposed by enemies (Pss 2, 110), and that he at some point does not stand his ground in battle, and so his splendor disappears: his throne is cast "to the ground" and his crown "in the dust," and finally the "days of his youth" are "shortened"—that is, his life is cut short (Ps 89:38-45). The suffering and death of the Servant are indicated by Isaiah to be a payment not for his own sins, but for the sins of mankind. "He was pierced through," says the prophet, "for our transgressions, he was crushed for our iniquities," and thus, "the LORD has caused the iniquity of us all to fall on Him."[275] I believe that the suffering and death of the Servant is the heel "bruise" that the "seed" of Eve sustains in the process of inflicting the mortal "bruise" on the head of Satan, as prophesied/decreed by God in Gen 3:15. As I said there, this death blow to Satan signals the reversal of the curse of death, which was at the first brought about by the first sin of man. There, we don't know *how* this reversal is accomplished, but we do get some idea how this is accomplished by what Isaiah says about the suffering servant: he bears the sins—i.e., *atones* for the sins—of all mankind. We deduce from this that men and women can then be reconciled to God and, it would strongly seem to be the case, that the "sting of death" that enslaved them can then be neutralized. That this is so is hinted at by the fact that the Servant himself, as revealed in Isa 53:10-12, appears to live on after his violent death. It could be that the Servant-Messiah is the first person to experience "salvation," and through his sacrificial act, he becomes a "light to

---

[272] Isa 42:1
[273] Isa 53:5-6 (KJV)
[274] Isa 53:8, 12 (KJV)
[275] Isa 53:5-6

the nations" in that God's "salvation may reach to the end of the earth."[276] And, thus, as was prophesied to Abraham, all the nations of the earth are "blessed."[277]

Another connection between Isaiah's Servant and what we already know about the Messiah is the "peace" connection. They both bring peace. Isa 53:5 (ESV) says that "upon him was the chastisement that brought us peace, and with his wounds we are healed." No doubt that this is permanent peace that comes from having the penalty of sin removed, the death curse annulled, and from being restored to God. From our previous study, we might think of the Messiah's possible name of "Shiloh," as prophesied by the dying Jacob as he blessed his sons (Gen 49:10), and also dwell upon the fact that Solomon—the "man of rest" (1 Chron 22:9)—was to some degree a type of the Messiah to come. But most of all, we should recall that Isaiah previously called the Davidic Messiah, among other wonderful things, the "Prince of Peace," and forecast that there would be "no end to the increase of His government or of peace."[278] In the process of bringing lasting peace to the earth, the Messiah (as is said of the Branch in Isa 11:4) judges in righteousness and "with fairness for the afflicted of the earth." He is a righteous judge. Isaiah says the same thing of God's Servant:

> Behold, My Servant, whom I uphold; My chosen one in whom My soul delights. I have put My Spirit upon Him; He will bring forth justice to the nations. He will not be disheartened or crushed until He has established justice in the earth; and the coastlands will wait expectantly for His law.[279]

The Messiah brings lasting peace and justice, and so does God's Servant. It is surely the case that they are one and the same. Finally, in consideration of what has just been said, the fact should not be overlooked that both the Messiah and the Servant bring tremendous blessing to not only Israel, but to the gentile nations as well. God promised Abraham that, in his seed, "all nations" would be blessed, and Jacob promised his son Judah that the "peoples" would one day be perfectly obedient to a distant descendant of Judah named "Shiloh."[280] Solomon said that "all nations" would one day serve the Messiah, and Isaiah prophesied that during the time of the "Branch," "all nations" would come to him and the whole earth would be "full of the knowledge of the LORD as the waters cover the sea."[281] Thus, Isaiah, in speaking of the Messiah-child at the

---

[276] Isa 49:6
[277] Gen 12:3; 18:18; 22:18
[278] Isa 9:6-7
[279] Isa 42:1, 4. See also Ps 72:2 and Isa 9:7.
[280] Gen 22:18; 49:10
[281] Ps 72:11; Isa 11:9

beginning of chapter 9, called him a "great light" for "those who live in a dark land." Isaiah spoke likewise of the Servant in chapter 42: He called him a "light to the nations"—a light that would bring God's "salvation" unto "the end of the earth."[282]

As can be seen, there are many reasons to understand that much of what Isaiah says about God's Servant rightly refers to an individual. Yes, this individual is part of Israel, and because of his excellence, may even be said to *be* "Israel" in that he perfectly embodies all that God ever wanted Israel to be. Israel, after all, began as the individual man, Jacob. So there is good evidence for the Servant's individuality; but is there evidence for his divinity?

There are indeed a couple of things worth mentioning that seem to hint at the Servant's divinity. First, at least there is a trajectory in this direction in that Isaiah shows us in 11:2 and 42:1 that the Spirit of YHWH infuses the Branch-Servant. Of course, God put his Spirit on many special people as recorded in the Tanakh; but this dispensing of the Spirit on the Servant may be so extensive that one is hard pressed to tell the difference between his human nature and the Spirit-supplied divine nature.

It surely appears to be the case that the Servant "redeems," although this particular word is not used of him by Isaiah. But the sacrificial work that he does certainly looks like a redeeming work, for he suffers and dies—"like a lamb to the slaughter"—obviously for a great purpose: That great purpose surely must be to redeem mankind (and thus allow him back into fellowship with God and back into God's blessings) by paying the penalty that all mankind had earned by their mountain of "transgressions." "The LORD caused the iniquity of us all," says Isaiah, "to fall on him," and so, "by his scourging, we are healed."[283] By saying "we are healed," Isaiah surely must mean that mankind is finally put back in God's good graces and is no longer subject to disease, fear, and death. Now the interesting thing is that, while Isaiah is silent regarding the question of whether or not the Messiah redeems,[284] he does say several times that God redeems, although the means of that redemption are not stated. For example, consider the following:

> Isa 49:26: And all flesh will know that I, the LORD, am your Savior and your Redeemer, the Mighty One of Jacob.

> Isa 52:9-10: Break forth, shout joyfully together, you waste places of Jerusalem; for the LORD has comforted His people, He has redeemed Jerusalem. The LORD has bared His holy arm In the sight of all the

---

[282] Isa 49:6
[283] Isa 53:5-6
[284] Perhaps the redeemer referred to in Isa 59:20 is the Messiah.

nations, that all the ends of the earth may see the salvation of our God.

Isa 43:14-15, 25: Thus says the LORD your Redeemer, the Holy One of Israel .... "I am the LORD, your Holy One, the Creator of Israel, your King .... I, even I, am the one who wipes out your transgressions for My own sake, and I will not remember your sins.

Notice in the last verse quoted that the LORD, Israel's redeemer, "wipes out" all of Israel's "transgressions." God is able to dismiss all of Israel's sins only because he *redeems* Israel, that is, he pays the redemption price that he himself demands—a payment, as he says in Isa 52:3, made "without money." Yet it is clearly the Servant-Messiah who pays the redemption price (Isa 53): he functions as a priest (see Ps 110:4), but offers himself up as a "guilt offering." By doing so, the "iniquity of us all" and the guilt are taken from us, and they "fall on Him," that is, they are transferred to him. And thus, "we are healed." So YHWH redeems, yet when the actual means of redemption is described, it is the Servant-Messiah who redeems, that is, who pays the price. Israel's redeemer must be one or the other—unless they are one and the same.[285]

If they are one and the same, perhaps Isaiah telegraphs this when he says in the suffering servant passage (52:13):

$$\text{הִנֵּה יַשְׂכִּיל עַבְדִּי יָרוּם וְנִשָּׂא}$$

Behold, my servant shall act wisely; he shall be high and lifted up. (ESV)

Now note what Isaiah says about God, whom he saw in his inaugural vision (6:1):

$$\text{וָאֶרְאֶה אֶת־אֲדֹנָי יֹשֵׁב עַל־כִּסֵּא רָם וְנִשָּׂא}$$

I saw the Lord sitting upon a throne, high and lifted up. (ESV)

Notice that the Servant *and* "the Lord"—who is clearly the LORD—are both "high and lifted up." The Hebrew verb stems in both texts are identical (*rum*,

---

[285] YHWH's "holy arm" (52:10) is "bared"—that is, his great power is displayed—in the process of redemption and salvation. Remarkable is the fact that "the arm of the LORD" is also "revealed" in the suffering and atoning death of the Servant (53:1). This is another indication that YHWH "has redeemed Jerusalem" through the suffering and death of the Servant-Messiah. That no mere man intercedes on the behalf of men, and that the work of redemption is from start to finish a work of God, are strongly indicated by Isa 59:16 and 63:5.

"be high"; *nasa*, "to lift"), although their MT inflected forms differ slightly.[286] What is Isaiah, through the Spirit, trying to tell us here? Can a mere man be "high and lifted up" like the Almighty? And we might also ask how the Servant, if a mere man, can take on himself the sins of the whole world? This is impossible, unless the Servant is not a mere man. Finally, what do we make of the fact that the Servant is "high and lifted up" in his dreadful suffering and death, and YHWH is "high and lifted up" in his holy glory? If the Messiah is divine, then it could be the case that God manifests his highest glory (and love) in the suffering and death of the Messiah.

One more commonality between YHWH and the Servant is worthy of note. The LORD says in Isaiah 51:4-5 in regards to himself:

> Pay attention to Me, O My people, and give ear to Me, O My nation; for a law will go forth from Me, and I will set My justice for a light of the peoples. My righteousness is near, My salvation has gone forth, and My arms will judge the peoples; the coastlands will wait for Me, and for My arm they will wait expectantly.

For our purposes let it be noted that the "coastlands" (אִיִּם, *ayeem*) wait expectantly for the LORD and all that he is and does, including his "law" and his "justice." Now the LORD in Isa 42:4 testifies something similar regarding his Servant:

> He will not be disheartened or crushed until He has established justice in the earth; and the coastlands will wait expectantly for His law.

I think that it can confidently be said here that if the "coastlands" (אִיִּם, *ayeem*) "wait expectantly" for the law of the Servant, they wait as well for the Servant himself. As with YHWH, the Servant's "justice" and "law" are universally established, and the "coastlands" at long last accept YHWH *and* his Servant, and they do it eagerly. My point here is that, as far as the "coastlands" are concerned, to accept the law and person of YHWH *is* to accept the person and law of the Servant.

Before moving on, let us ponder another portion of Scripture that deals with the messianic "Servant" subject, Ezekiel chapters 34 and 37. Ezekiel, who served his exiled people in Babylonia at the end of Judah's history, and for a short time after, had a prophetic life somewhat similar to Isaiah. Both prophesied the downfall of Judah, but Ezekiel lived when that downfall occurred (although he didn't experience it firsthand like Jeremiah did). We will see that Ezekiel's concept of the Servant of God is closely bound up with the

---

[286] Isa 53:13: Qal imperfect and Niphal perfect; Isa 6:1: Qal participle and Niphal participle.

concept of the great Shepherd of God's people who will rule righteously over them forever.

"In the year that King Uzziah died," 740 BC, Isaiah had his inaugural commissioning vision of God, whom he saw "high and lifted up" (Isa 6:1 ESV). As part of the commissioning ceremony, a Seraph touched his lips with a hot coal after Isaiah confessed that he felt "ruined" because he had seen "the King, the LORD of hosts." Ezekiel, about a century and a half later, had his inaugural commissioning vision (593 BC) five years after he had been exiled to Babylonia (Ezek 1:1-2). He saw YHWH as the "semblance of a human form" sitting upon a throne—which seemed to be made of "Sapphire"—with the blinding appearance of fire and rainbow around him.[287] In the course of Ezekiel's commissioning, an event that involved the mouth also happened to him: YHWH gave him a scroll to eat that was full of "lamentations, mourning, and woe."[288] Like Isaiah, Ezekiel was all but "ruined" by the spectacle: The Spirit brought him back to his fellow exiles at Tel-Abib, and there the prophet sat for seven days, "overwhelmed."[289] In both cases, God commissioned them to speak to their fellow countrymen—people who were "sinful," "unclean," "obstinate," and "rebellious."[290] The pattern of what they prophesied is roughly similar in that they both warned the people and their leaders, but then comforted them with the news that, even though (to once again employ my own metaphor) the "rug" would be pulled out from under them, God would nevertheless in the long run take compassion and bring them back to their land where they would be blessed with a permanent peaceful existence under a righteous Davidic king ruling under the conditions of an entirely "New Covenant." Isaiah's comforting prophecies begin in earnest in chapter 40 ("Comfort, oh comfort My people"), and Ezekiel's begin after chapter 33—the chapter that records (v. 21) the arrival of fugitives from Jerusalem who brought the news to Ezekiel and his fellow exiled Jews that Jerusalem had fallen to the Babylonians and was in the process of being destroyed (thus fulfilling a number of Ezekiel's prophecies, and Isaiah's and Jeremiah's too).

The prophetic life was not easy for Ezekiel. Only a few days after his inaugural vision, God had made him unable to speak except for the words that God gave him directly by revelation.[291] He was all but mute for seven years. During this time, the prophet carried out a number of difficult sign-acts at the LORD's command. Among these was the requirement to lay motionless—first on his left side, and then on his right—for a total of fourteen months. The

---

[287] Ezek 1:26-28 (JPS '85)
[288] Ezek 2:8-3:3
[289] Ezek 3:15 (ESV)
[290] Isa 1:4; 6:5; Ezek 2:4, 8
[291] Ezek 3:26

purpose of this was to symbolize the years of Israel's and Judah's iniquity, and to "bear the iniquity" of these nations. During this ordeal he was given only enough bread and water to keep him alive—a diet that symbolized the meagre diet of the Jews in Jerusalem during Nebuchadnezzar's siege that would come a few years later.[292] When the news finally came that Jerusalem had fallen, God re-opened Ezekiel's mouth.[293] He then began to speak words of comfort to the "lost sheep" of Israel, but not before he gave two more words of criticism: The first criticism was of those who believed that God would deliver the Jews from the Babylonians simply because they were sons of Abraham;[294] the second criticism was given to the "shepherds" of Israel, i.e., the leaders, who didn't really care about the sheep under their care, but only took advantage of them.[295] Speaking to these shepherds, the Lord YHWH said through Ezekiel:

> Woe, shepherds of Israel who have been feeding themselves! Should not the shepherds feed the flock? ... Those who are sickly you have not strengthened, the diseased you have not healed, the broken you have not bound up, the scattered you have not brought back, nor have you sought for the lost; but with force and with severity you have dominated them.[296]

In view of the fact that the "shepherds," preeminently represented by the kings of Israel, had by and large failed to provide their people righteous and wise leadership, the LORD decided to take matters into his own hands, and so said this:

> Behold, I Myself will search for My sheep and seek them out. As a shepherd cares for his herd in the day when he is among his scattered sheep, so I will care for My sheep and will deliver them from all the places to which they were scattered on a cloudy and gloomy day.... I will feed My flock and I will lead them to rest. [297]

That YHWH was the ultimate shepherd of Israel was a fact known by what had already been said here and there in Scripture: "The LORD is my shepherd," David had said; but not only his shepherd, but the "Shepherd of Israel," and in fact the whole world.[298] So here YHWH commandeers the helm of Israel from, so to speak, the sub-shepherds who had fallen far short of expectations (Ezek 34:11-31). Before proceeding on to the critical verse in this passage, we would

---

[292] Ezek 4
[293] Ezek 33:22
[294] Ezek 33:24-29
[295] Ezek 34:1-10
[296] Ezek 34:2b, 4
[297] Ezek 34:11, 12, 15
[298] Pss 23:1; 80:1. See also Gen 48:15; Ps 78:52; Isa 37:16; 40:11; Mic 5:2-4; etc.

do well to remember that the most excellent situation—and the one that *must* be in the final state—is for God to be *the* King of Israel and of all mankind. When the Israelites asked Samuel for a human king to rule over them and fight their battles, God considered this to be an affront to his royal authority that would result in an ongoing "evil" situation.[299] At some point, unless "evil" is to persist into the eschaton, God must become king over all mankind, and remain so forever.

So, in view of the failure of the kings (and other leading men) of Judah and Israel, YHWH, out of compassion and out of what is rightfully his due, reasserts himself as the great Shepherd of all Israel. But then he says this, in chapter 34, through Ezekiel:

> I will deliver My flock, and they will no longer be a prey .... Then I will set over them one shepherd, My servant David, and he will feed them; he will feed them himself and be their shepherd. And I, the LORD, will be their God, and My servant David will be prince among them; I the Lord have spoken.[300]

So important is this word, that in chapter 37 YHWH repeats it in similar wording:

> My servant David will be king over them, and they will all have one shepherd.... David My servant will be their prince forever. I will make a covenant of peace with them; it will be an everlasting covenant with them.[301]

It is readily apparent here that God is speaking about the Messiah: David ("your kingdom shall endure before Me forever"—2 Sam 7:16), God's "Servant," in the restoration will rule as king (= "Prince") "forever" under the conditions of a totally new covenant. Now notice here that David, God's Servant, will "feed them [i.e., God's "flock"] *himself*" (34:23), and that YHWH says the same of his own shepherding in 34:15: "I [*myself*] will feed my flock." In both of these texts, there is a pronoun ("he," "I") in the Hebrew just before the verb *rahah* ("to feed," "to pasture"), which gives emphasis to the person doing the action (*He himself will feed the flock; I myself will feed my flock*). Understood literally, there seems to be two shepherds, the Messiah and YHWH, who lead and feed the sheep in the eschaton. And in consideration of the fact that "shepherd" here is just another way of saying "king," and of the fact, already mentioned, that YHWH has every right to be king of Israel and all other nations "forever," it seems to be the case that in the long run, there will be two kings ruling Israel

---

[299] 1 Sam 12:20. See 1 Sam 8 and 12.
[300] Ezek 34:22-24
[301] Ezek 37:24-26

forever—YHWH and the Messiah. Yet YHWH says that he alone, and no one else, will feed his own sheep. This is another way of saying, "I myself—and no one else—will be king over my own people." But if YHWH is the sole shepherd-king of Israel, how can the Messiah be that also? I believe that the Lord telegraphs the solution to this conundrum with what he says twice (34:23 and 37:24): "Then I will set over them one shepherd"; "they will all have one shepherd." What does this mean?

It could be said that YHWH acts temporarily as an emergency shepherd in order to rescue the scattered sheep of Israel, and then once the flock is back in the Promised Land, he turns over the shepherd-king duties to the Messiah, who from that time on will be Israel's "one shepherd." But 34:13-14 indicates that YHWH not only leads his flock back to Israel, but also tends his flock *in* Israel. "For thus says the Lord GOD":

> I will feed them on the mountains of Israel, by the streams, and in
> all the inhabited places of the land I will feed them in a good pasture,
> and their grazing ground will be on the mountain heights of Israel.

In any case, if YHWH turns over the reins to the Messiah, a substandard condition will forever exist on earth from then on (and on the "new earth"—Isa 65:17). But how can this be in view of what God said to Samuel? And how can this be in view of the fact that in many places in the Tanakh, God is called Israel's "king" and Israel's "shepherd"? No, I don't think that YHWH will turn "over the reins" to a merely human Messiah. And this is what is indicated by God's repeated emphatic declaration: they will have "*one* shepherd."[302] Yes, YHWH should be Israel's shepherd-king, and he will be such in the final state: In bestowing the kingdom upon the Messiah, he will pour out so much of himself "upon" the Messiah that both the human Davidic "Servant" and the Holy God will be experienced by the world in one person, one man, or in—as Daniel, to whom we turn to now, called him—one "Son of Man."

THE MESSIAH IS THE "SON OF MAN"

In general the prophets of the divided monarchy period foresaw the downfall and exile of Israel and Judah, a return from exile, and a glorious reestablishment of the nation of Israel led once again by the Davidic monarchy. They saw, so to speak, these mountain tops, but could not discern that there

---

[302] Regarding these two shepherds, Wright says: "Here Ezekiel is certainly not contrasting the two, but binding them together as two dimensions of the same overall rule." (Christopher J. H. Wright, *The Message of Ezekiel*, the Bible Speaks Today [Downers Grove: Intervarsity Press, 2001], 280.)

was to be a wide valley between the second and third peaks—that is, between the return from the Babylonian exile and the commencement of the Eden-like Israelite kingdom led by the Messiah. The course of history since the Babylonian exile has made this, needless to say, obviously true: A Davidic kingdom in which the wolf lies down with the lamb, everyone knows the LORD, and no one fears outside enemies, has yet to exist. But the prophet and royal counselor to Babylonian and Persian kings, Belteshazzar—whose Jewish name was Daniel—did provide some prophetic insight about this "valley" era: It is then that the Messiah will come and soon thereafter be "cut off," but then come again in conquering glory.

Daniel, who may have been of royal Davidic blood,[303] was taken away to Babylon when Nebuchadnezzar conquered Jerusalem the first time, in 605 BC. King Jehoiakim, who had callously burned Jeremiah's scroll, was killed at that time or in a later Babylonian siege.[304] Daniel, along with his three friends, Hananiah, Mishael, and Azariah (their names were changed by the Babylonians to Shadrach, Meshach, and Abed-nego), were then schooled for three years, and after that became personal servants to Nebuchadnezzar when he discerned that the boys' learning and wisdom was far above others who had also gone through the same training.[305] Soon thereafter Daniel was elevated to ruler of the province of Babylon (in a series of events reminiscent of the events that brought Joseph to the right hand of Pharaoh) as a result of his correctly knowing and interpreting Nebuchadnezzar's dream of the awesome statue of "extraordinary splendor."[306] The prophet served in the administrations of at least four Babylonian and Medo-Persian kings, a total of about eighty years, down through at least the first year of Cyrus. It may be that he prompted this last king to issue the edict that allowed the Jews to return to Jerusalem and rebuild the temple.[307] In any case, he served these kings from the start of the Babylonian exile to its end. Because he served these superpower kings, his prophetical focus was upon the destiny of their kingdoms and subsequent superpower kingdoms, including the final kingdom of God and of the "Son of Man" which would supersede and destroy all previous kingdoms. Other than Daniel's chapter nine prophecy about the "seventy weeks" timeline of the Jews and Jerusalem, there are only occasional references to the Jews or to the physical Promised Land. In Daniel, the concern about the return from exile and the establishment of a permanent and idyllic earthly Jewish nation is greatly attenuated compared to other prophets. What matters most is that God will one day rule all nations

---

[303] Daniel may have been a member of the "royal family" mentioned in Dan 1:3.
[304] See Jer 22:18-19 and Josephus, *Jewish Antiquities*, 10:96-98.
[305] Dan 1:17-20
[306] Dan 2
[307] M. G. Easton, *Easton's Bible Dictionary* (New York: Harper & Brothers, 1893), "Daniel."

unopposed, and this kingdom will be an "everlasting kingdom" which will "never be destroyed."[308]

Daniel, thankfully, gives us quite a lot of prophetic information about the time between the second and third mountain peaks just mentioned, that is, between the return from exile and the establishment of the eternal messianic kingdom. Now the details that Daniel gives us are quite diverse and something like pieces of a jigsaw puzzle that are a challenge to fit together. Despite this challenge, some very interesting details about the Messiah and the time of his coming can nevertheless be discerned.

A rough outline of world history from Daniel's time to Messiah's kingdom can be appropriated from the awesome statue of Nebuchadnezzar's dream and Daniel's interpretation of that dream recorded in Dan 2, and also from Daniel's dream/vision of the four great beasts recorded in Dan 7. From these we learn that, from Daniel's time onward, four great empires would exist in succession: Babylon, Medo-Persia, Greece, and Rome. These first three are sure because the identity of them is given in the Daniel text.[309] Rome, symbolized by the iron legs of Nebuchadnezzar's statue and the fourth ferocious beast of Daniel's dream, is not identified as such in Daniel, although there can be little doubt—given the fact that the Greek kingdoms finally succumbed to the iron fist of the Romans—that the Roman empire is prophetically in view. Ten kingdoms (represented by the ten horns on the fourth horrible beast of Dan 7:7, and perhaps by the ten toes on the Dan 2 statue) would then arise out of the Roman empire, and out of those ten kingdoms would emerge a final wicked king (represented by the "Little Horn" coming up from the ten horns, Dan 7:8) who would oppose God and who would persecute God's people unmercifully for three and a half years (7:25). At the end of that time, God would pass judgment upon this final ruler: He and his kingdom would be destroyed, and all previous kingdoms/empires would also come to an end. This final annihilation of earthly human rule is depicted in Dan 2 by a "stone ... cut out without hands" striking and destroying the awesome statue, and in Dan 7 by the heavenly supreme court—presided over by the "Ancient of Days"— passing judgment upon the "Little Horn" and consigning this awful "beast" to "burning fire" (7:9-11). Once this wicked king is destroyed, and all previous kingdoms disappear, the stone that struck and destroyed all the kingdoms/empires (that are represented in Nebuchadnezzar's statue) becomes a "great mountain" that fills "the whole earth." As Daniel tells Nebuchadnezzar, "The God of heaven will set up a kingdom which will never be destroyed," a kingdom which "will itself endure forever."[310] In Dan 7, the same establishment

---

[308] Dan 2:44; 4:3, 34; 6:26; 7:14, 27
[309] See Dan 2:38; 8:20-21.
[310] Dan 2:44

of God's eternal kingdom is depicted, with the addition that the "Son of Man," who comes "with the clouds of heaven," plays a vital role in this establishment (more will be said about this a little later).

So to review, the history from Daniel's time to the end includes four known kingdoms coming in succession (Babylon, Medo-Persia, Greece, Rome) followed by ten kingdoms (it seems, not in succession; there has been endless speculation about who these kingdoms were/are/will be) followed by a final wicked king (whom Christians call "Antichrist") who rages against God and his saints for three and a half years before being killed. Only then is God's kingdom permanently established on earth. Now it should be noted that this portrait does not show us the actual time involved. The "seventy weeks" prophecy of Dan 9 on the other hand does give some chronological information. This chronology, as we will see, still leaves us perplexed regarding the question of how much *total* time elapses between Daniel and the end; on the other hand, it does give us fascinating time information about the Messiah: it provides an approximate timespan from when Daniel received the prophecy (from the angel Gabriel) to the time when Messiah first appears and is then killed. So it is worth our time to consider this "seventy weeks" prophecy in some detail.

After Daniel gave his prayer of praise and thanksgiving upon the occasion of the expiration of the seventy years of Babylonian exile as earlier prophesied by Jeremiah, the angel Gabriel appeared to Daniel and said (v. 24):

> Seventy weeks have been decreed for your people and your holy city,
> to finish the transgression, to make an end of sin, to make atonement
> for iniquity, to bring in everlasting righteousness, to seal up vision
> and prophecy and to anoint the most holy place.

First to notice is that "seventy weeks" means seventy *sevens of years*—totaling 490 years. That "weeks" of *years* are meant is strongly indicated by the fact that this time period follows immediately (or nearly so) the seventy years of Babylonian exile.[311] 2 Chron 36:21 (in conjunction with Lev 26:14-15, 32-35)

---

[311] Hengstenberg says that this has always been the standard view. Some commentators believe that the "weeks" are sevens of denominations of time that no one knows, except God. If this is the case, it seems to me that the prophecy loses most of its force and becomes mainly only a statement of future disasters for the Jews. Plus the fact that Jerusalem would be rebuilt, Messiah would come, and Messiah would be cut off, were facts already discernable in previous prophecies. New here is the news that Jerusalem and the Temple would again be destroyed. Thus, the prophecy is in general quite negative. But it appears to be the case that Gabriel brought the prophecy to Daniel as somewhat of a reward, and an encouragement, because of Daniel's faithfulness and his prayer and concern about his fellow Jewish people. There is something momentous about the presentation of the prophecy: It is brought by the mighty angel Gabriel as a great sign of God's concern and grace, and one has the feeling that it contains momentous content that will greatly bless Daniel and his fellow Jews then and in later generations. But this could only be the case if the "weeks" could be understood as a definite

explains why the exile lasted seventy years: Israel had failed to let the land rest (which was supposed to occur every seventh year, as commanded by Moses in Lev 25:1–7) a total of seventy times during her history. So God decreed that the people would be ejected from the land for a total of seventy years—a sum which would allow the land to get the rest that it should have had, that is, one year of rest for each "Sabbath" rest that Israel had failed to provide. So given the fact that Moses' command regarding land Sabbaths was denominated in *years*, and that the exile was denominated in *years*, then it is very likely the case that Dan 9's "seventy weeks" are meant to be understood as seventy weeks of *years*. We should notice next that the introduction to this prophecy clearly tells us that the timeline extends all the way to the end, for the ultimate things that must be accomplished to solve the human cursed condition are indeed solved: sin is ended and atoned for, and "everlasting righteousness" is forever established. Now, of course, readers may immediately question all this, noticing that two and a half millennia have transpired since Gabriel appeared to Daniel: either the "weeks" must be sevens of something more than years, or the timeline does not go to the end of time. I hope that as we proceed on through the prophecy, it will become clearer as to why the "weeks" are weeks of years, and that the prophecy encompasses (approximately) the time of Daniel all the way to the end, or, more precisely, all the way to the occasion of the death of the "Little Horn."

Gabriel continues (v. 25):

> So you are to know and discern that from the issuing of a decree to restore and rebuild Jerusalem until Messiah the Prince there will be seven weeks and sixty-two weeks; it will be built again, with plaza and moat, even in times of distress. (NASB)

> And you shall know and understand that from the emergence of the word to restore and to rebuild Jerusalem until the anointed king [shall be] seven weeks, and [for] sixty-two weeks it will return and be built street and moat, but in troubled times. (Judaica)

Here we are told that "Messiah the Prince" (Judaica: "the anointed king") will appear after a certain amount of time. The Hebrew here—in view of all that has prophetically gone before—is obviously messianic: מָשִׁיחַ נָגִיד, *mashiach*

---

period of time. Assuming that this is the case, then later generations could look forward to what good was in store (like the coming of Messiah and the rebuilding of the city), and ponder and prepare for the bad that was to come. In other words, with a definite time element understood, the prophecy would help future generations stand a better chance of ordering their lives around God and his will for their lives. The prophecy is a blessing because it is evangelistic, and thus an act of God's grace.

nagid, literally, "Anointed one, Prince,"[312] certainly must be *the* Messiah who has been the subject of so much previous Scripture. Also, given the fact that the prophecy concerns the final history of the Jews and their ultimate concerns about sin, the atonement for sin, and bringing all to salvation through finally becoming righteous in God's eyes, it must be the case—especially in view of the role that Messiah plays in the salvation of man already learned from previous prophets—that *mashiach* here must identify *the* Messiah who will one day rule forever on David's throne. Going on, Gabriel says that this Messiah will appear immediately after a span of time that begins with "the issuing of a decree to restore and rebuild Jerusalem." This decree is probably the decree which King Cyrus of Persia issued (ca. 536 BC—Daniel might have influenced him to do this) shortly after Gabriel's prophecy, or it may have been an order issued by one of the later Persian kings allowing first Ezra, and then Nehemiah, to go to Jerusalem. In any case, for the present purposes, it is enough to say that the timeline begins *about* the time that the Jews returned to Jerusalem from the Babylonian exile—roughly five centuries before the Christian era began.[313]

The time period between the Jerusalem rebuilding decree and the appearing of Messiah is said by the NASB to be seven weeks and sixty-two weeks, which is the usual translation in Christian Bibles. During this total of 69 weeks (483 years) Jerusalem will be rebuilt, and right afterward, Messiah will appear. But the Judaica and other Jewish Bibles understand the MT to say that it will take only seven weeks for Messiah to show up, and then another 62 weeks to rebuild the city. Grammatically speaking, there are pros and cons for each of these two translations. As a Christian, of course, I favor the Christian view that Messiah came after 69 weeks, for that is close to the time when Jesus of Nazareth came on the scene. It seems that when this critical prophecy first speaks of a "Messiah-Prince" in v. 25, it speaks of the same person when it says a verse later that "Messiah" is "cut off." If Jewish translations like the Judaica are correct, then a Messiah comes after seven sevens (49 years), and then another Messiah is "cut off" at the end of another sixty-two sevens (another 434 years). But why would a highly messianic prophecy like this—after all that has been said about *the* Messiah—now speak of two Messiahs? It is highly unlikely. So if this prophecy has only one Messiah in view, then, given the fact that he is "cut off" right after the 69th week, it is probably the case that his first appearing was not long before that.

---

[312] If *mashiach* were to function as an adjective (as the Judaica understands it does—"anointed king"), it would come after *nagid*, not before it.

[313] Cyrus's decree, as recorded in 2 Chron 36:22-23 and Ezra 1:1-4; 6:3-5, allowed the Jews to go to Jerusalem and rebuild the Temple. Nothing is said about rebuilding the city. On the other hand, Isaiah prophesied that Cyrus would rebuild both temple and city (Isa 44:28; 45:13). The only post-exile decree recorded in the Tanakh ordering the rebuilding of the city was made by King Artaxerxes (Neh 2:1-8) in 445 BC.

So far we have learned a lot about the Messiah: He is the son of David and also the Son of God who will one day rule all nations forever. But we've also learned that he must first suffer and die for "the iniquity of us all."[314] Now, thanks to Gabriel's prophecy, we find out *when* this suffering and atoning death takes place (v. 26):

> Then after the sixty-two weeks the Messiah will be cut off and have nothing, and the people of the prince who is to come will destroy the city and the sanctuary. And its end will come with a flood; even to the end there will be war; desolations are determined.

After seven and then 62 weeks—that is, a total of 69 weeks, or 483 years—Messiah will be "cut off and have nothing." Those who try to figure out an *exact* date of the cutting off (based upon the years since their choice of when the original decree was made) have to deal with many complex historical and calendrical issues. For our purposes, let us simply notice that Gabriel reveals that Messiah will be "cut off" roughly five centuries after the return from the Babylonian exile. While the Gospels indeed show that there was much expectation of the Messiah when Jesus came on the scene, they also show that there was next to no expectation (other than with Jesus himself) that the Messiah would be "cut off."[315] Jesus' disciples, for example, were well aware of the third "mountain peak" that I mentioned a few pages ago: They anticipated the wonderful messianic kingdom, and they believed that in that soon-to-arrive kingdom they would rule and reign alongside Jesus, for Daniel had also said that the saints would inherit the kingdom along with the "Son of Man" (Dan 7, which we'll soon consider).[316] They saw the last glorious peak that the prophets had seen, but failed to notice the great valley in between the second (return from exile) and third peaks that the prophets had spoken little about, although spoken just enough for men to know that at some point, the Messiah was to suffer and die (Ps 89:38-45; Isa 52:13–53:12) for the sins of mankind.

So Gabriel's great prophetic word to Daniel tells us of the approximate date of Messiah's death, which is bad news that in hindsight becomes "good news" in that his death provides the atonement for the sins of mankind. Now hurrying on through the prophecy, we notice that there is a lot that goes on *after* the 69th week but *before* the 70th week that is mentioned in the next verse:

---

[314] Isa 53:6

[315] John the Baptist had some knowledge of this, as he called Jesus "the lamb of God who takes away the sin of the world" (John 1:29). On the other hand, Jesus' disciples seemed to have had no expectation of the Messiah's suffering and death (Matt 16:22; 17:23; Mark 8:32; 9:32; Luke 18:34). It seems the High Priest Caiaphas was at least vaguely aware of the notion of the Messiah dying for the good of God's people (see John 11:49-52).

[316] The disciples' eagerness to participate in kingdom leadership is shown in Matt 19:28; 20:21; Mark 10:37.

Messiah is killed, the city and sanctuary are destroyed by "the prince that will come," and wars and desolations occur "even to the end." It would seem that all this would take a long time to happen. In view of the fact that the Messiah came and then was shortly thereafter "cut off," and also in view of the fact that the seventieth week (up to the present day) has not yet occurred (if it had, the Messiah would have by now set up his permanent perfect kingdom), it must be the case that there is a time-gap—now spanning nearly two millennia and increasing every day—between the end of the 69th week and the start of the 70th week. This "gap" of time contains the Messiah's death, war, desolations, and destruction of Jerusalem and the Temple. The stopwatch of Daniel's people does not start ticking again (at the beginning of the 70th week) until Jerusalem is intact enough again to host a temple and its Mosaic temple rites. This can be deduced from what is said in the final verse of the prophecy (v. 27):

> And he will make a firm covenant with the many for one week, but in the middle of the week he will put a stop to sacrifice and grain offering; and on the wing of abominations will come one who makes desolate, even until a complete destruction, one that is decreed, is poured out on the one who makes desolate.

The "he" who "will make a firm covenant with the many for one week" on one hand seems to be the "prince" of the previous verse whose "people" (his followers or soldiers) destroy the city and the Temple. The Roman general Titus destroyed Jerusalem and the Temple in AD 70; but this was nearly two millennia ago, and the 70th and final week "decreed" for the Jewish people is yet to happen. So Titus could not possibly be the "he" of v. 27 (otherwise he'd be 2,000+ years old!). This "he" of the 70th week is no doubt the "Little Horn" of Dan 7 who appears just before God's kingdom is permanently established. The end of Gabriel's prophecy to Daniel indicates that the "he" (of 9:27) will make a seven-year covenant with Israel (and perhaps with other nations), but 3 ½ years later break that covenant, and thereafter (for 3 ½ years) commit much evil (indicated in 9:27 by the "he" closing and defiling the Temple). We can infer from this that the "he" of 9:27, after breaking the covenant with God's people, comes down hard on them for 3 ½ years until the 70th week is finished. This inference is confirmed in Dan 7: The "Little Horn" persecutes the saints unmercifully for 3 ½ years, then (like the end of 9:27 seems to allude to) is "annihilated and destroyed forever" (7:26). Human and Satanic domination over the earth is over at that point, and divine domination begins.

In summary, Gabriel's prophecy in Dan 9 does not tell us anything new about the Messiah, although the notice of the time of his coming and death is of great value (especially to those who lived then).[317] In the great dream-vision that Daniel received as recorded in Dan 7, we as well do not learn anything particularly new about the Messiah, but we do get great confirmation regarding his divinity and future dominion. And we get the wonderful and surprising news that his "saints" will participate in his royal administration.

When Jesus of Nazareth said, "You shall see the Son of Man sitting at the right hand of Power, and coming with the clouds of heaven" in response to Caiaphas's question, "Are You the Christ, the Son of the Blessed One?"[318] he identified himself with David's "Lord" who sits at the right hand of YHWH (Ps 110:1) and also with the heavenly "Son of Man" of Dan 7 who is given dominion over the whole earth. Although Jesus was about to be "cut off" by the decision of the High Priest and the Sanhedrin, he here telegraphed to them that after his suffering, all his enemies would be put under his feet, and he would thereafter rule the world with an authority and power that Nebuchadnezzar—represented by the golden head of the awesome statue of his dream—could only dream of. That Jesus meant this is quickly realized when Dan 7 is read and understood. For in Daniel's great dream-vision, the Son of Man is given dominion over the world when, or shortly after, God judges the final wicked world ruler (the "Little Horn"). The Son of Man is given "a kingdom, that all the peoples, nations and men of every language might serve Him" (7:14). At the same time, God's absolute dominion *over the same domain* is established, never again to be overthrown (7:27). This final judgment of the earth and the establishment of God's messianic kingdom comes right after the Little Horn runs amok over God's people for 3 ½ years, as is testified in 7:25:

> He will speak out against the Most High and wear down the saints
> of the Highest One, and he will intend to make alterations in times
> and in law; and they will be given into his hand for a time, times,
> and half a time.[319]

---

[317] Perhaps Jesus alluded to the Dan 9 "time" of his first coming when he lamented over Jerusalem: "For the days will come upon you when your enemies will throw up a barricade against you, and surround you and hem you in on every side, and they will level you to the ground and your children within you, and they will not leave in you one stone upon another, because you did not recognize the time of your visitation" (Luke 19:43-44).

[318] Mark 14:61-62

[319] That "time, times, and half a time" is roughly 3 ½ years is strongly indicated by the contextual connections to Dan 9:27, where the wicked Prince defiles the Temple at the 3 ½ year mark of the seventieth "week," and by the depiction of the "Little Horn" commandeering and defiling the Temple for "2,300 evenings and mornings" as recorded in Dan 8:14. As the wicked "Prince" of Dan 9 made us first think of Titus who destroyed the Temple in AD 70, the "Little Horn" of Dan 8 allows us to first think of the Greek Seleucid king Antiochus IV who defiled the Temple and ended its Jewish rituals for a season (ca. 165 BC). But in both cases, these individuals are typical of the wicked final ruler of the world, that is, *the* Little Horn who persecutes the saints terribly just before the messianic eternal kingdom is established.

And if we continue back in time, Dan 7 tells us that the Little Horn came out of ten horns that were upon the horrible fourth beast, Rome, that "devoured and crushed and trampled down" the previous three beasts that represented (continuing back in time) Greece, Medo-Persia, and Babylon. So Dan 7 plainly covers the entire time from Daniel's day to the end. There is no need for us in this case to understand the Little Horn to have been some ancient historical figure, who then typifies the final wicked world ruler: in Dan 7, the Little Horn *is* that final wicked world ruler, plain and simple.

Now one might at this point question the legitimacy of so quickly identifying the Son of Man in Dan 7 with the Messiah. What can give us confidence that they are one and the same? All we have to do is notice that there is much said about the Son of Man in vv. 13-14 that we already know to be true about the Messiah:

> I kept looking in the night visions, and behold, with the clouds of heaven One like a Son of Man was coming, and He came up to the Ancient of Days and was presented before Him. And to Him was given dominion, glory and a kingdom, that all the peoples, nations and men of every language might serve Him. His dominion is an everlasting dominion which will not pass away; and His kingdom is one which will not be destroyed.[320]

First of all, the Son of Man comes "with the clouds of heaven." In the Bible, only God is said to come within or upon clouds (see Pss 18:9-13; 104:3; Isa 19:1; Jer 4:13; Nah 1:3), and so, the Son of Man's divinity is most likely indicated here. The Messiah is also human, and, of course, Daniel's designation of this person as the "Son of Man" is meant to emphasize his humanity. Lest we think of the Messiah as only God, his name here reminds us that he is human; lest we think of him as only human, his coming "with the clouds of heaven" shows us that he is God.

The identity with the Messiah is probably best indicated here in the fact that the Son of Man is given a worldwide kingdom: "to Him was given dominion, glory and a kingdom, that all the peoples, nations and men of every language might serve Him." It should first be observed that this scene takes place in heaven where the Son of Man is presented before the Ancient of Days. This should bring to mind David's words: "The LORD says to my Lord, sit at my right hand until I make your enemies a footstool for your feet" (Ps 110:1). Apparently, all of the Son of Man's enemies are now subdued (or will soon be subdued) and YHWH is about to give him the kingdoms of the world. With this kingdom that he is given, the Son of Man bridges, as it were, God's realm

---

[320] The Babylonian Talmud, Sanhedrin 98a, takes the Son of Man here as the Messiah.

of the infinite and the human realm of the finite. In this regard, he is a high priest—a thought that takes us to v. 4 in Ps 110 where the Messiah is called "a priest forever according to the order of Melchizedek."

We have covered many Tanakh verses that speak of the future dominion of the Messiah. Just to recall a few: Jacob said regarding the Messiah, "The scepter shall not depart from Judah, nor the ruler's staff from between his feet, until Shiloh comes, and to him shall be the obedience of the peoples" (Gen 49:10); YHWH said to his Son, his Messiah, as recorded by David, "Ask of Me, and I will surely give the nations as Your inheritance, and the very ends of the earth as Your possession" (Ps 2:8); Solomon, through the Spirit, said of the Messiah, "May he also rule from sea to sea and from the River to the ends of the earth. And let all kings bow down before him, all nations serve him" (Ps 72:8, 11); and in speaking of the Messiah, Isaiah said that there would be "no end to the increase of His government or of peace" (Isa 9:7), and that one day the nations would flock to the "root of Jesse" (Isa 4:10), that is, to the son of David who would one day rule on David's throne forever. In these texts God gives the Messiah worldwide rule; in Dan 7:13-14 God bestows worldwide rule upon the Son of Man. Important to notice here is that the Son of Man's kingdom "is an everlasting dominion that will not pass away; and His kingdom is one which will not be destroyed." Of the Messiah, as just noted, Isaiah said that the "increase of His government" would have "no end." We should also remember that God (through the prophet Nathan) told David that he would establish the throne of David's son "forever" (2 Sam 7:13; 1 Chron 17:12). So the Messiah and the Son of Man are both given worldwide kingdoms, and in both cases the kingdoms bestowed are eternal. There can be only one conclusion to draw from this: David's son and the Son of Man are the same person.

There is one other feature of the book of Daniel that I'll mention now that will also attest to a mysterious unity between God and the Son of Man. But let us start this by going back again to Nathan's prophecy to David. In the 1 Chron 17 version of it, let us recall that God said regarding David's son: "I will settle him in My house and in My kingdom forever, and his throne shall be established forever" (v. 14). With this in mind, let us note the following. The Son of Man is given a worldwide kingdom, by God, that is "everlasting" and that "will not be destroyed" (Dan 7:14). But Daniel has already said this of God's coming eternal kingdom. When Daniel interpreted Nebuchadnezzar's dream, he said to the great king,

> [T]he God of heaven will set up a kingdom which will never be destroyed, and that kingdom will not be left for another people; it

will crush and put an end to all these kingdoms, but it will itself endure forever.[321]

And then some time later when Nebuchadnezzar had perceived that the God of Shadrach, Meshach, and Abed-nego had preserved the young men in the fiery furnace, he exulted regarding the God of the Hebrews:

> How great are His signs and how mighty are His wonders! His kingdom is an everlasting kingdom and His dominion is from generation to generation.[322]

Some time later, after Nebuchadnezzar had come back to his senses after God had taken his sanity away from him for a season, the king—finally seeing the full light of God—testified:

> I, Nebuchadnezzar, raised my eyes toward heaven and my reason returned to me, and I blessed the Most High and praised and honored Him who lives forever; for His dominion is an everlasting dominion, and His kingdom endures from generation to generation.[323]

And, finally, after the Medo-Persian King Darius pulled Daniel out of the lion's den, and was profoundly relieved that he had not been harmed, the king gave this command:

> I make a decree that in all the dominion of my kingdom men are to fear and tremble before the God of Daniel; for He is the living God and enduring forever, and His kingdom is one which will not be destroyed, and His dominion will be forever.[324]

God wants us to know, by what he reveals through the book of Daniel, that God's kingdom will surely come, and that it will be an *indestructible and eternal kingdom.* Let us ponder once again what God said regarding David's son (1 Chron 17:14): "I will settle him in My house and in My kingdom forever, and his throne shall be established forever." And let us read one more time what is recorded by Daniel (7:14) regarding the Son of Man:

> And to Him was given dominion …. His dominion is an everlasting dominion which will not pass away; and His kingdom is one which will not be destroyed.

---

[321] Dan 2:44
[322] Dan 4:3
[323] Dan 4:34
[324] Dan 6:26

What is said of God's kingdom is exactly what is said of the Son of Man's kingdom. These kingdoms are both worldwide, eternal, and never to be destroyed. In other words, they are one and the same kingdom. The Son of Man is "given" this kingdom, and thus he is "settle[d]" in God's "house" and "kingdom forever." God is the king, and yet the king whom mankind will see is the Son of Man. If any are unsure of the truth of this mystery, the principle made clear by God and Samuel should be soberly remembered: in the long run—especially the *eternal* long run—only God should, and will, be our king.[325]

Thus we have confirmed what we learned earlier in the study: the Messiah, who is the Son of Man, becomes king of the world, and this king, who will rule forever, is divine. But the amazing things revealed in Dan 7 are not yet exhausted in this study. We should notice something else that is amazing and profoundly encouraging for those "who long for his appearing." Before saying what this is, let us first consider the infinitely wonderful (for the righteous) fact that God reveals to Daniel as recorded in chapter 12—a fact that has been only partially revealed in a few places of previous Scripture, but here is stated overtly. We learn (from what God's strange messenger says to Daniel, vv. 2-3) that *there will be a resurrection of the dead*:

> Many of those who sleep in the dust of the ground will awake, these to everlasting life, but the others to disgrace and everlasting contempt. Those who have insight will shine brightly like the brightness of the expanse of heaven, and those who lead the many to righteousness, like the stars forever and ever.

I might note on the occasion of presenting this text that this was the purpose of the Messiah—to suffer and die so that "the iniquity of us all" might be laid upon him, and so that we might be "healed," that is, *saved* from death and damnation. So we learn from this precious portion of holy Scripture that the saints are saved from "disgrace and everlasting contempt" to "everlasting life" in which the saints "shine … like the stars forever and ever." Now as we turn back to Dan 7, we get an idea, from what is said in vv. 18, 22, and 27, what will be the position and occupation of these saved saints. And so now we come to what is "amazing and profoundly encouraging." This last verse sums up what will happen once the Little Horn is killed and God establishes his kingdom on earth:

> Then the sovereignty, the dominion and the greatness of all the kingdoms under the whole heaven will be given to the people of the

---

[325] 1 Sam 8:7; 12:17

saints of the Highest One; His kingdom will be an everlasting kingdom, and all the dominions will serve and obey Him.

God's eternal kingdom will be ruled by the Messiah, and Messiah's eternal kingdom will be administered worldwide by his resurrected saints. There will be much for them to do! But given the context of Dan 7, as well as what has previously been said about the Messiah, it is obviously the case that the "people of the saints" will only be those who "kiss the son," for he is the face of the One who will be their great Shepherd and Lord forever and ever.

THE MESSIAH IS JOSHUA

We now come to the last book of the Tanakh that we will consider in some detail, the book of the prophet Zechariah. This great prophet lived near the end of the prophetic epoch, and then the prophetic light soon went out.[326] Although he is considered one of the twelve "minor" prophets, he is certainly not to be seen as "minor" among the prophets. He did not produce as much prophetic information as, say, Isaiah, but what he did produce—through the Spirit of God—was densely packed and eclectic. So with him (along with Malachi), the prophetic sun sets, and like the setting sun often produces an explosion of colors in the western sky, so Zechariah gives us an explosion of prophetic information that both dazzles and baffles. While there are straightforward prophecies about present and future events, there are others that are just plain hard to understand. Among this latter group are several prophecies that come in the form of visions that contain many enigmatic symbols, like, for example, myrtle trees, horns, craftsmen, feces-splattered high priest vestments, olive trees, a stone with seven eyes, a giant flying scroll, a wicked woman in a basket, and a women with stork wings. There are plain and encouraging prophecies concerning the regathering of God's people to their Promised Land, and of the edenic conditions that will exist there "in that day"; yet there are disturbing prophecies of a future time when God's people will endure horrible tribulation. Zechariah is both encouraging and deeply disturbing. In the midst of this prophetic maelstrom, the Messiah makes his appearances, first in symbolic form as a priest clothed in filthy garments and as a priest who is crowned as king, then as a donkey-mounted king appearing for the first time to his people, thereafter as a shepherd who is "detested" by his flock, and finally as YHWH "whom [his own people] have pierced."[327]

---

[326] Malachi probably prophesied not long after Zechariah and Haggai.
[327] See, respectively, Zech 3, 6, 9, 11, and 12.

Zechariah prophesied during the last few years of the building of the post-exilic temple, ca. 520 BC. About two decades before, King Cyrus, the Persian, had given permission for the Jews to return to Jerusalem in order to rebuild the Temple. The prophet Daniel died about that time or shortly thereafter. Compared to the vast number of Jews then living in the Persian empire, only a small remnant returned. These were under the leadership of the Persian-appointed governor, Zerubbabel, and the High Priest, Joshua, who together directed the Temple rebuilding that began about a year after their arrival in Jerusalem. But soon opposition from the local leaders and people arose, and so the work on the Temple stopped due to that, as well as due to general lack of motivation.[328] God, however, was still motivated, thus he raised up two prophets whose mission it was to re-energize the Jewish leaders and workers: Haggai spurred them on to finish the construction of God's house, and warned them not to work on their own houses at the expense of God's house; Zechariah also encouraged the Jews to finish the job, but not by admonishments as Haggai had done, but by simply prophesying that the job would indeed be completed—mainly through the leadership of Zerubbabel and Joshua, but also by "those who [were] far off."[329] Haggai's admonishments and prophecies have to do with the rebuilding of the Temple in his day; Zechariah's do too, but they also symbolically point to realities that are far in the future and are far more important than the physical Temple.

So let us now consider how Zechariah contributes to our messianic "forensic picture." I must confess up front that this is not an easy task. Many things are pretty clear in the book, but many things are inscrutable and difficult to place neatly in a messianic context, unless one already has some preconceived notion of what the Messiah should look like. Analogous to Zechariah are the many pieces of a complex jigsaw puzzle scattered on the floor, but the puzzle does not come with a clear picture on the box-top giving us some idea of how the parts fit together. Fortunately, what we have learned so far about the Messiah in the Tanakh does give us a rough picture by which we can begin to make sense of the many scattered pieces of Zechariah. But there is so much that is new and symbolic in the book that for our purposes here, I think it best at this point to do what I have mostly avoided, that is, to bring in some knowledge from the New Testament in order to give us at least some template—some puzzle box-top picture—by which we can make sense of the many disparate and mysterious parts of the book. I have tried my best up till now to let the Tanakh interpret itself, that is, I have built the "forensic picture" of the Messiah solely from the Tanakh. But now we are very near to the end of my case, so I

[328] See Ezra 1-6.
[329] Zech 6:15

hope that you, the reader, will tolerate a little bit of an appeal to the NT as I struggle with finding meaning in Zechariah. As far as my mission to demonstrate the divinity of the Messiah, my use of an organizing template based loosely upon the life of Christ in the NT will be somewhat (as philosophers say) "question begging"; but it seems to me that the case for the Messiah's divinity has already been pretty much made, and this last burst of sunset glory contained in Zechariah will serve as a transition to the book's conclusion which does connect what we have learned so far with what is taught about the Messiah in the Gospels of the NT. The "template" is simply this: the Messiah comes in humility to build his church (his "temple"), but he is rejected and killed; the Messiah comes again, but this time as a conquering king, and successfully defeats all his enemies and finally establishes his church upon earth. That's it. It sounds like the life of Jesus of Nazareth, but, really, it's simply the basics of what the Tanakh has already told us about the Messiah. Now in what follows, I will briefly mention a number of Zechariah prophecies, and do so without much or any exegetical justification. There is just so much in the book that is symbolic and subject to varying interpretations, that justifying my views in each case would involve multiple debatable assumptions and make this section on Zechariah way too long. On the other hand, several of the prophecies mentioned below will be so clear that they do not need detailed explanation. So here we go: this is my messianic take on the book.

To begin, Zechariah says that the Messiah will indeed come and build his temple—although he doesn't use the term "Messiah," but uses another term that we've already become familiar with, "the Branch."[330] In chapter 3, the Angel of the LORD, relaying the words of the "LORD of hosts," says to the High Priest Joshua, "I am going to bring in My servant, the Branch" (v. 8).[331] Note that the Branch is also God's "Servant." From what we have said earlier about the Angel of YHWH, and from what the Angel says here about the future coming of the Savior of mankind, it is entirely fitting that the Angel was seen just before by Zechariah (in the same night's vision) pleading with God to have mercy on Jerusalem (1:12).[332] Later, in chapter 6, Joshua, after being crowned,

---

[330] צֶמַח, *tzamach*, takes on messianic meaning in Zechariah as well as in Isa 4:2; Jer 23:5; 33:15.

[331] George Klein offers this interesting information: "Joshua the high priest appears also in Ezra 2:2 and Neh 7:7 as 'Jeshua.' The name means 'Yahweh saves.' Joshua also figures prominently in Hag 1:1, 12, 14; 2:2, 4, as well as in Zech 6:11. We know that Joshua was the son of Jehozadak (2 Kgs 25:18; 1 Chr 6:40-41; Jer 52:24), who was the son of Seraiah, the chief priest when the exile began in 587 BC. The Babylonians executed Seraiah, and presumably Jehozadak fathered and raised Joshua in Babylon. Joshua was probably an old man by the time of Zechariah's vision." (George Klein, *Zechariah: an Exegetical and Theological Exposition of Holy Scripture*, The New American Commentary [B & H Publishing, 2008], Kindle e-book, 182-83.)

[332] The Angel of YHWH's appearance in chapter 3 is his last actual appearance in Tanakh history, although it is given to us through the medium of Zechariah's prophetic vision. Regarding the Angel of the LORD's appearance in Zech 1:8, 11, Baron wrote: "The 'man' …

is named "Branch" by YHWH, and YHWH declares that Joshua "will branch out from where He is; and He will build the temple of the LORD" (more about the context and details of chapters 3, 4, and 6 a little later). While it is the sixth century BC High Priest Joshua who is the subject of these prophecies, and the physical temple that he was trying to build is in view, it is obvious that Joshua is only symbolic of the far greater "Branch" to come, and that the Temple is simply a symbol of the far greater reality of "God with us," that is, the fact that one day God will permanently reside with his people.[333]

Malachi, who prophesied not long after Zechariah, said that the "Lord," whom he also called "the angel of the covenant," would surely one day "come to his temple" (Mal 3:1). But as Zechariah shows, he would first come not as a conquering king riding a proud horse, but as a humble king riding a donkey—in fact a step lower than that: riding "a colt, the foal of a donkey" (Zech 9:9).[334] Not only would this king be a king, but, as represented by the crowning of the High Priest Joshua in chapter 6, he would be a priest as well. "Thus," as Zechariah says in 6:13, "He will be a priest on His throne, and the counsel of peace will be between the two offices." That is to say, there will be peace between the royal and priestly offices because they are combined in one man. This, of course, reminds us of the decree of YHWH, as recorded in Ps 110:4, that tells the world that the Messiah is not just a king, but a priest as well—and not only that, but a priest not of the order of Aaron, but of the order of Melchizedek.

So the humble Messiah comes, but instead of being loved and accepted by his people, Zechariah shows us that he is despised and rejected by a people and leadership who are greatly inclined to evil. In chapter 3, we get the first indications of this, although in highly symbolic form. Zechariah sees in his night vision the High Priest Joshua in filthy clothes being viciously accused by Satan. Joshua, as the High Priest, is here representative of the people in general who, like Joshua, are "filthy" with sin, and as such are subject to the accusations of the Accuser, the Devil. He is also representative of the Messiah (this is made

---

was the *Malakh Yehovah*—the Angel of Jehovah, who is none other than the 'Angel of His face,' the Divine 'Angel of the Covenant,' the second person in the Blessed Trinity, whose early manifestations to the patriarch and prophets, as the 'Angel' or Messenger of Jehovah in the form of man, were anticipations of His incarnation and of that incomprehensible humiliation to which He would afterwards condescend for our salvation." (David Baron, *The Visions and Prophecies of Zechariah* [London: Morgan and Scott, 1918], 23, accessible at www.archive.org.)

[333] In the NT, the Temple is symbolic of Christ's body (John 2:18-21), and his body is symbolic of the Church (Eph 1:22-23).

[334] The first time he comes on a foal of a donkey. The next time, as Zech 9:14 says, he "will march in the storm winds of the south," or as Isa 66:15 says: "the LORD will come in fire and His chariots like the whirlwind, to render His anger with fury, and His rebuke with flames of fire." Regarding the king coming on a donkey (Zech 9:9), the Babylonian Talmud in general understands this messianically. See Sanhedrin 98a and 99a.

plain in chapter 6 where he is called the "Branch") who will, by and by, be given as an atonement for the people—an atonement by which the "iniquity of us all" (in this case symbolized by filthy clothes) will be laid upon him. Satan here, even though rebuked by the Angel of the LORD, accuses Joshua before God, knowing that God must mete out justice for sin. Satan obviously wants Joshua, and all he represents, condemned and destroyed.[335] But the Angel of the LORD says that Joshua and all Israel will one day be seen as clean: Joshua will receive clean vestments, and the sins of Israel will be at long last totally removed.[336] But to do this, says the Angel, will require the coming of the Branch—also described as a "stone [with] seven eyes"—through whom YHWH "will remove the iniquity of that land in one day" (3:9).[337] That it will take the death of the "stone" in order to accomplish this is strongly hinted at by the fact that YHWH, in the process of the removal of sin, will "engrave an inscription" upon the stone. This is to say what has already been said: he will be "pierced through for our transgressions" and "crushed for our iniquities" (Isa 53:5). And this is also to say what Zechariah will say later regarding the sight that will cause all Israel to repent: "They will look upon [YHWH] whom they pierced; and they will mourn for Him, as one mourns for an only son" (Zech 12:10). The distain for the Messiah is also indicated in chapter 11 where three shepherds—i.e., the political, priestly, and prophetical leadership classes—oppose him, and the nation considers him worth no more than a common slave.[338] The situation, according to what Zechariah says in chapter 13, is so bad that the good Shepherd is subject to the sword (he is killed), and the sheep of his flock are scattered.[339]

---

[335] This reminds us of Satan's vicious attack against Job in Job 1 and 2. Feinberg here says that the filthily be-clothed Joshua is representative of all Jewish people—a people whom Satan wants to destroy. Important to notice is that the Angel takes away Joshua's iniquity (3:4)—something that only God can do—and then declares that the LORD will remove the sins "of this land in a single day" (3:9). We might recall that the Angel who went ahead of Israel in the wilderness (Exod 23:20-21) had the authority to forgive the sins of those Israelites who chose to "obey his voice." (Charles Feinberg, God Remembers: a Study of Zechariah [Wheaton: Van Kampen Press, 1950], 54-55.)

[336] The Angel of the LORD commands the removal of Joshua's filthy clothes, then says: "I have taken your iniquity away from you and will clothe you with festal robes" (3:4). But only God can remove sins (see also Exod 23:20-21).

[337] Regarding seven eyes, see Rev 5:6.

[338] These "three shepherds" despised the good shepherd, and the people valued him at only 30 pieces of silver, which was the price of a slave (Joseph was sold by his brothers for 20 pieces, Gen 37:28; and Exod 21:32 put the price of a slave at 30 pieces). The good shepherd, perceiving the insult, threw the silver "to the potter in the house of the LORD" (Zech 11:13). This act is meant to remind us of Jeremiah's breaking of the clay jar in the Valley of Ben-Hinnom which represented the coming destruction of Jerusalem (Jer 19:10, 11; see also Jer 18). The Sanhedrin paid Judas 30 pieces of silver to betray Jesus (Matt 26:14-15). About forty years later Jerusalem and the Temple were destroyed by the Romans and most Jews there either killed or enslaved.

[339] Zech 13:7-8

So the "Shepherd," who is also called "Joshua," "Branch," God's "Servant," and "High Priest," will be a king who is killed, and through this, the sins of the people will be removed by that atoning act all "in one day." And the cleansed people will be not just Israelites, but people from all over the world:

> Many nations will join themselves to the LORD in that day and will become My people. Then I will dwell in your midst, and you will know that the LORD of hosts has sent Me to you.[340]

And they will assist in the building up of God's house:

> Those who are far off will come and build the temple of the LORD. Then you will know that the LORD of hosts has sent me to you.[341]

People from all nations will be seen as clean in the eyes of God, for all nations will go up to Jerusalem in order to participate in the Feast of Booths (14:16-19).

The Messiah, even though "struck" and "pierced," will overcome death and return to Jerusalem, not like the first time in poverty and humility, but as a saving warrior who delivers his sheep from the marauders who will fall upon them in the last days:

> Then the LORD will appear over them, and His arrow will go forth like lightning; and the Lord GOD will blow the trumpet, and will march in the storm winds of the south. And the LORD their God will save them in that day as the flock of His people; for they are as the stones of a crown, sparkling in His land.[342]

Furthermore,

> the LORD will be king over all the earth; in that day the LORD will be the only one, and His name the only one.[343]

How do we know that the Messiah who suffers and dies is the "LORD" who will one day rule "over all the earth"? Before noticing two things in Zechariah that seem to point this way, we might recall Ezekiel's teaching, found in chapters 34 and 37, that YHWH is Israel's Shepherd, and David is Israel's Shepherd, and that in the restored state, Israel will have "one Shepherd." We should also remember that in the long run, only God alone should be Israel's king, as YHWH's lament to Samuel has shown us.[344]

Now let's look at a couple of interesting things in Zechariah that prompt us to ponder the Messiah's divinity. First of all, the coming eternal omnipotent

---

[340] Zech 2:11
[341] Zech 6:15
[342] Zech 9:14
[343] Zech 14:9
[344] 1 Sam 8:7

king is first referred to by YHWH (in Zech 9:10) as a person separate from YHWH, yet possessing the worldwide dominion of YHWH:

> I [i.e., YHWH] will cut off the chariot from Ephraim and the horse from Jerusalem; and the bow of war will be cut off. And He [i.e., the Messiah] will speak peace to the nations; and His dominion will be from sea to sea, and from the River to the ends of the earth.

This should sound familiar, for Solomon (Ps 72:8) used nearly the same words to describe the Messiah's "dominion" ("May he also rule from sea to sea and from the River to the ends of the earth"). And yet, in the long run, as already mentioned just above (Zech 14:9), it will be the LORD who "will be king over all the earth." Does the Messiah possess a universal kingdom, but at some point, he will give this kingdom up to God? To answer this, the words of God to David regarding the Messiah should not be forgotten: "I will establish the throne of his kingdom forever."[345] And let us recall Isaiah's words regarding the Messiah:

> There will be no end to the increase of His government or of peace, on the throne of David and over his kingdom, to establish it and to uphold it with justice and righteousness from then on and forevermore.[346]

In some mysterious way, the Messiah rules forever and YHWH rules forever; yet there is only one Shepherd-King in the eschaton.

Let us consider one other feature of Zechariah that may point to the identity between the Messiah and YHWH. This brief argument will admittedly be speculative, and involve interpretations of certain elements of Zechariah that will seem on the face of it somewhat fantastic. Earlier in the book I provided biblical evidence that strongly shows that there is a mysterious identity between the Angel of YHWH and YHWH, and that this Angel appeared from time to time in order to help preserve, in one way or another, the "Holy Seed," that is, preserve the bloodline that would one day lead to the Messiah. In view of the fact that there is this identity between the Angel of YHWH and YHWH—and, as I have striven to show through this book, that there is mysterious identity between the Messiah and YHWH—then it follows that there is mysterious identity between the Angel of YHWH and the Messiah, for they are both divine, and there can only be one God. Now in Zechariah, the case for the Angel of YHWH's identity with YHWH is reinforced by the fact that the Angel of YHWH in chapter 3 speaks both *of* YHWH and *as* YHWH. In the chapter

---

[345] 2 Sam 7:13
[346] Isa 9:7

3 courtroom scene in which the High Priest Joshua is accused by Satan, there are four persons present: Joshua, Satan, the Angel of YHWH, and Zechariah observing. Here, the Angel of YHWH is actually called "YHWH" by Zechariah (vv. 1-2):

> Then he [i.e., the angel who had been guiding Zechariah through his visions in Chapters 1-6] showed me Joshua the high priest standing before the angel of the LORD, and Satan standing at his right hand to accuse him. The LORD said to Satan, "The LORD rebuke you, Satan! Indeed, the LORD who has chosen Jerusalem rebuke you! Is this not a brand plucked from the fire?"

Notice that Zechariah records that YHWH spoke to Satan, yet when he speaks, he refers to YHWH in the third person: "The LORD said to Satan, 'The LORD rebuke you, Satan!'" Because of the way that the scene is set up, it is most likely the case that the person speaking the rebuke is the Angel of YHWH before whom Joshua and Satan stand. If so, then the Angel of YHWH speaks as YHWH, and then speaks of YHWH as a separate person.[347]

One more text out of Zechariah should be mentioned that seems to connect the person of the Messiah to the divinity of YHWH. Speaking of God's final victory over all of Israel's enemies, Zechariah says:

> In that day the LORD will defend the inhabitants of Jerusalem, and the one who is feeble among them in that day will be like David, and the house of David will be like God, like the angel of the LORD before them.

The last clause is easy to understand in the Hebrew:

$$\text{וּבֵית דָּוִיד כֵּאלֹהִים כְּמַלְאַךְ יהוה לִפְנֵיהֶם}$$

And the house of David—like God, like the Angel of YHWH
before them.

First to notice here is that "God" and "the angel of the LORD" both appear as exemplars of omnipotence. In that day when God and God's people fight

---

[347] "[W]e are given here further proofs of the deity of the Angel. In the first place, He is distinctly spoken of by the Spirit of God as Jehovah in verse 2. In the second place, He is seen forgiving sins (vs. 4), a work that God has never delegated to mere man." (Feinberg, *God Remembers*, 54.) The Jewish Study Bible text of Zech 3:1-2 indicates that the speaker is the Angel of the LORD: "He further showed me Joshua, the high priest, standing before the angel of the LORD, and the Accuser standing at his right to accuse him. But [the angel of] the LORD said to the Accuser, 'The Lord rebuke you, O Accuser; may the Lord who has chosen Jerusalem rebuke you! For this is a brand plucked from the fire.'" (Fishbane, *The Jewish Study Bible*, Zech 3:1-2 [brackets theirs].)

against their enemies, and finish them off once and for all, the weak among them will fight as skillfully as the great warrior David, and the "house of David," that is, the Messiah, will fight as powerfully as God, as powerfully as the Angel of YHWH. "Like" usually means "similar to," although the qualitative similarity can be understood as more or less, depending on the context. In view of what we know already about the Messiah, it is probably the case here that Zechariah intends for us to understand that the Messiah will be very much "like" God and the Angel of YHWH. This is said of no one else in the Tanakh, i.e., that one is like both God and the Angel of YHWH. It is no coincidence that the only person that this is said of happens to be the one person that is elsewhere in the Tanakh spoken of in divine terms, that is, the Messiah.

Let us now proceed on according to our "template" borrowed loosely from the NT. So the Messiah comes the second time as a conquering king,[348] as I've already shown from Zechariah, and he comes to his people under the conditions of a new covenant—according to 9:11 a covenant "for the sake of the blood," as the JPS '85 has it. Whose blood this is, is not stated; but we can be sure that, like the Mosaic covenant, it is based upon the idea of substitutionary atonement. Now when the Messiah comes, he will complete the building of his temple. Like the post-exilic temple construction began, then stopped for a time (about fifteen years), then was completed, so will the greater temple—God's people among/in whom he dwells—see two major phases of building that correspond to the Messiah's first and second comings. The Messiah doesn't just come to his temple, he builds it. This is symbolized by Zerubbabel (the Jewish governor at the time of the return from exile who was a descendant of David) being told by God that he (Zerubbabel) would surely complete the rebuilding task by the power of God's Spirit (chap. 4), and also symbolized by the High Priest Joshua who is also informed that he (Joshua) would build the Temple (chap. 6). There is a subtle difference in these two visions worth noting: It is said of Zerubbabel that he, who had laid the foundation of the Temple, would surely complete the rebuilding of "this house" (4:9); but with Joshua in chapter 6—who embodies the more robust messianic symbol, for he is a priest who is also crowned as king—YHWH informs him (via the mouth of Zechariah) that he would surely "build the temple of the LORD," these exact words being said twice (6:12-13). At that time the Temple had already been partially built. Especially in view of the fact that Joshua in this vision of his crowning is named the "Branch," it is most likely the case that Joshua is symbolic of the Messiah, and that his building of the Temple of YHWH is symbolic of the Messiah's building of his covenant people—a group

---

[348] Zech 2:5-13; 9:13-16; 12:1-9; 14

that the NT calls "church," which is simply the English way of saying "assembly" (in Greek, *ekklesia*).[349]

In the end phase of building this spiritual temple, great affliction will come upon God's people: in fact, two-thirds of them will be killed (13:8). But in the end as the nations make their final attack upon Israel, God will protect his people (chapters 12 and 14) in such a miraculous fashion that their enemies' flesh will rot upon them even while they are standing (14:12). At the apex of the Day of the LORD, the LORD-Messiah will appear and stand upon the Mount of Olives (14:4) just east of the Temple, and that hill will be split in half. It should not be missed that he will *stand* upon the Mount of Olives.[350] Once enthroned in Jerusalem, "living water" will flow from that city, half to the east and half to the west (14:8). In Ezekiel's vision of the eschatological Temple (Ezek 47), that "living water" emanates as a trickle from under the Temple and grows rapidly into a large river that cascades into the Dead Sea and brings it back to life.[351]

The coming of YHWH-Messiah will be witnessed by every person on earth, and when they see him, the LORD testifies (Zech 12:10):

$$\text{הִבִּיטוּ אֵלַי אֵת אֲשֶׁר־דָּקָרוּ}$$

they will look on Me whom they have pierced (NASB)

they shall look unto Me because they have thrust him through (JPS '17)

they shall lament to Me about those who are slain (JPS '85)

they shall look to me because of those who have been thrust through [with swords] (Judaica)

they will look toward Me because of those whom they have stabbed (Artscroll)

In this case the NASB easily has the most literal and accurate translation. The Jewish versions add words that are not in the Hebrew text ("because," "about," "those," "him") so that someone/some group is mortally injured, and not YHWH. But the direct object marker, *et*, is just before the relative pronoun, *asher*, showing that the object of the verb "they pierced" is "whom," which obviously refers back to "Me"—i.e., YHWH. When they see YHWH-Messiah

---

[349] Targum Jonathan has for Zech 6:12: "Behold the man, Messiah is his name." Compare Pilate's words to Jesus recorded in John 19:5.

[350] The LORD and the Angel of the LORD in other Bible passages are described as *standing*. For example, Gen 18:2; Exod 34:5; Num 12:5; 22:23; Josh 5:13; 1 Chron 21:16.

[351] "Living Water": see Ezek 47:1-12; Joel 3:18. Also Jer 2:13; John 4:7-15; 7:37-39; Rev 22:1-2, 17.

whom they pierced (killed), God, through his "Spirit of grace and supplication," will prompt them to mourn and weep bitterly, "like the bitter weeping over [the death of] a firstborn."

From then on YHWH-Messiah will rule the world. His people will be the jewels in his crown (9:16). Who is this king who will rule the world? David himself gives us the answer:

> Lift up your heads, O gates, and be lifted up, O ancient doors, that the King of glory may come in! Who is the King of glory? The LORD strong and mighty, the LORD mighty in battle. Lift up your heads, O gates, and lift them up, O ancient doors, that the King of glory may come in! Who is this King of glory? The LORD of hosts, He is the King of glory. Selah.[352]

The LORD of hosts is the great "King of glory" who will rule the entire creation forever and ever. Yet both Zechariah (9:10) and David's son Solomon (Ps 72:8) say that the Messiah will rule "from sea to sea and from the River to the ends of the earth." Pondering this, we might recall YHWH's words to his Son, as recorded by David in Ps 2: "Ask of Me, and I will surely give the nations as Your inheritance, and the very ends of the earth as Your possession." From that time on all of God's people will live in peace (Zech 14:11) and all the people and the things of earth will be "Holy to the LORD": There will be no distinction between what is holy and what is not, because everyone and everything will be holy, even (previously unclean) horses and household pots and pans (14:20-21). One might even say that the entire world will be a Holy of Holies, because God will dwell in the midst of his people.[353]

When all these things come to pass, then will occur what the Angel of the LORD predicted several times in Zechariah: "Then you will know that the LORD of hosts has sent me to you."[354] Who is the "me" whom the people will

---

[352] Ps 24:7-10

[353] "[A]t the time of the completion of the kingdom of God the distinction between Jerusalem and the temple will have ceased, and the whole of the holy city, yea, the whole of the kingdom of God, will be transformed by the Lord into a holy of holies (see Rev. 21:22, 27)." (Keil and Delitzsch, *Commentary on the Old Testament*, Zech 14:20-21.)

[354] Zech 2:9, 11; 4:9; 6:15. Jonathan Edwards said: "[W]hen we read in sacred history what God did, from time to time, towards his church and people, and how he revealed himself to them, we are to understand it especially of the second person of the Trinity. When we read of God appearing after the fall, in some visible form or outward symbol of his presence, we are ordinarily, if not universally, to understand it of the second person of the Trinity. John 1:18: 'No man hath seen God at any time; the only begotten Son, which is in the bosom of the Father, he hath declared him.' He is therefore called 'the image of the invisible God,' Col. 1:15, intimating, that though God the Father be invisible, yet Christ is his image or representation, by which he is seen." Regarding the Angel of the LORD in the burning bush, Edwards said: "Jesus Christ ... appeared to Moses in the bush, and sent him to redeem that people, as is evident from his being called the Angel of the Lord, Exod. 3:2, 3." (Jonathan Edwards, *The*

ERIC E. ENGLEMAN

finally believe is sent from the LORD? He is the same One whom they previously "pierced": the Branch, God's Servant, the Angel of YHWH, even YHWH, and, if you please, יְהוֹשֻׁעַ the Messiah.

History of the Work of Redemption Comprising an Outline of Church History [New York: American Tract Society, 1816], 29-30, 77, accessible at www.archive.org.)

CONCLUSION

Today we say "Jesus" when speaking about the one whom Christians believe in and worship. The earliest manuscripts of the New Testament are in the Greek language, and Jesus' name there is Ἰησοῦς, pronounced *ee-hey-soos*. This was the Greek way of saying the Hebrew name יְהוֹשֻׁעַ, *yuhhoshua* (or the post-exilic shortened form, יֵשׁוּעַ, *yeshua*), which is the name of Moses' successor (as well as others) whom we now know in English as "Joshua." When we speak today of Moses' successor, we say "Joshua"; when we speak of the Christian Savior, we say "Jesus." But back in Jesus' day and before, these names were the same. Did the Tanakh somehow predict that the Messiah's name would be *yuhhoshua*? Moses' successor Joshua was something like the Messiah in that he led his people from the terrible wilderness into the Promised Land "flowing with milk and honey"—a type of messianic leadership and a type of messianic salvation. It is interesting to note that *yuhhoshua* in the Hebrew literally means "YH is salvation." The shortened form of the name, יֵשׁוּעַ, *yeshua* (used several times in Ezra and Nehemiah), sounds very much like the Hebrew word for "salvation," יְשׁוּעָה, *yuhshuah*. By leading Israel into the Promised Land, Joshua provided "salvation" for his people. It is, of course, more accurate to say that YHWH (in the form of the "Commander of the LORD's army," Josh 5:13-15 [CSB], who went before Joshua and Israel) saved his people. This, of course, is not a prophecy of the Messiah's name, although we should not be surprised if the Messiah is named after him. Coming close to a prophecy of his name, however, are the words that God commanded Zechariah to speak to Joshua the High Priest in the course of his symbolic crowning (Zech 6:11): "Behold, a man whose name is Branch, for He will branch out from where He is; and He will build the temple of the LORD." Obviously, the High Priest Joshua was meant by the prophecy to be typical of *the* "Branch," i.e., the Messiah. But this may have indeed been a direct indication of what the Messiah's name would be.

Be that as it may, it is surely the case that Jesus, or "Joshua," of Nazareth vigorously laid claim to being the Messiah so amply prophesied about in the Tanakh.[1] He claimed to be the fulfillment of all that "Moses and ... all the

---

[1] Michael Rydelnik (*The Messianic Hope* [Nashville: B & H Publishing, 2010]) believes much of the OT points directly or symbolically to the Messiah, such that the Messiah is its central theme. This is somewhat based upon Jesus' and Peter's statements that could be interpreted to mean that "all" that the prophets had said pointed to the Christ (Luke 24:27; Acts 3:24). But this clearly overstates the reality. Even if God meant the Tanakh to chiefly be concerned with the Messiah, this is very far from obvious when the OT text is straightforwardly read. Compared to the NT direct concern about the Messiah, the OT seems relatively unconcerned. The same could be said about the question of what happens after death, and how

prophets" (Luke 24:27) had said about the Messiah. So now that we have thoroughly filled in the "forensic picture" that the Tanakh builds of the Messiah, we can now ask ourselves if Jesus of Nazareth fits the picture. Before answering that in some detail, it should be mentioned that there were several other Messiah-like leaders who arose more or less around the time of Jesus.[2] Very little has been recorded about them (mainly by Josephus), and we really

---

one can have a good outcome if there is an afterlife. The NT is engrossed with the question, the OT only speaks of it overtly in a few places. The two subjects are inextricably linked. It seems to me that the OT, through various mostly subtle and often enigmatic signs, leads one slowly to an awareness of the Messiah and of an awareness that having a good outcome after death has something to do with him. The OT subject of the Messiah is not set on a golden platter for us, better, not thrown as pearls before swine, but the wonderful and hallowed subject is metered out sufficient for men to come to a knowledge of the truth, believe, and be saved. God made the OT as it is, and had it slowly come together, such that evil men would have their reasons for not believing, and good men would have their reasons for believing. To borrow partially from Leibniz, it was the "best of all possible" Old Testaments that precipitates the greatest number of saved souls. If the OT had been much more overt in its messianic emphasis, there is no telling what evil men would have done to defile his word and thwart God's plans. Herod himself might have been waiting with sword in hand in Bethlehem at the moment of Jesus' birth, and there would have been no gospel history of Jesus. Or maybe the Messiah would have been so universally expected, that he would have been enthusiastically made Israel's king, and we would all still be lost in our sins because he avoided death and thereby failed to atone for our sins. In any case, the OT does have a messianic theme (as this book shows!), but it does require some effort to discern it.

    [2] Gamaliel, a Pharisee and member of the Sanhedrin, mentioned two religious men who had lived not long before (sometime before ca. AD 30), Theudas and Judas the Galilean, who attracted many followers. But they were opposed and killed and their followers dispersed (Acts 5:35-37. Judas is also mentioned briefly by Josephus, *War*, book 2, chap. 8, as having "prevailed with his countrymen to revolt" during the Procuratorship of Coponius, ca. AD 5). During the time of Cuspius Fadus' government, procurator of Judah about AD 45, a man named Theudas gathered a large following and convinced them to join him at the Jordan River. Fadus sent soldiers after them, who slew many, and brought Theudas back to Jerusalem where he was beheaded (Josephus, *Antiquities*, book 20, chap. 5). About ten years later, an unnamed Egyptian, whom Josephus calls a "false prophet" and a "cheat," incited 30,000 men to follow him and to attempt a takeover of Roman-controlled Jerusalem. He was successfully countered by the army of the Roman Procurator, Felix. The Egyptian disappeared, and many of his followers were captured or killed (*Jewish War*, book 2, chap. 13; *Antiquities*, book 20, chap 8). The chief energizing factor of the Jewish revolt against the Romans, says Josephus (*War*, book 6, chap. 5), "was an ambiguous oracle that was also found in their sacred writings, how, 'about that time, one from their country should become governor of the habitable earth.'" It could be that some of the leaders of the various Zealot factions at that time may have fancied themselves as being that "governor," thus fulfilling messianic prophecy. The leader of the Bar-Kochba revolt (ca. AD 132-135), Simon bar Kosiba, was understood by some leading rabbis as the fulfillment of the messianic Num 24:17 text—"a star [*kochab*] shall come forth from Jacob" (thus, Simon was called Bar-Kochba, Aramaic for "son of the star")—and was perceived by many as the Messiah. It is not clear if he understood himself as such, although he did call himself "Prince of Israel." Half a million or more of his followers died in the unsuccessful revolution, and countless others were enslaved by the Romans (John J. Collins, *The Scepter and the Star* [Grand Rapids: Eerdmans, 2010], 225-227). History does not record if any of these thought of themselves as *the* Messiah. The only messianic figure around the time of Jesus of Nazareth that history records plainly as having a self-understanding as *the* Messiah was Jesus of Nazareth.

don't know if they even thought of themselves as *the* Messiah. They all seemed to have this in common: They were charismatic and religious, they accumulated followers, they tried in differing ways to overthrow the established (Roman) order, and they were usually killed. What the original history records about them fits on a few pieces of paper; but the original NT history of Jesus takes up far more space than that. And as far as impact upon the world, little could be said about them; but Jesus changed the world.

To an amazing degree, Jesus of Nazareth looks like the "forensic picture" of the Messiah developed in the Tanakh. Now, of course, it could be said (and has been said) that he was really not the Messiah, but an imposter who acted out the part so as to appear like the Messiah, and his disciples only further contributed to the deception. In puzzling over this question, I sometimes ask myself how—if this were true—God could allow millions to be deceived by someone who otherwise appeared to be love incarnate, and who offered a means of salvation that is rational, sacrificial, and in accordance with Scripture. Well, I don't think that God in all his holy and loving perfection would ever have allowed it. He squashed the false Messiahs mentioned just above long before they or their followers got anywhere close to first base.[3] In any case, in the case of the *real* Jewish Messiah, whoever he might be, skeptics could claim that he lived his life so as to *appear* like the Messiah of the Tanakh, or, as time goes on, skeptics could assert at any time that the whole story was concocted much later by dishonest men. So simply making the claim that Jesus lived out his life so as to make it appear that he was fulfilling OT prophecies, is no valid argument, but only an assertion. If he really did at least appear to fulfill those prophesies, this should be compelling to us, for when the true Messiah comes upon the scene, this is just what he will do. So does Jesus "at least appear" to have fulfilled the Scripture?

Our "forensic picture" that we have sketched from the testimony of the Tanakh shows us that the Messiah would come on the scene, according to the prophet Daniel, about five centuries after Cyrus' decree that allowed the Jews to return to Jerusalem in order to rebuild the Temple.[4] That is approximately when Jesus was born. And Micah prophesied that the place of his birth would be the little town of Bethlehem.[5] Although Mary and Joseph lived about seventy miles north of that in Nazareth, Caesar Augustus' census prompted them to register in a town of their Judean ancestral tribe, Bethlehem, and so, Jesus was

---

[3] Simon Bar Kochba (d. ca. AD 135) is an exception. He led Judah to an initially successful revolt against the Romans, but was finally killed and the revolt put down. Little of Jewish presence remained in Judah after that.

[4] Dan 9:24-27. Gabriel told Daniel when the Messiah would come, so it was very fitting for Gabriel to announce to Mary his coming (Luke 1:26-38).

[5] Mic 5:2

born there.[6] Several Tanakh prophets, especially Isaiah, indicated that the Messiah would come the first time not as a conquering king, but as a humble, impoverished, and suffering servant.[7] Jesus' parents could not even afford the customary lamb to offer when he was consecrated at the Temple,[8] and by Jesus' own testimony, he was "gentle and humble": even though foxes and birds had places to lodge, "the Son of Man [had] nowhere to lay his head."[9]

Isaiah said that the Messiah would have the seven-fold Spirit of God (something said of no one else in the Tanakh).[10] At Jesus' baptism the Spirit of God came upon him in a form visible to the man who baptized him, John the Baptist, and Jesus went on to exhibit the power of that Spirit in many ways.[11] His knowledge of God was amazing: Moses had shown that God is "compassionate and gracious ... abounding in lovingkindness";[12] Jesus' coming revealed to us that, in fact, "God *is* love."[13] The Tanakh taught that the hearts of men are "more deceitful than all else and ... desperately sick" and that "the soul that sinneth, it shall die."[14] Jesus, through the Spirit, could read the thoughts of men,[15] understood perfectly well that their thoughts were "only evil continually,"[16] and revealed to us that "No one can come to [Jesus] unless the Father who sent [Jesus] draws him."[17] All men, Jews included, are sinners and guilty before God,[18] and thus the Tanakh taught that "God will bring every act to judgment, everything which is hidden, whether it is good or evil."[19] God's redemption of his people was mentioned at several points in the Tanakh,[20] but Jesus revealed to us how it would be accomplished: His blood would atone, and God's Holy Spirit would "circumcise" men's hearts such that they could put their faith in God and God's Son in order that the blood of the Son would, on judgment day, cover their sins.[21] In sum, Jesus knew God and he knew men,

---

[6] Luke 2:1-7
[7] Ps 89:38-45; Isa 42:1-4; 52:13-54:12; Zech 11:12. Several Old Testament saints were types of the Messiah, like Joseph, Moses, Joshua, and David. After early difficulties, they were all exalted by the power of God.
[8] Luke 2:21-24
[9] Matt 11:29; Luke 9:58
[10] Isa 11:2-3
[11] Matt 3:16; Mark 1:10; Luke 3:22; John 1:32
[12] Exod 34:6
[13] 1 John 4:8
[14] Jer 17:9; Ezek 18:20 (KJV)
[15] Matt 9:4; 12:25; Luke 9:47; John 2:24. See also 1 Kings 8:39.
[16] Gen 6:5. See also Matt 7:11; 17:17; John 2:24-25.
[17] John 6:44
[18] 1 Kings 8:46; Ps 14:2-3; Eccl 7:20; Rom 3:23
[19] Eccl 12:14
[20] E.g., Ps 49:15; Isa 43:1; 52:3; Hos 13:14.
[21] Matt 20:28; Deut 30:6; Jer 31:33; 32:39; John 3:3; 6:44; Matt 26:28

and he knew how to reconcile God to man, and most amazing, he accomplished this reconciliation himself.

It was indicated in more than a few places in the Hebrew Scriptures that the Messiah would provide atonement for our sins through his own suffering and death. Isaiah said that "the LORD has caused the iniquity of us all to fall on Him," when he is "cut off out of the land of the living," and that through this death and atonement, "we are healed."[22] Daniel too told us that the Messiah would come and then be "cut off."[23] Jesus, of course, suffered greatly in life, then was killed. He was, as John the Baptist called him, "the Lamb of God who takes away the sin of the world."[24] During his three-year ministry he was greatly resisted, and at the end, was beaten, flogged, and tortured to death on a Roman cross. Just before giving up the ghost, he said with his last ounce of strength, "It is finished."[25] Thus, he gave "his life a ransom for many"[26] and thereby fulfilled the Law's requirement that blood must be shed for sins if there is to be any possibility of forgiveness for those sins.[27] The Mosaic Law, and the custom of patriarchal sacrifice before that, required ongoing sacrifices because of ongoing sins. In general, sacrifices under the Mosaic Law only covered *unintentional* sins. Sins done intentionally—i.e., with a "high hand"—would result in one being "cut off from among his people."[28] Some believe that the sacrifice made by the High Priest on the Day of Atonement covered all the people's sins, intentional and unintentional, for the foregoing year; but even if this were so, right after this sacrifice was made, the people (and the priests) would sin again and be guilty again. And so it can be argued—especially in view of the fact that all hearts were "desperately sick" all the time—that there never was a time when anyone, even the most righteous, was seen as pure in God's eyes.[29] In any case, the blood of animals, to put it simply, had only limited ability to satisfy YHWH for the sins of human beings, especially for intentional sins. It could be said that the sacrifices under the Mosaic system *covered* sins to some extent, but in the eyes of God, did not *eliminate* them. If (as Ps 49:7-9 says) a man cannot redeem another man—"or give to God a ransom for him for the redemption of his soul

---

[22] Isa 53:5-6, 8
[23] Dan 9:26
[24] John 1:29
[25] John 19:30
[26] Mark 10:45
[27] Lev 17:11; Heb 9:22
[28] Num 15:22-31; Heb 9:7
[29] Heb 9:7 says that the blood sprinkled on the Mercy Seat on the Day of Atonement only covered unintentional sins. We might note that when Israel was about to enter the Promised Land, they were considered frightfully unclean—"rebellious" and "stiffnecked" as they were—by God. Yet, God in his grace and mercy allowed most of them to cross the Jordan and enter in. But he held Moses (the humblest man in the world—Num 12:3) to a higher standard, and as a result did not allow him to lead his people in (Num 20:12; Deut 1:37).

is costly"—how can his soul be redeemed by the blood of a goat or lamb? But Jesus—being divine, sinless, and infinitely valuable—provided a sacrifice wholly pleasing to God that had the atoning potential to eliminate the sins of all mankind.[30] In doing so, the sacrificial system of the Mosaic Law and the Aaronic priesthood was arguably rendered obsolete.[31]

The reason I say "arguably" is this: Inasmuch as the sacrifices practiced under the Law propitiated (satisfied) God's demand for justice *temporarily*, God might continue to accept the sacrifices brought by unbelievers after the time of Jesus' atonement in order to provide them some "breathing room" until that time when they hopefully would believe in the Messiah and thereby have his blood "remove" all of their sins—past, present, and future. But for those who believe God and "kiss" his Son now, God applies his Son's blood, so to speak, to the "doorposts" of their lives permanently, and so there is no further need of the temporary covering of the Law's bloody animal sacrifices. Now inasmuch as it was understood that the Law's sacrifices could completely atone for the sins of Israelite men and women, and thereby propitiate God completely such that they would be declared innocent in the final judgment, the atonement provided by Jesus rendered these sacrifices "obsolete," because under the "New Covenant" men and women have no further need to bring any bloody animal sacrifices, but only the need to believe in the Son of God and through that claim for themselves the sacrifice that he provided when he was crucified and died upon the Roman cross. Regarding this last scenario, I say "inasmuch" as this is the case; but, in truth, this never was—as I have already said—the case, for nowhere in the Law of the Tanakh, and nowhere in the NT, is it taught that the sacrifices demanded by God, and offered by the people, ever propitiated God *permanently*, and thereby eternally saved (from eternal damnation) the souls of the offerors. Stepping back from all these details in order to sum up, it can be simply said with confidence that Jesus' work on the cross renders the sacrifices of the Law obsolete, and so it is a matter of time till, as the writer of the book of Hebrews puts it, the (expiatory rites and value) of the Law will "soon disappear."[32]

---

[30] But a man must claim this atonement, so to speak, for himself by exercising faith in Christ, and thankfulness to Christ for his unspeakably wonderful gift. Otherwise the payment Jesus made on his behalf will not be credited to his account.

[31] See Heb 8-10.

[32] Heb 8:13 (ISV). My understanding of the function of Mosaic Law sacrifices, both before and after Jesus' death, is based on the following articles: Jerry M. Hullinger, "The Compatibility of the New Covenant and Future Animal Sacrifice," *Journal of Dispensational Theology* 17:50 (Spring 2013): 47-66. "The Function of the Millennial Sacrifices in Ezekiel's Temple, part 1," *Bibliotheca Sacra* 167:665 (Jan 2010):40-57. "The Function of the Millennial Sacrifices in Ezekiel's Temple, part 2," *Bibliotheca Sacra* 167:666 (Apr 2010): 166-79. Charles C. Ryrie, "Why Sacrifices in the Millennium?" *Emmaus Journal* 11:2 (Winter 2002): 229-310. John C.

This claim, of course, has stuck in the craw of most Jewish men and women through the ages, especially in view of the several Tanakh indications that the Mosaic Law would be of eternal duration.[33] But let me say, as I have alluded to before, that there were many indications in the Tanakh that the Law was eroding in its force as time went along. The Mosaic Law itself was conditional, that is, the fulfillment of the blessings promised depended upon the submission of the people to it.[34] But Israel never did fully submit to the Law, not even close.[35] The Israelites, we might recall, were allowed into the Promised Land not because of their righteousness (they were, as Moses said, a "defiant and stiff-necked" people), but only because of the unconditional promises that God had previously made to the patriarchs.[36] Complicating their situation was the unpardonability of, as just mentioned, intentional sins, which all men are apt to make. Even if all types of sins of the previous year were forgiven on the Day of Atonement, once the Ark of the Covenant was lost (in the Babylonian destruction, or perhaps sooner), with its all-important Mercy Seat (the "Throne" of YHWH upon which the High Priest sprinkled the blood), there was no means by which the rite could be carried out, and thus the people's year of sins remained.[37] And it was not like there was any hope that the Ark would be one day found and once again installed into service, for Jeremiah had said plainly that the day would come when the Ark would no longer be remembered or come into anyone's mind anymore.[38] As the prophets said, God was in fact really not so concerned about the strict observance of all the rites of the Law, rather, he cared much more about men's hearts: were they true towards him, and were they merciful?[39] So the Mosaic Covenant eroded in power and authority, and this is why Isaiah, Jeremiah, and Ezekiel spoke about a New Covenant to come, a covenant that would be much more about men's hearts and not so much about outward deeds and rituals.[40] Or, to put it another biblical way, the New Covenant would be more concerned about the circumcision of the heart rather than the circumcision of the flesh.[41] The Old

---

Whitcomb, "Christ's Atonement and Animal Sacrifices in Israel," *Grace Theological Journal* 06:2 (Fall 1985): 201-28.

[33] E.g., Exod 31:16; Lev 16:31; Ps 119:159-160; Mal 4:4.

[34] Deut 4, 28

[35] Isa 1:2-9

[36] Deut 9:4-6

[37] Lev 16:14-16

[38] Jer 3:16

[39] Kaiser lists these OT texts that show that God is more concerned about love/obedience than sacrifice: Exod 15:26; Deut 10:12, 20; 1 Sam 15:22; Pss 50:8, 14; 51:16; 69:30-31; Prov 15:8; 21:3; Isa 1:11-18; Jer 7:21-23; Hos 6:6; Amos 5:21; Mic 6:6-8. (Walter C. Kaiser, *The Messiah in the Old Testament* [Grand Rapids: Zondervan, 1995], 124-5.)

[40] Isa 55:3; Jer 31:31-34; 32:40; Ezek 16:60-62; 37:26

[41] The Tanakh speaks about the New Covenant change of heart in several places, e.g.,: Deut 30:6 ("the LORD your God will circumcise your heart and the heart of your

Covenant was founded in the blood of animals, and the New Covenant was founded in the blood of Jesus.[42] When Jesus took the cup on the night that he was betrayed, he said, "This cup is the new covenant in my blood, which is poured out for you."[43] The next day Jesus' blood was spilled on the cross, and the New Covenant was initiated. As Daniel said, Messiah came, and then he was "cut off."[44] And not long after, as predicted by that prophet, the nation and its temple and priesthood were destroyed.[45]

The Tanakh shows that the Messiah suffers and dies, yet he is resurrected. Isaiah told us that the Messiah is "cut off out of the land of the living," and yet, he "sees" the "anguish of his soul" and is "satisfied."[46] Let us also recall the proto-good news of this way back at the beginning: the Messiah's heel was bruised by the devil, but the devil's head was bruised by the Messiah.[47] In other words, the Messiah would die temporarily, but the devil would die permanently. Plenty of Tanakh texts show the eventual triumph of the Messiah.[48] In general, though he suffers and dies, yet he comes in glory and rules the world forever. Jesus suffered and died, and rose again on the third day, a fact disputed over the ages, but one that has the weight of the disciples' testimony behind it, as well as the testimony of the five hundred or so people who encountered Jesus after the resurrection and before his ascension to God.[49] The NT testifies that after his ascension, he has been ever since at the right hand of God the Father in heaven where he continues to intercede for his saints.[50] One man who testified to this was Stephen (Acts 7:55-56): As he was being stoned to death after making his defense before the Sanhedrin, he, full of God's Spirit, saw God's glory and Jesus standing at God's right hand. As he died he cried out, "Lord, do not hold this sin against them!"[51] It is probably the case that the Son was standing instead of sitting at God's right hand because of his

---

descendants"); Jer 24:7 ("I will give them a heart to know me"); Jer 31:33 ("I will put My law in their minds and inscribe it on their hearts"); Jer 32:40 ("I will put My fear in their hearts so that they will never turn away from Me"); Ezek 11:19 ("I will give them singleness of heart and put a new spirit within them; I will remove their heart of stone and give them a heart of flesh"); Ezek 36:26 ("I will give you a new heart and put a new spirit within you; I will remove your heart of stone and give you a heart of flesh").

[42] Exod 24:8; Matt 26:28

[43] Luke 22:20 (CSB)

[44] Dan 9:26.

[45] Dan 9:26 is fulfilled, at least partially, in the events of AD 70 and AD 135.

[46] Isa 53:8, 11. Verses 10-12 of Isa 53 are admittedly difficult to understand, but it seems clear enough that the suffering servant lives on and is greatly blessed by God.

[47] Gen 3:15

[48] E.g., Gen 49:10; Ps 2, 72, 110; Isa 9:7; 42:4; Dan 7:14, 27; Zech 9:10.

[49] 1 Cor 15:3-8

[50] Mark 16:19; Luke 22:69; John 20:17; Acts 2:33; 7:55; Eph 1:20; Col 3:1; Heb 1:3; 8:1; 10:12; 12:2. See also Ps 110:1.

[51] Acts 7:60

concern for what was then happening to his beloved Stephen. God the Father has been putting all of his enemies, one by one, under Jesus' feet for the last two millennia, and will continue to do so until the day comes when "at the name of Jesus every knee will bow, of those who are in heaven and on earth and under the earth."[52] That it will be this way should not be a surprise, for God had commanded long ago:

> Now therefore, be wise, O kings; be instructed, you judges of the earth. Serve the LORD with fear, and rejoice with trembling. Kiss the Son, lest He be angry, and you perish in the way, when His wrath is kindled but a little. Blessed are all those who put their trust in Him.[53]

And Solomon through the Spirit testified of the Messiah:

> May he also rule from sea to sea and from the River to the ends of the earth. Let the nomads of the desert bow before him, and his enemies lick the dust. And let all kings bow down before him, all nations serve him.[54]

How do we know that this is not just bombastic talk similar to that of ancient near eastern kings who spoke similarly about themselves and about their gods?[55] Because the Messiah will, according to God's promise given to David, rule forever;[56] and this son of David, as Isaiah told us, will rule on David's throne forever and be known as "Mighty God," and even more amazing, as "Everlasting Father."[57]

And this brings us back to the main question of the book: viz., is the Messiah divine? The NT, needless to say, teaches this as I will discuss briefly in a moment. But it is not as if the NT teaching comes out of left field, so to speak. If it did—that is, if the OT had nothing to say about this—then it would be a very tough doctrine to swallow. The truth is (as I've tried to show in this book) that the Tanakh sets several precedents for the NT idea of the Messiah's divinity, although, admittedly, they are quite veiled in comparison to the NT. The two great precedent-setting truths regarding this subject that the Tanakh reveals are these: first, that God does come to earthly man in the form of a man, and, second, that God has a son. God visited men as a "man" in the past, and more important for our purposes, God in the future, according to the Tanakh

---

[52] Phil 2:10. See Isa 45:23.
[53] Ps 2:10-12 (NKJV)
[54] Ps 72:8-9, 11
[55] The plentiful autobiographical annals of the Assyrian kings, for example, are full of bombast. They typically claimed to be "king of the four corners of the world" and "king of the universe." See Luckenbill, *Ancient Records of Assyria and Babylonia*, accessible at www.archive.org.
[56] 2 Sam 7:13; 1 Chron 17:12, 14
[57] Isa 9:6-7

prophets, will visit men as God's "Son"—who is also the son of King David and goes by such names as "Branch," God's "Servant," "YHWH our Righteousness," and, of course, the "Anointed One," i.e., the "Messiah." Let us review several of these precedents regarding the Messiah's divinity that are found in the Tanakh.

The first precedent—that God can and has come in the flesh—began right away in Scripture. YHWH is recorded as "walking in the garden in the cool of the day" looking for the freshly sinful Adam and Eve.[58] About two millennia later he, as one of "three men," came to Abraham and Sarah who were camped near Hebron.[59] There, YHWH "ate" (and probably drank) what Sarah prepared. Two generations later, YHWH wrestled all night with Jacob—"man" versus man—and, amazing enough, the man Jacob prevailed.[60] The enigmatic Angel of YHWH appeared to Moses as a constantly burning bush, and later he showed up several times in the form of a man.[61] In several of these appearances, the Angel sometimes speaks *of* YHWH in the third person, and sometimes *as* YHWH in the first person. The OT teaches that no one can see God and live, and the NT teaches that no one can see God at all;[62] yet, in both Testaments, men did see God and live. In order to preserve Moses' life, YHWH did not allow him to see his face;[63] yet Moses on many occasions on Sinai and at the Tent of Meeting spoke with God "face to face, as a man speaks with his friend."[64] How can this be?

That God comes to man under several names, and that these names are connected with the idea of God's "Son," is amply demonstrated in the Tanakh. Just mentioned are YHWH's epiphanies to men as "man" and "the Angel of YHWH," which occurred during patriarchal times, the Exodus, and the conquest under Joshua. At David's time and afterward, appearances of God are less frequent; on the other hand, prophecies begin to appear regarding future times when God will be manifested to men in the form of the Messiah. Does the Tanakh say that the early epiphanies were appearances of the Messiah? No, not in any direct way. But there surely must be some kind of correspondence between them, because the Tanakh reveals that they are both manifestations of God. That the Messiah spoken of at David's time and afterward is divine is shown by these basic facts: David's son is, as God said to David through the prophet Nathan, also God's Son, and he will rule on the throne of David

---

[58] Gen 3:8
[59] Gen 18
[60] Gen 32
[61] Exod 3; Num 22; Judg 6, 13
[62] Exod 33:20; John 1:18
[63] Exod 33:20
[64] Exod 33:11; Num 12:7-8

forever;[65] Psalm 2—most surely a psalm of David—says that this Son of God is God's "Messiah" who will one day rule over all kings and nations; this Son, whom Isaiah says will sit on David's throne forever, will, as that prophet says, be "Mighty God" and "Everlasting Father";[66] a "Branch" will be raised up from the seed of David and, according to Jeremiah, will one day be called "YHWH our righteousness"—the only name in the Tanakh given to a man that includes the whole name of God;[67] and Ezekiel tells us that in the time of the final and permanent restoration, Israel will have YHWH as their Shepherd, and that they will have David as their Shepherd, and that they will from that time on have One Shepherd.[68] So within the Tanakh, the precedents are there for the NT revelation of a human-divine Messiah who is the Son of God.

The NT, of course, has much more to say about Christ's divinity. Here are just a few highlights from the Gospels: His disciple John testified that Jesus was the "Word" of God that was "with God" and "was God" from the beginning.[69] He was conceived in the womb of the virgin Mary via the intercession of God's Holy Spirit—a stupendous "sign" that indeed revealed the truth, "God [is] with us."[70] Jesus was born in Bethlehem, which fulfilled the prophecy of Micah, who said concerning the king to be born there, "His goings forth are from long ago, from the days of eternity."[71] At twelve years old, Jesus already could interact with the teachers in the Temple, and later as an adult his understanding of God, man, and the Scriptures caused the Pharisees, Scribes, and Sadducees to be no match for him in debate.[72] John the Baptist understood himself as preparing the way for Jesus in fulfillment of Isaiah's prophecy, "Clear the way for the LORD in the wilderness; make smooth in the desert a highway for our God."[73] Jesus had the authority to claim that he fulfilled the Mosaic Law and to revise the Law to better reflect the "gracious and compassionate"

---

[65] 2 Sam 7:13-14; 1 Chron 17:12-14

[66] Isa 9:6-7

[67] Jer 23:5-6

[68] Ezek 34; 37:24. Gaebelein is right when he says: "It is not David, but He who is according to the flesh the Son of David and David's Lord as well. The one Shepherd can only be the Messiah. Numerous passages show that David's name is used in a typical sense. Jeremiah announced, 'They shall serve the Lord their God, and David their King, whom I will raise up unto them' Jeremiah 30:9. Here David stands typically for Christ, the Messiah of Israel, for He is raised up unto them when Jacob's trouble is ended (Ezekiel 34:1-7)." (Arno C. Gaebelein, *The Annotated Bible* [1919], Ezek 34:20-26, accessible at www. biblehub.com.)

[69] John 1:1

[70] Matt 1:18; Luke 1:35. The virgin birth was the fulfillment of the "sign" that God (through Isaiah) gave to King Ahaz (Isa 7:14)—a sign that went completely over his head.

[71] Mic 5:2. Compare with Ps 93:2.

[72] Luke 2:41-52; Matt 22:21-22, 33, 45; Mark 12:34; Luke 20:40

[73] Isa 40:3

heart of God and the hopelessly wicked heart of man.[74] Of course, he worked many miracles, even healing blind men and raising men and women back to life who had just died.[75] His miraculous authority extended over nature, human bodies, and even demons.[76] He had the power and authority to forgive sins, something only God can do.[77] Jesus said to his disciples, "I and the Father are one"; and to his disciple Philip who asked Jesus, "show us the Father," Jesus replied, "Have I been so long with you, and yet you have not come to know Me, Philip? He who has seen Me has seen the Father."[78] Jesus said that he is Israel's "Good Shepherd," and, in fact, the "One Shepherd" of both Jews and gentiles.[79] And Jesus repeatedly called himself "the Son of Man," thereby invoking identity with the "Son of Man" who, in Daniel's vision, was seen being presented before YHWH in heaven and as coming as YHWH in judgment upon the clouds of heaven.[80] Jesus revealed this identity (and sealed his fate) when he stood before the Sanhedrin and in response to the High Priest's question, "Are you the Christ, the Son of the Blessed One?" said, "I AM, and you will see the Son of Man seated at the right hand of the Power and coming with the clouds of heaven."[81] The High Priest understood perfectly what Jesus said, and tore his clothes. Much more could be said regarding the NT's witness of Jesus' divinity, but it is best now to bring the book to a close.

Why did the eternal King wind up before the High Priest and Sanhedrin to stand trial as a criminal?[82] *There* was the crossroads of what is of ultimate interest to God, men, and Satan: God requires justice for men's sins, but is unwilling that any of them perish; men are hopelessly enslaved to wickedness,

---

[74] Matt 5:17-18. See Jesus' "Sermon on the Mount," Matt 5-7. See also Mark 3:1-5; Luke 6:1-11 (esp. v. 5); 14:1-6.

[75] Matt 9:27-31; Mark 8:22-26; Luke 18:35-43; John 9; Luke 7:11-17; 8:40-42, 49-56; John 11:1-45. In many cases, Jesus did what the Tanakh says only God can do. E.g., he: calmed the sea (Ps 107:29); walked upon the sea (Job 9:8); fed the multitude (Deut 8:16); perceived men's thoughts (Amos 4:13); raised the dead (Ps 68:20); opened the eyes of blind men (Ps 146:8); healed sickness (Ps 103:3); healed bodily immobility (Ps 146:8). (This list is from Jonathan Edwards, *The History of the Work of Redemption*, 231-232.)

[76] E.g., Mark 4:39; John 21:6; Luke 17:11-19; Matt 8:28-33.

[77] Matt 9:2-7; Luke 7:36-50. It appears that the Angel of YHWH also had the power and authority to forgive sins. See Exod 23:21.

[78] John 10:30; 14:8-9

[79] John 10:11, 14, 16. See Ezek 34; 37:24. That salvation would go to both Jews and gentiles is indicated in many places in the Tanakh. In Ps 22:27 David said, "All the ends of the earth will remember and turn to the LORD, and all the families of the nations will worship before You." His son Solomon, at the Temple dedication, said that it was good for Israel's religion to prosper, "so that all the peoples of the earth may know that the LORD is God; there is no one else." See also especially Isa 56:3-8.

[80] E.g., Matt 8:20; 16:27-28; 19:28; Mark 8:31; Luke 22:48. The "Son of Man" is depicted in Daniel in Chap. 7.

[81] Mark 14:61-62 (ISV). Jesus had previously said to the Pharisees, "Before Abraham was, I AM," a statement that revealed his self-understanding of his own divine pre-existence.

[82] Matt 27:57-68; Mark 14:53-65; Luke 22:66-71

yet many hope for some way to escape God's judgment and eternal punishment; Satan wants God defied, the Son of God killed, and all mankind to be damned. At the trial, on one side, was Caiaphas, representing sinful man. Yet he had enough knowledge of Scripture and circumstances to prophesy that Jesus would die for the good of Israel. It is not likely that he thought about this in a messianic sense, but in the sense that Jesus' death would make it less likely that the Romans would come and take away their nation.[83] Standing across from Caiaphas was Jesus, the perfect Lamb of God, who represented in one Man all that God intended Israel to be. Previous to this, Jesus had lamented, "Jerusalem, Jerusalem, who kills the prophets and stones those who are sent to her! How often I wanted to gather your children together, the way a hen gathers her chicks under her wings, and you were unwilling."[84] Caiaphas was not willing—although he knew better—and most of the rest of the Counsel were as well not willing. But there were two (and might have been one or two more) who dissented: Joseph of Arimathea and the Pharisee Nicodemus. The latter had some time previous come to Jesus in the night and spoken to him about ultimate matters. But he could do nothing at the trial—a trial in which occurred a partial yet significant portion of the fulfillment of Ps 2: "Why do the nations rage and the kings of the earth take their stand against the LORD and his Messiah?" And Ps 89: "His crown is cast to the ground." Isa 53: "He was esteemed not." And Zech 11: They "despised" him.

Jesus knew what was in their minds and hearts, for, as John said, "He Himself knew what was in man," and as Solomon said, "[God] alone know[s] the hearts of all the sons of men."[85] He knew the thoughts of men and he knew those thoughts long before they thought them. Based on this knowledge, his infinite wisdom, and what God the Father, the Son, and the Holy Spirit had conceived out of infinite love countless ages before, Jesus knew at that moment that he was perfectly in God's will and in the right place at exactly the right time in order to fulfill his mission of providing the atonement that would satisfy God's wrath and thereby give men and women the opportunity to escape eternal condemnation.[86] Here was in action the superlative act of God, in love, *working all out for good*: the devil appeared the victor when, for example, Joseph was sold into slavery by his brothers; but through this he was elevated to the right hand of Pharaoh and turned out to be the savior of his brothers; likewise, the devil appeared the victor when Jesus was condemned and killed, but he turned out to be the loser when that death was accepted by God as the price that was sufficient to pay for the sins of his Jewish brothers and everyone else.

---

[83] John 11:47-53
[84] Matt 23:37
[85] John 2:24-25; 1 Kings 8:39. See also Matt 9:4; 12:25; Luke 9:47.
[86] Luke 13:31-33

To put it another way, Satan bruised Jesus' heel, but in that act, Jesus bruised Satan's head.

Was Jesus' sacrifice really valuable enough to pay the penalty that all men owe God on account of their sins? A mere man, had said the psalmist, could not pay for the sins of his fellow man.[87] But Jesus was not a mere man. Being the Son of God, God the Son, he was valuable enough for God to accept him as a "ransom for many." Any sin against the infinitely holy God is of infinite measure, so only the sacrifice of the infinitely valuable Son of God would suffice to cover such sin. This is why repeatedly throughout the OT God claimed to be the one who would one day redeem Israel from her sin.[88] So when Jesus replied to Caiaphas, "I AM," he understood that this would guarantee his death; but he knew that God would work it out for stupendous good. And by uttering those words, he let Caiaphas, the Sanhedrin, and the whole world know that it is God who pays for the sins of mankind—for "without the shedding of blood there is no forgiveness."[89]

Jesus' blood was sufficient to atone for the sins of all mankind; but does it free every man and every woman of their guilt "in that day" when "thrones [are] set up and the Ancient of Days [takes] his seat" in order to judge the living and the dead?[90] To answer this question, and to close this book, let us consider the conversation between Jesus and Nicodemus.[91] This "elder of Israel," as Jesus called him, came to Jesus because he, and a few others, had observed that no one could do what Jesus had done unless God were with him. Nicodemus only expressed curiosity and perplexity; but Jesus, caring that Nicodemus might quickly learn what is most urgently needed (i.e., what he must know and do in order to be saved), got right to the point: "Truly, truly, I say to you, unless one is born again he cannot see the kingdom of God."[92] Speaking Rabbi to Rabbi, Jesus first wanted Nicodemus to know that even the "work" of seeking God and desiring to put one's faith in God could not be reckoned to the credit of the seeker—for even that most fundamental element of true religion is, truth be known, a work of God.[93] Emphasizing this thought, Jesus said, "The wind blows where it wishes and you hear the sound of it, but do not know where it comes from and where it is going; so is everyone who is born of the Spirit."[94]

---

[87] Ps 49:7-8

[88] E.g., Pss 49:15; 130:8; Isa 43:1; 48:20; 52:3; Hos 13:14.

[89] Heb 9:22. See Lev 17:11.

[90] Dan 7:9. See also Matt 25:31; Rev 1:7; 20:11.

[91] John 3:1-21

[92] John 3:3

[93] Prov 16:9; Isa 6:10; Jer 31:33; John 6:44

[94] John 3:8. This is an echo of the truth spoken by Solomon a thousand years before: "Just as you do not know the path of the wind and how bones are formed in the womb of the pregnant woman, so you do not know the activity of God who makes all things" (Eccl 11:5).

Nicodemus first needed to know that his own efforts to seek truth and obtain a change of heart were hopeless, for hopelessly sinful men first need to be given a "heart of flesh" in order to truly believe. With this out of the way, Jesus then gave to Nicodemus this great statement about God's love and about how men can be reconciled back to God:

> For God so loved the world, that He gave His only begotten Son, that whoever believes in Him shall not perish, but have eternal life.[95]

Nicodemus needed to know, and we all need to know, that "God is love" and that God is "not wishing for any to perish but for all to come to repentance."[96] God made us all and loves us all, but we, being made in his image and likeness, are able to discern right from wrong, and to choose one or the other. Using this freedom, we all sinned—which is not God's fault, but our own fault: for "God made man upright, but they have sought out many schemes."[97] God, being "merciful and gracious, slow to anger, and abounding in steadfast love and faithfulness,"[98] gave his "only begotten Son," whom he loved, as a sacrifice in order to pay the sin debt of all mankind. The sacrifice is *sufficient* to pay for the sins of all men and women; but for it actually to apply to them, there is a simple condition: we must repent and "believe" in the Son of God—and, of course, in God also.[99] Even this, as Nicodemus learned, is a gracious gift of God, "lest any man should boast."[100] Jesus' atonement will not pay for the sins of a man who does not repent and believe. Why does God require this? Why shouldn't he, considering all that he has done for us? Jesus gave his life for us; all God asks is that we give our allegiance to him. He is God after all, and apart from him, we would be nothing. But, really, what pleases God now is no different than what pleased God when he came in the form of a man to Abraham, and Abraham "bowed himself to the earth," called him "Lord," and was graciously hospitable.[101] May we all show the same love and reverence for the One whom God appointed to reveal God to man, and whom he commissioned to save men and women from eternal condemnation.

> Who has ascended into heaven and descended? Who has gathered the wind in His fists? Who has wrapped the waters in His garment? Who has established all the ends of the earth? What is His name or His son's name? Surely you know! (Proverbs 30:4)

---

[95] John 3:16
[96] 1 John 4:8; 2 Pet 3:9
[97] Eccl 7:29 (ESV)
[98] Exod 34:6 (ESV)
[99] Matt 3:2; John 14:1
[100] Eph 2:9 (KJV)
[101] Gen 18:2

Your throne, O God, is forever and ever; a scepter of uprightness is the scepter of Your kingdom. You have loved righteousness and hated wickedness; therefore God, Your God, has anointed You With the oil of joy above Your fellows. (Psalm 45:6-7)

Who is like the LORD our God, Who is enthroned on high, Who humbles Himself to behold The things that are in heaven and in the earth? (Psalm 113:5-6)

The End

BIBLIOGRAPHY

A Select Library of Nicene and Post-Nicene Fathers of the Christian Church. Edited by Philip Schaff and Henry Wace. 28 vols. in 2 series. 1886–1889. Repr., Grand Rapids: Wm. B. Eerdmans. Accessed Mar 13, 2021. https://www.ccel.org/ccel/schaff/npnf207.iii.xiv.html.

Assyrian and Babylonian Literature. New York: D. Appleton and Co., 1901. Accessed Apr. 9, 2021. https://archive.org/stream/AssyrianBabylonian Literature1901/Assyrian%20%26%20Babylonian%20Literature%201901 #page/n7/mode/2up.

Avot of Rabbi Natan. Accessed Mar 13, 2021. https://www.sefaria.org/Avot_ D'Rabbi_Natan.25.3?lang=en&with=all&lang2=en.

Baron, David. *Rays of Messiah's Glory.* Originally published 1886. Kindle e-book, 2017.

Baron, David. *The Visions and Prophecies of Zechariah.* London: Morgan and Scott, 1918. Accessed May 26, 2021. https://archive.org/details/thevisions 00barouoft.

Berlin, Adele, Marc Zvi Brettler, and Michael A. Fishbane. *The Jewish Study Bible.* New York: Oxford University Press, 2004.

Bimson, John J. "1 and 2 Kings." In *New Bible Commentary: 21st Century Edition,* edited by D. A. Carson, R. T. France, J. A. Motyer, and G. J. Wenham. Downers Grove: Inter-Varsity Press, 1994.

Brenton, Lancelot C. L. *The Septuagint Version of the Old Testament: English Translation.* London: Samuel Bagster and Sons, 1870.

Calvin, John. *The Penteteuch.* Vol. 1 of Calvin's Commentaries. Grand Rapids: Associated Publishers.

Collins, John J. *The Scepter and the Star.* Grand Rapids: Eerdmans, 2010.

Dorner, Isaac A. *A System of Christian Doctrine.* Edinburgh: T & T Clark, 1883. Accessed May 25, 2021. https://archive.org/details/systemofchristia 01dorn/page/n1/mode/2up.

Easton, M. G. *Easton's Bible Dictionary.* New York: Harper & Bros., 1893.

Edersheim, Alfred. *Life and Times of Jesus the Messiah*. New York: E. R. Herrick and Co., 1886. Accessed Feb 22, 2019. https://archive.org/details/lifetimesofjesus01eder/page/n11.

Edersheim, Alfred. *Prophecy and History in Relation to the Messiah*. New York: Anson D. F. Randolf, 1885. Accessed Feb 22, 2019. https://archive.org/details/prophecyandhisto00ederuoft/page/n7.

Edwards, Jonathan. *The History of the Work of Redemption Comprising an Outline of Church History*. New York: American Tract Society, 1816. Accessed July 24, 2018. https://archive.org/details/historyofworkofr00edwa.

Feinberg, Charles L. *God Remembers: a Study of Zechariah*. Wheaton: Van Kampen Press, 1950.

Fruchtenbaum, Arnold G. *Ha-Mashiach*. San Antonio: Ariel Ministries, 2017.

Frydland, Rachmiel. *What the Rabbis Know about the Messiah*. Messianic Publishing Co., 1991.

Gaebelein, Arno C. *The Annotated Bible*. 1919. Accessed May 25, 2021. https://biblehub.com/commentaries/gaebelein/ezekiel/34.htm.

Gesenius, Wilhelm, and Samuel Prideaux Tregelles. *Gesenius' Hebrew and Chaldee Lexicon to the Old Testament Scriptures*. Bellingham WA: Logos Bible Software, 2003.

Hengstenberg, Ernst W. *Christology of the Old Testament*. Translated by Theodore Meyer. Vol. 1. London: T. and T. Clark, 1868. Accessed Apr 11, 2019. https://archive.org/details/christologyofold01heng.

Hengstenberg, Ernst W. *Christology of the Old Testament*. Translated by Theodore Meyer. Vol. 2. Edinburgh: T. and T. Clark, 1861. Accessed Oct 22, 2019. https://archive.org/details/christologyofold02heng.

House, Paul R. *1, 2 Kings*. Vol. 8 of *The New American Commentary*. Nashville: Broadman and Holman, 1995.

Hullinger, Jerry M. "The Compatibility of the New Covenant and Future Animal Sacrifice." *Journal of Dispensational Theology* 17:50 (Spring 2013): 47-66. Galaxie e-journal.

Hullinger, Jerry M. "The Function of the Millennial Sacrifices in Ezekiel's Temple, part 1." *Bibliotheca Sacra* 167:665 (Jan 2010):40-57. Galaxie e-journal.

Hullinger, Jerry M. "The Function of the Millennial Sacrifices in Ezekiel's Temple, part 2." *Bibliotheca Sacra* 167:666 (Apr 2010): 166-79. Galaxie e-journal.

Josephus, Flavius. *The Works of Josephus: Complete and Unabridged.* Trans. by William Whiston. Peabody: Hendrickson, 1987.

Kaiser, Walter C. *The Messiah in the Old Testament.* Grand Rapids: Zondervan, 1995.

Keil, Carl Friedrich, and Franz Delitzsch. *Commentary on the Old Testament.* Peabody MA: Hendrickson, 1996.

Klein, George. *Zechariah: an Exegetical and Theological Exposition of Holy Scripture.* The New American Commentary. B & H Publishing, 2008. Kindle e-book.

Kugel, James L. *The Bible as it Was.* Cambridge MA: Harvard Univ. Press, 2001.

Luckenbill, Daniel D. *Ancient Records of Assyria and Babylonia.* Vol. 1. Chicago: Univ. of Chicago Press, 1926. Accessed May 22, 2021. https://archive.org/details/LuckenbillAncientRecordsAssyria01/page/n3/mode/2up.

Luckenbill, Daniel D. *Ancient Records of Assyria and Babylonia.* Vol. 2. Chicago: Univ. of Chicago Press, 1927. Accessed Oct 20, 2021. https://archive.org/details/in.ernet.dli.2015.532630/page/n7/mode/2up.

Rydelnik, Michael. *The Messianic Hope.* Nashville: B & H Publishing, 2010.

Ryrie, Charles C. "Why Sacrifices in the Millennium?" *Emmaus Journal* 11:2 (Winter 2002): 229-310. Galaxie e-journal.

Shedd, William G. T. *Dogmatic Theology.* Vol. 1. New York: Charles Scribner's Sons, 1888. Accessed Aug 17, 2018. https://archive.org/details/dogmatictheology01sheduoft/page/n1/mode/2up.

The Ante-Nicene Fathers: Translations of the Writings of the Fathers Down to A.D. 325. Edited by Alexander Roberts and James Donaldson. 10 vols. 1885–1887. Repr., Grand Rapids: Wm. B. Eerdmans. Accessed Mar 13, 2021. https://ccel.org/ccel/schaff/anf03/anf03.v.ix.v.html.

Thiele, Edwin R. "The Chronology of the Kings of Judah and Israel." *Journal of Near Eastern Studies* 3, no. 3 (Jul 1944): 137-186. Accessed Apr 21, 1921. https://archive.org/details/E.r.ThieleTheChronologyOfTheKingsOfJudahAndIsrael1944/page/n19/mode/2up.

Whitcomb, John C. "Christ's Atonement and Animal Sacrifices in Israel." *Grace Theological Journal* 06:2 (Fall 1985): 201-28. Galaxie e-journal.

Wolters, Al. "The Messiah in the Qumran Documents." In *The Messiah in the Old and New Testaments*, edited by Stanley E. Porter. Grand Rapids: Eerdmans, 2007.

Wright, Christopher J. H. *The Message of Ezekiel*. The Bible Speaks Today. Downers Grove: Inter Varsity Press, 2001.

Young, Edward. *The Book of Isaiah*. Vol. 1. Grand Rapids: Wm. B. Eerdmans, 1992.

SCRIPTURE INDEX

Printed in the USA
CPSIA information can be obtained
at www.ICGtesting.com
LVHW070223080124
768390LV00037B/1240